Cricket's 300 Men

And One 400 Man

Cricket's
300 Men
And One 400 Man

CHRISTOPHER HILTON

breedon **books**
PUBLISHING

First published in Great Britain in 2005 by
The Breedon Books Publishing Company Limited
Breedon House, 3 The Parker Centre, Derby, DE21 4SZ.

ISBN 1 85983 450 7

Printed and bound by CPI Group, Bath Press, Lower Bristol Road, Bath.

Contents

Introduction

There is a misleading symmetry about the 18 men in this book and the recreation of the 20 triple-century innings they played. At the obvious level, these are the only men to have played such innings in Test matches, and at an even more rarefied level, only two have done it twice, Sir Donald Bradman and Brian Lara. Lara is more rarefied still by having broken the record (held by Sir Garfield Sobers since 1958) when he scored 375 against England at Antigua in 1994 and then, a decade later, becoming the only man to reach 400. Hence the title of this book.

The misleading part is that scoring a triple century is not only a matter of ability but a conjunction of circumstances. Many great players have enjoyed long and prosperous careers but never found themselves at such a conjunction. Test matches in England were played over three days until 1930, which put a premium on time. It can be no coincidence that the first triple centurion, Andy Sandham, made his in a timeless Test in the West Indies in 1930. It lasted nine days. Walter Hammond, the next English man to do it, flayed a weak New Zealand attack all over Auckland but arguably that cost England the match because, replying to the New Zealand total of 158, England went as far as 548 for seven declared – hugely more than they would have needed and taking up time, however fast Hammond scored. New Zealand were 16 for no wicket when the rain came and washed the match away. This is not a criticism of Hammond (who got the runs in 5 and a quarter hours) or Bob Wyatt, the England captain, but merely a way of illustrating that all too often no Test batsman had a realistic chance of fitting a triple century into the context of a match and even more so because the era was one, we are assured, of chivalry and the true spirit of the game itself. To distort a Test match in order to accommodate one batsman gorging himself would not have been contemplated.

Put another way, at The Oval in 1938, Leonard Hutton scored 364 and batted until 'after lunch on the third day'. It would have rendered a three-day match farcical but of course Hutton was playing in a timeless Test.

For these reasons, some of the very greatest are missing: W.G. himself and all the others from the early days through the golden age, Victor Trumper included. His highest test score was 214 not out against South Africa, although in 1899 he did score 300 not out against Sussex in 6 hours and 20 minutes. That was a three-day game, it was unaffected by the weather and drawn, and the Sussex bowling certainly represented no Test attack.

However, Test matches in Australia were played to a finish (in effect, they were timeless Tests) until the Fifth Test of the 1928–9 series which lasted eight days. When it limped to a close just about everybody had had enough. It has been called 'the match that ended the timeless Tests in Australia'. Consider that as this Fifth Test, played over 8, 9, 11, 12, 13, 14, 15 and 16 March, limped towards a close (Australia won by 5 wickets), the last Australia v England Test to be drawn in Australia had been in Melbourne in March 1882. All the rest had been played out although, one way or another, they tended to last three or four days. Whether that was for reasons of technique (or the lack of it), whether it was that cautious, defensive thinking didn't exist or whether there was not much point in defending in a timeless Test is unclear and probably unprovable.

For our purposes, before Melbourne 1928–9, batsmen had as much time as they needed and the consequence was that the heaviest scoring was done in Australia. That fourth day, which was so often played, opened up all sorts of possibilities.

You can drown cricket in a sea of statistics and it is all too easy to lose sight of the shoreline, but between 1876–7 and 1928–9 there were 67 Ashes Tests in Australia, producing 97 centuries, and 52 Tests in England, producing 54.

From 1876–7 to 1928–9 only six innings of 200 and over were played: one in England and four in Australia (including R.E. Foster's 287 at Sydney in 1903–4, a record which stood for 26 years in all Tests). The fact that only two batsman got to 200 before Forster may be interpreted in a variety of ways but, inescapably, it demonstrates that runs were harder to get. A century was a genuine feat, and Forster's innings were a peak that might never be scaled again. Hammond, dining out on the Australian bowling in 1928–9, scored 905 runs at an average of 113.12, with four centuries – 251, 200, 119* and 177, so even he didn't get past Forster and by now centuries were common currency. Seventeen were made in this series alone.

You might confidently expect that triple hundreds were a logical progression from this and that Australia's true wickets would be a natural home to them, not least because of Bradman and what he might do over his long career. The first triple-hundred on Australian soil was in fact made by Bob Cowper in 1966.

In 1930 Test matches in England were extended to four days and also Bradman played for the first time. That extra day allowed him to score a triple century without distorting the match, something he'd do again on the tour four years later.

Bradman was the first batsman to 'think' in immense terms because he knew he was capable of immensity. C.L.R. James has written: 'By 1928, when he began, big cricket was being played everywhere with the same ruthlessness that Bradman is saddled with. He never knew any other kind of cricket. [...] His gifts and his cricket personality matured at a time when the ethics, the morals, the personal impulses and desires of cricketers were quite different from those who had played the game in the decades that had preceded. Cricketers already mature when Bradman appeared might want to play like Bradman. They couldn't. They hadn't the outlook. They hadn't the temper. They had inhibitions Bradman never knew.'[1] If you ally this to pitches that might have been problematical in the early days, batting techniques which must have been less refined than now and the outlook pre-Bradman that they had, you can understand why the first triple hundred did not come along until Test cricket had been played for 54 years, whereas in the year that I am writing this – 2004 – we have had scores of 309 and 400 within a month.

A further misleading aspect is that a triple century does not necessarily reflect the quality of the player making it. However, no batsman is going to get anywhere near it unless he is good, whatever the conjunctions bring.

The fascination of cricket is that it proceeds one ball at a time. Hutton could have been dismissed by the first ball he faced at The Oval in 1938 or the second or any before the 847th that did dismiss him. From ball to ball, nobody knew what the next ball would bring, including Hutton.

The list of 20 innings and 18 batsmen might be much longer if a lot of other batsmen in other places had done no more than survive the ball that got them, but none of them did from 1876 all the way to the present.

That is a mischevious way of embracing so many who were arguably better than many on the list but aren't on it themselves: Hobbs and Sutcliffe, cavalier Charles Macartney, Bill Ponsford who scored almost as heavily as Bradman in the 1930s, Compton and May and Cowdrey, Neil Harvey of the beautiful balance, the three Ws, princely Viv Richards and explosive Rohan Kanhai, Supercat Lloyd with a bat the size of a supertanker, little Sunny Gavaskar building, building, building, Graeme Pollock and Barry Richards who were trapped and lost within a political conjunction, burly Allan Border and the Waugh twins, Greg Chappell who batted like an artist and his brother Ian who batted like a yeoman.

Martin Crowe, a deeply accomplished batsman, really did need to survive the ball that had him caught behind off Arjuna Ranatunga at Wellington in 1990–1. He was 299 and although only three balls of the match remained he'd have found that extra run all right. The only other batsman to score 299* in a Test was Bradman against South Africa at Adelaide in 1931–2. The last man was run out.

As the triple-hundreds depended so much on the conjunction of circumstances, the list of batsmen is in a certain sense the creation of chance (apart from Bradman). That lends it a much more egalitarian feel as well as the element of surprise. You'd have to pick a lot of World XIs before you got down to Andrew Sandham opening but there he is, forever the first triple centurion. The list, to me, is much more interesting because of this element of chance. It involves batsmen from all the Test playing countries except New Zealand and South Africa (leaving aside Bangladesh and Kenya).

The triple hundreds are fascinating not just because of their rarity and the quality of the 'ultimate' but because they could bring with them many curious tensions. This was graphically illustrated by the dilemma of Mark Taylor who, against Pakistan in 1998, made 334* by close of play on the second day. He was captain and could easily have given himself enough time next morning to score the single that would have taken him past Bradman and made him Australia's highest scorer. He chose to put the interests of the side first, reasoning that his bowlers would need all the time they could get to bowl the Pakistanis out. Initially, Taylor's decision was read as a sort of homage to Bradman – that, even by implication, Taylor did not want anyone to think he was better than Bradman. It was reinforced by the knowledge that if anyone would hew a chivalrous gesture out of the bleakly pragmatic modern game, Taylor was that man. He put the side first.

A word about the structure of this book. The innings are recreated in chronological order. It was initally tempting to do it in ascending order – for dramatic reasons – starting with the lowest, the 302 of Lawrence Rowe, and working up to Lara's 400, but that was entirely artificial because it implied a competition with successive batsmen hauling themselves ever upwards: Bradman at Leeds in 1930 beating Rowe by two runs, then Bob Cowper beating Bradman by three runs, and so on. It didn't work, because

Rowe made his 302 in 1974, 40 years after Bradman's 304, and Cowper made his eight years before Rowe. The highest innings, Lara's, might have been the perfect culmination, had Chris Gayle not batted his way to 317 in May 2005 as this book went to press.

The chronological approach has an inherent drama of its own in that each of the 17 batsmen after Sandham knew what the record was and, therefore, what they had to do to beat it (if they cared to try, which not all did). After the scorecards beneath the recreation of each innings, I have set out by how much the batsmen failed to beat the record or, if they did beat it, how long it had stood for. It has only been beaten seven times: Bradman 334 in 1930, Hammond 336 in 1933, Hutton 364 in 1938, Sobers 365 in 1958, Lara 375 in 1994, Matthew Hayden 380 in 2003, Lara 400 in 2004.

In recreating the innings I have used as wide a variety of sources as I can but in particular have used the local newspapers that actually covered the matches as they were happening. For example, *The Gleaner* in Jamaica devoted several thousand words a day to the Sandham Test and, more than that, set out the play in meticulous detail, beginning at the beginning.

All the local papers were the same in England, Australia and New Zealand too, and before television or radio this was how people 'saw' the day's play. There was no other way. A by-product of this, however meticulous the reporting seems, is that it is easier to have a full idea of what happened during Sandham's innings than, say, that of Matthew Hayden in 2003. By the 1960s the wordage of Test match reports (and everything else) was being reduced and it now seemed pedantic to expect a ball-by-ball account the following morning, especially when it had all been on television, with highlights in the evening, and on the radio, and there were quotes to be gathered in, press conferences to be attended, angles to be followed up. Nor is it at all clear whether the reading public had the time or inclination to read those several thousand words.

I have included plenty of strokes played – the cover boundaries, the singles on the leg side and so on – because, however matter-of-fact these may seem in the narrative, they were the fabric of what each batsman was doing.

I have leant heavily on many players' autobiographies, which are of varying standards and accuracy and, as a general rule, the further back you go the less revealing (in any sense) the book and the less human the author.

When I was working on the *Daily Express* I was commandeered to give the monthly talk to the Wombwell Cricket Society in Yorkshire (the Sports Editor couldn't go) and when it was over there was a question-and-answer session. One questioner explained that E.W. Swanton of the *Daily Telegraph* had given a talk shortly before, and during it he had explained that throughout his long reporting career he had never quoted any player, and what did I think of that? It seemed to me then (and now) that you can report what happens on the field as it all happens in front of you, and at that one ball at a time, but you can scarcely explain why players did what they did without asking them.

I sensed the Wombwell audience didn't agree with me. They didn't want quotes and they certainly didn't want clever angles, they just wanted to know what had happened. They'd have liked *The Gleaner*, c.1930, a lot more than some cricket row being dealt with in 30 seconds on *Sky News*.

There is a bibliography at the back of the book, but I record my gratitude here to the other sources and that must begin with *Wisden Cricketers' Almanac*. The *Wisden* quotations are reproduced by kind permission of John Wisden & Co. Ltd (Christopher Lane, the Managing Director, was particularly prompt and helpful). No praise is too high and if you're writing cricket history you can't really begin without it. The extent and accuracy of its coverage over, as I write this, 141 years is without parallel in any other sport – or most human activities. This standard has been maintained in their *cricinfo* website, http://www.cricinfo.com/, which is an astonishingly deep and up-to-the minute mine of information. I used it more and more and the ball-by-ball commentary transcriptions allowed me to recreate the Inzamam-ul-Haq and Sehwag innings. Sincere thanks for that. CricketArchive, http://www.cricketarchive.co.uk, is another valuable source and thanks to them too.

I thank the following for permission to quote: Telegraph Group Limited for coverage in the *Daily* and *Sunday Telegraphs;* Christopher Martin-Jenkins for his book *Testing Time*, the story of the MCC in the West Indies in 1974; Frank Tyson for the Bob Cowper extract from *The Century Makers;* HarperCollins for *My Autobiography* by Graham Gooch; *The Age* and *Sunday Age,* Melbourne; Random House for *Beyond A Boundary* by C.L.R. James, *Beating The Field* by Brian Lara, *Runs In The Family* by John Edrich and *With England in Australia* by John Clarke.

I have used the reporting of *The Gleaner,* Jamaica; *The Yorkshire Post* and *Yorkshire Evening Post,* Leeds; *The Auckland Star; The Hindu* magazine website of 31 March, 2002; *The Daily* and *Sunday Gleaner,* Jamaica; *Sheffield Telegraph; Advocate-News* and *Sunday Advocate-News,* Barbados; *Evening Standard,* London; *Daily News,* Colombo; *The Times of India,* Delhi; *The New Zealand Herald* and the *NZPA; Sydney Morning Herald* website, 14 October 2003, http://www.smh.com.au/articles/ 2003/10/13/1065917348483.html;*Cape Times* website 30 March 2004, http://www.capetimes.co.za/index.php?fArticleld=387011&fSectionld=307&fSetId=258; *NewKerala.com,* New Delhi, 29 March 2004, http://www.newkerala.com/ newsdaily/news/features.php?action=fullnews&id=7959; *The Independent on Sunday,* London. A DVD, *400 not out!,* Sky Sports/Green Umbrella Co. helped me bring Brian Lara's quadruple century to life. Former Test player Mike Selvey, now cricket correspondent for *The Guardian,* has a fine eye for detail (and whimsy) in his reporting. Colin Bateman, a former colleague on the *Daily Express,* reads the game as well as any and has perfected the art of explaining all its complexities in everyday simplicities – deceptively difficult to do. Their reporting helped.

Note: the symbol * means Not Out throughout.

Note also that until the winter of 1977–8 touring sides from England were MCC sides and styled like that for all the matches except the Tests, when they became England. This ended with the tour to Pakistan and New Zealand when the tourists were called England all the way through.

Notes
[1]   *Beyond A Boundary,* James.

England in West Indies, Kingston, April, 1930

Andrew Sandham, born Streatham, London 6 July 1890, died Westminster, 20 April 1982.

Test career 1921–30: 14 Tests, 879 runs, 2 centuries, average 38.21.

In the winter of 1929–30 the MCC decided to send out two touring parties, one to New Zealand and the other to the West Indies. Both would play Test matches, something which had not happened before.

The MCC, an austere club that ran the game within very traditional rigidities, was also a custodian of its values as well as assuming a missionary function. They saw it as their duty to protect the game and spread it, hence the two tours. However, it was not as simple as that because Britain was a great imperial power – one person in every three on the planet in its Empire and Commonwealth – and the mother country. Certainly Australia and New Zealand regarded it as such, and the West Indian islands wouldn't be getting their independence for another three decades. If you even glance at the West Indian newspapers of the time they read as if they were recording the activities of some English provincial town. Here are some of the headlines from *The Gleaner,* Jamaica, as the English tourists arrived to play what was described by *Wisden* (1931 Almanac) as the Fourth Representative Match in early April:

PROPOSED ADDITIONS TO RULES AND ORDERS OF THE JOCKEY CLUB

MASONIC
over a paragraph: 'A regular meeting of the Royal Lodge No. 207, will be held at the Masonic Temple, 20 Hanover Street, Kingston, on Monday, 7th April commencing at 7:30 p.m.'

TOURIST TRADE: MORE TOURS FROM ENGLAND AND WINTER TOURS FROM CANADA A DESIRABILITY

THREE BRITISH EXPERTS DOUBT NEW PLANET

CHARITY ORGANISATION

The tourists to the West Indies were travelling a great distance and in another very real sense no distance at all. By definition, neither of the two touring sides that winter could be fully representative and, more than that, several leading players declined to go on either tour. The result was, from a historical perspective, something of a devaluation.

Bob Wyatt, a future England captain, went to the West Indies and would remember the average age of the team as 32, making it, he estimated, one of the oldest touring parties to leave England. He ticked off some of the ages: Nigel Haig 42, Wilfred Rhodes 52, Patsy Hendren 40, George Gunn 50, Ewart Astill and Andy Sandham both 39.[1] All of these were very good players and Rhodes was a great one. He had made his debut for England against Australia in 1899 as a slow left-arm bowler and matured into an effective, efficient opening batsman as well. The party was 14 strong and also included Les Ames, who had himself matured into the leading batsman-wicketkeeper in the world, and Bill Voce, an ox-like, left-arm pace bowler who within two years would be slaying Australians with his fearsome deliveries.

Wyatt, incidentally, would thoroughly enjoy the topography and tenor of the West

Indies, not least sailing across the blue Caribbean Sea from island to island to play the matches. It meant that if the players didn't feel far from home they certainly saw that this particular part of home was different, and delightful.

There were four Tests, as we'd style them now: the First at the Kensington Oval had been drawn, England won the Second at Port of Spain by 167 runs, West Indies rallied at Georgetown and won by 289 runs with George Headley, a master batsman, scoring 114 and 112. The Fourth, at Kingston, would be fought to the finish however long that took. Andrew Sandham had met his conjunction of circumstances.

The side was one very much of its time. Captained by the Hon. F.S. ('Freddie') Gough-Calthorpe of Warwickshire, it included an Army Captain, R.T. Stanyforth, another amateur but one who had led England in South Africa in 1927–8. Stanyforth was the right stuff, being from Eton and Oxford. When he led that side in South Africa he had not yet played a county match for his native Yorkshire and in fact only ever played three. He was evidently a capable wicketkeeper.

Thereby hangs a tale of this tour. After the Georgetown test, the tourists went to Jamaica for four consecutive matches against a Jamaica Colts XV, against Jamaica twice and then the Test. Stanyforth would remember a bizarre incident during the second match against Trinidad. He was keeping wicket and found himself being accused of what he believed was called 'picking the bails' by the 'coloured editor of a daily paper.' The last wicket fell, bowled by Calthorpe, and, as Stanyforth remembered, the ball had struck the off-stump hard enough to send both bails flying. Quite by chance, the ball came on into his gloves after that. Everybody trooped off and Stanyforth 'thought nothing more about it' until he read the newspaper the following morning. The reporter said that he had seen the ball miss the wicket and the bails were dislodged by Ames's hands. Whether this annoyed Stanyforth or amused him he does not say but he points out that if the reporter's eyesight was so keen that he could see a cricket ball miss the stumps by an inch, how come it wasn't keen enough to see that while Ames had kept wicket all morning, Stanyforth had been keeping it all afternoon?[2]

You can, however, feel Stanyforth's righteous indignation and not least because the editor of the paper was Black, although whether Stanyforth was wielding that as a way of saying no judgement by a Black person was of value cannot be proven. However, it certainly seems so because otherwise why would he have pointed it out at all? The MCC was the austere custodian, white men ruled the empire and the globe was etched in swathes of red for each colony. Whether old hands like Haig, Rhodes, Hendren, Astill and Sandham cared about this except in a passive, accepting way is unclear, but for West Indians to do well against them was of a different order altogether.

A flavour of the times. The old professionals, including Rhodes the wily who had deceived several generations of batsmen and Hendren who had scampered his way to a mountain of runs for Middlesex, would do the hard work. That included Sandham, an opener who had made his Surrey debut as long ago as 1911. Strangely, it seemed that circumstances had conspired against him. He was, according to Wisden, (1983 Almanac, Obituaries, page 1254) slow to develop and, although he began to realise his promise with 196 against Sussex in 1913, he was dropped. World War One meant that when cricket resumed he was almost 30. He scored 175 not out against Middlesex, although batting at number four – Hobbs and the amateur D.J. Knight opened. Sandham played beautifully for some four hours and the innings was enough to give him a regular place in the Surrey side until his retirement in 1937. He'd made more than 40,000 runs at an average of 44.

On this West Indian tour the amateurs of course would make the decisions. (No professional captained England until Len Hutton in 1952.)[3]

The West Indies had been playing Test cricket for only two years. The authoritative *A History of Cricket* would speak of West Indian cricketers as suffering from 'temperamental weaknesses'[4] and Bradman would describe how the West Indies was almost like a team of 'big children', with great elation when they were doing well and utter despair when they weren't. This was an impression that lasted into the 1950s: naturally explosive and gifted players – wonderful entertainers – who lacked the stamina and stomach for a prolonged fight. The writer C.L.R. James, who will be quoted often in this book, has comprehensively demolished this conception of calypso cricketers with no backbone – and, indeed, the West Indian players would demolish it themselves too.

Again, however, what the old hands in the England party thought of their opponents is unclear. (James, an erudite Marxist, settled in Accrington, and one day, while sat on a park bench, a boy came up and asked him where his spear was. Don't read too much into that but see what Test matches must have meant to whole islands finding themselves and their self-respect; Sandham's innings must be set into that context.)

Calthorpe won the toss from Karl Nunes, a left-handed Jamaican who'd captained the West Indies to England in 1928. Another flavour of the times, Nunes was austere looking and white. No Black player captained the West Indies until Frank Worrell in 1960.

Calthorpe decided to bat on a dull, cloudy morning with a hint of rain in the air. A little rain had already fallen. Evidently Calthorpe was so delighted he chuckled audibly – he knew that England wouldn't have to bat last on a wicket which, however well prepared, would have deteroriated by then. The fourth innings, after all, could be many, many days away in a timeless Test.

Sandham opened with Gunn, another old professional but a quixotic one, whose personality and doings provided a rich seam for Neville Cardus. Gunn characteristically wore a white sun hat, while Sandham satisfied himself with the England cap.

H.C. Griffith opened the bowling to Gunn. Griffith, a Barbadian, was fast and, according to one authority, disliked batsmen hitting his deliveries to such a degree that he took extreme care to ensure that it did not happen or, if it did, was as infrequent as possible.[5] Griffith was fast this day, starting with a couple of balls outside the off stump before Gunn took a single to cover. The timeless Test had clicked into motion.

That single, of course, brought Sandham into strike and he played out the over in the most unhurried way. There was, truly, no hurry. O.C. (Oscar Constantine) Da Costa, making his debut, bowled from the other end and rain did fall but only briefly. Gunn, typically, began to spread his shots around the wicket and had made five scoring strokes before Sandham cut Da Costa past point for a single to launch his innings; but all these runs were singles except a couple of overthrows when Headley tried to run Gunn out from point after he – Gunn – had cut the ball there.

Sandham cut Griffith past point for another single, Gunn cut Griffith again and Headley again conceded a couple of overthrows. England had needed a full 20 minutes to reach 10. Truly no hurry. Sandham steered Da Costa to the leg side boundary, the first four of the match. Across the following nine days it was not to be the last. Griffith worried Sandham, who countered with another single past point.

George Gladstone, who'd taken four wickets for the Jamaica Colts XV when the tourists started their mini-tour of Jamaica, replaced Da Costa who couldn't find his length and line. Sandham took a single to leg off him. Tommy Scott, a spinner, replaced Griffith and Sandham cut him to the boundary. Gunn went down the wicket and made the ball into a full toss, hitting it to the long-on and raising the total to 30.

They were constructing a foundation, just as old hands would. Gunn would be the engine room, Sandham – best known for his partnerships with Jack Hobbs at Surrey – would steer the ship, although only after surviving a leg-break which turned so sharply that he had to deflect it away using his pad. After that he proceeded circumspectly, picking up singles and twos as the 50 came up. At lunch it had moved on to 69.

After lunch both batsmen dealt in singles and twos, although Sandham was beaten by Scott and then, two balls later, survived an lbw appeal. He moved to 50, made out of 96, by snicking Martin through the slips. The 100 soon after had taken two hours and 15 minutes, which was respectable enough and very respectable for a timeless Test.

Sandham accelerated. He hammered a full toss from Griffith to the long-on boundary and pulled a short ball for a couple. Gunn accelerated. He late-cut a boundary and hooked Da Costa for two successive boundaries, which brought England up to 150. Gunn moved briefly ahead of Sandham, then Sandham moved back ahead of him. Then, on 85 and coming down the wicket to attack Martin, Gunn missed the ball and was stumped. Sandham was on 86 and England, 173. It represented much more than a good start: from here England could build an impregnable position and Sandham still had all the time in the world.

Bob Wyatt came in and, as if to welcome him, Sandham off-drove Gladstone to the boundary then clipped him to leg for another. At tea he was 96 and after it went to his century with a cover drive off Scott.

It was, in many ways, a precise expression of the man who had had the misfortune to be a contemporary of Hobbs and Yorkshire's Herbert Sutcliffe. Sandham might be the perfect complement to Hobbs at The Oval, but Sutcliffe was the perfect complement to Hobbs at international level and their opening partnership had become almost a mythical thing. This rationed Sandham's England appearances to 14. He has been memorably described as having 'suave discretion at the wicket. The fast ball that searches for the leg stump is forced silkily beyond long leg off feet that ought to be wearing dancing pumps. The out-swinger that seeks to touch with poisoned kiss the edge of the bat, is guided with the full blade through the slips to the boundary. Now and then the trim feet come forward, the bat is pushed gently down the pitch; and the ball flows away noiselessly, past the bowler.'[6]

Wyatt batted freely and the 200 came up. Amazingly, the first bye was not conceded until 211, when the new ball had been taken. Still Sandham proceeded circumspectly, mingling the judicious singles with boundaries on the leg side and strong driving to the cover boundary. There was one moment of genuine alarm. Sandham cut Gladstone into the covers and Clifford Roach threw the wicket down with Sandham only just safe. Roach, at medium pace, came on himself but both batsmen were untroubled. Sandham drove Griffith through the covers for 4 to reach 150 shortly before the close of play, which came at 289 for 1 (Sandham 151, Wyatt 47).

The Gleaner, summing up the day's play, said that Sandham was at ease all the way through against all the bowlers and showed accurate judgement in which balls to hit, and, when he'd made the decision to hit, he knew precisely where to place the ball. He was, *The Gleaner* added, 'even neater and more workmanlike than usual in the execution of his shots,' scoring with equal facility to either side of the wicket. The bulk of his runs had come from the cover driving, but he'd harvested plenty through point and down to third man. The reporter was describing, unconsciously, an old hand who knew precisely what he was doing, how and why. The reporter ruminated aloud on quite what Sandham might do on the morrow refreshed by a good night's sleep.

On the second day, *The Gleaner* reported that among the large crowd (strangely slightly smaller than the opening day) was His Excellency the Governor, Sir Edward Stubbs and Lady Stubbs, Admiral Fuller of HMS *Despatch* and Lady Fuller, Miss Fuller, Hon. A.S. Jelf, Colonial Secretary, and Mrs Jelf, and Captain Curtis of HMS *Despatch* as guests of Sir William Morrison.

Wyatt bustled back into his innings, and Sandham flowed back into his, turning Gladstone to the boundary and then striking a full toss past cover for a single. He was constructing a foundation again. Wyatt pushed a ball to mid-off for a single, and that was the 300. The first half an hour, however, yielded only 15 and after a Sandham flurry – a couple past point off Griffith, drives for a couple and a boundary off Da Costa – Wyatt went, caught at the wicket, for 58.

Hendren, a great favourite in these parts, was given a tremendous ovation as he made his way to the wicket. He wasn't tall but he was bulky – chunky, anyway, and merry like an English yeoman. Hendren was going to do a bit of hustling, or, as *The Gleaner* put it rather diplomatically, he was playing in a 'very lively fashion, not at all carefully'. The change in tone seemed to reach Sandham, who drove Scott to the cover boundary and, stepping back, pulled him for 4. Hendren drove Griffith to the mid-on boundary and then cut him past point for another 4. A little later Hendren steered Griffith to the leg side, Sandham running so hard to complete the second run that one of his boots came off. There is a story, obscure and extremely mysterious, that for some reason Sandham was playing in borrowed boots that were too big for him, and, incidentally, using a borrowed bat whose handle may have been too long for him. Why? Time has closed in on this and we hear only silence.

Hendren 'broomed' – swept! – Tommy Scott to the boundary, Sandham cut him for a couple and stole a single to move to 193. He turned Martin to the leg side boundary, and, after Hendren cut airily through the slips to bring up the 400, Sandham drove Martin into the covers and that was his 200.

After lunch, Hendren drove a no-ball out of the ground (the first 6 of the match),

CRICKET

SPORTING PAGE

RACING

ENGLAND CLOSE FOR 849, AND WEST INDIES 141 FOR 3

Griffith Bowls Sandham for 325, and Scott Accounts for Four More Wickets to Close the Record-Making Innings of the English Side. Astill, Haig and Voce Make Useful Scores.

WEST INDIAN INNINGS STARTS BADLY.

Roach Loses His Wicket on an Unfortunate Decision, and Headley Gets Out at 10 to a Risky Stroke, Frank Martin and F. I. DeCaires Now Batting.

VOCE BOWLING WITH A LOT OF KICK.

The problem of getting out the English side was chiefly the blem of getting out Sandham—and this was solved, rather unexpecte... early, in Saturday's play, by Griffith, who deceived him with lever change of pace ball after he had added 16 to his overnight re. This wicket was all the more creditable to the Barbadian wler as Sandham did not appear in any way affected by his two s of batting, and, in fact, looked very likely to remain for aner day.

The ball was not only a change of pace but also a yorker, and combination defeated the great little Surrey batsman, the ball t touching the edge of his bat but not sufficiently to deflect its rse onto the wicket.

The rest of the innings might have been said to be mostly Tom. Scott; he was not bowling any better than he had done on the vious days, for he had bowled his best throughout, but the bats- n had more difficulty in dealing with him—and he got four more kets for 56 more runs, aided thereto by fine catches by Griffith d DaCosta. Griffith bowled excellently—faster than the previous s, and employing his change of pace ball more frequently—and is fairy sae to say that no other bowler in the side coud have l Sandh..n's great innings.

Barrow was keeping wicket at the close of the innings as well as had done at the beginning, and came out with only 6 direct byes total of 849 runs—it would be interesting to know if this is a rd, or, if not, how nearly it approaches one.

Talking about records—the next best innings total in a Test ch to the present one made by the English side was given in Satay's account as 600—this was only approximate, the actual fig- ..eing 636; made by England against Australia in the last tour.

The West Indies Side Start Badly.

Faced with this formidable total, the West Indian side comnced their first innings at 2.25 p.m.—Nunes and Roach facing e and Haig—and it was soon evident that the fast bowler was g to give trouble. He was sending them down at a great pace, varying his good length balls with shorter ones which were kick- a lot— Nunes giving a chance to Ames beind the wicket off his over, which was, very fortunately not accepted. After good for- , however, came bad fortune. Roach was batting in confident , and showng us some very pretty shots on the off—he had de 15 when he was given out lbw. on a decision which, in my ion, and in the opinion of others in a far better position to e than myself, was an absolute mistake, as he played the ball re it hit his pads. This, if the general opinion on the decision correct, was bad luck for the side—but there was worse to e, with no "if" whatever about it—when George Headley took a ce on hitting a fast one from Voce for four to leg, and, the ball g more than he had expected, was easily caught at square leg 10.

Consdering the state of the game, and Headley's ability and erience, none of us would have anticipated that he would have e anything else but leave this ball alone—so that we may call al bad luck for the side that he had a go at it.

here however bad luck—if it may be so called, ended for the —and, let us hope, for the innings—Nunes associated with k Martin then batting carefully yet confidently until the former dismissed by Voce on almost exactly the stroke with which he given the chance in his first over.

estion of Light.

This was about two minutes to five, and the light was rather , the sky being heavily overcast—but there is no reason to sup- that this was responsible for Nunes losing his wicket, since, as ady shown, he was not too certain in his play to the fast bowler the start of his innings. He had made some delightful strokes atch, especially through the slips, and scored his runs at a pretty rate.

Frank Martin was batting with his usual patience; and was lly at home to both the fast and spin men.

There are good men to come such as DeCaires, Passailaigue— ow, Scott—but they are, to some extent, uncertain quantities— at, as far as known possibilities are concerned, when play re- s to-day the responsibility of saving the side from something like disaster will rest on Martin's shoulders.

With the position as it is, it could not rest in any better place.

G. St. C. S.

ere was the largest attendance tour so far on Saturday, fully 0 being on the ground.

ongst those seen in the pav- and Stands were His Excel- the Governor Sir Edward s and Lady Stubbs, Sir Will- Morrison and Hon. A. S. Jelf Mrs. Jelf, His Honour Mr. e Adrian Clark and Mrs. , Hon. F. C. Wells Durrant, W. H. Fraser, Hon. J. H. all, Hon. D. T. Wint, Mr. F. . G. Austin, Mr. L. T. Year- , Mr. J. Scheult (representing ricket Boards of Barbados, the ard Islands, and Trinidad, res- ely), Messrs. C. S. Burton, Nethersole, . J. O'L. Brad- P. L. Carder, L. V. D. Sam- Major G. S. Cox, Messrs. V. eCormack, R. H. Fletcher, D. acy, V. G. Sasso, Major W. Messrs. G. Harvey Clark, ille DaCosta, Hon. Leonard dova, Messrs. C. S. Morri- Ellis Levy, Ken Pringle, Lind- owner, Edwin Charley, Michael dova, Lewis Ashenheim, Owen el, Herbert McDonald, H. F. vell, Frank Lyons, H. V. Al- ler, O. K. Henriques, William n, Dr. Eugene Gideon, Dr. U. urray, Dr. L. Crooks, Dr. O. arsh, Dr. E. V. Smith, Dr. E. Bronstorph, Dr. C. H. pson, Dr. L. M. Moody, Dr. rutchley, Dr. E. Constantine, . Anderson, Dr. E. H. Evans, W. A. S. Browne, Dr. D. J. ops, Dr. Dickenson, Dr. E. . Mellad, Rev. Canon Harry- Rev. Canon Ramson, Rev. rst Hall, Messrs. R. H. Mel- A. A. Melhado, A. O. Thomp- C. R. Crosswell, J. L. King, . Campbell, A. D. Goffe, Ar- Foote, Robert Marley, U. Theo. y, H. Cresswell Powell, Cecil deCordova, G. J. deCordova, Geoff Gunter, C. C. Pascoe, Claude deS. Pinto, Leslie Robison, Norman Marsh, C. M. daCosta, W. J. Palmer, Captain Hamilton, H. E. Allan E. V. Muschette, F. and L. Roper, E. Wells Elliott, C. Hope Panton, E. R. D. Evans, Lewis Kelly, D. C. Tavares, E. S. Beek, B. Boggis, Inspectors of Schools, S. L. Burey, Neilson, P. Williams, J. F. Parkinson, A. J. Myers, the majority of the gentlemen being accompanied by their wives and party.

Resuming on Saturday morning Griffith started at the south, Sandam taking the bowling. Sandy looked fresh and fit in spite of this being his third continuous day of batting. Griffith sent down a fine maiden. Gladstone came on at the top and O'Connor drove him to cover for a single. Sandham turned him neatly to fine leg for 3. Passailaigue running well to save the boundary. O'Connor cut him square for two. Gladstone was pitching up rather far this over. Sandham had trouble with a rising one from Griffith, end this he put to cover for two and again for a very short one to cover, Headley having a good try to throw him out, the ball just missing the wicket and going for 4 overthrow. O'Connor cut to 3rd slip. Passailaigue fielding well. Sandham drove Gladstone hard past point for 4, and O'Connor got a single to mid leg, and Sandham another. Sandham drove to extra cover for one—both men scoring freely off Gladstone.

GRIFFITH BOWLS SANDHAM.

Off the fourth ball of Griffith's next over, he sent up his change of pace ball to Sandham as practically a yorker and bowled him, the bat just touching the ball [illegible] much as to deflect it, for 325. The total being 720 for 5.

It was a great surprise to everybody, as he looked perfectly confident—and was due to the excellent way in which the bowler had disguised the change of pace. The Hon. F. S. G. Calthorpe came in next, and cut for two to cover. DeCairies misfielding. Both men got singles off Gladstone and O'Connor hit him in the air to leg for 2. Calthorpe drove for 2 to cover. O'Connor hooked a rising one from Griffith over the slips for 4—a very lucky shot. Another very good over by Griffith, fast and well on the wicket. O'Connor put Gladstone to 3rd for 4—the bowler then sending down 4 good balls.

Scott came on for Griffith, and Calthorpe cut to cover for one. Tommy nearly beat O'Connor with a good one, the batsman just edging it off the wicket for a single in the slips. O'Connor got 2 to point off Gladstone, and pulled a full toss to leg for 4. Scott beat Calthorpe with a good ball, the over going for a maiden, and Gladstone bowled one to O'Connor.

748 FOR 6.

Calthorpe hit Scott hard to leg, for Griffith, standing fairly near in to bring off a fine catch and dismiss him for 5—total being 748 for 6.

Haig came in next and survived a most confident appeal for lbw off his first ball—he looked well in front. O'Connor got Gladstone to cover for a single, to send up his 50. Another by Haig sent up the total to 750. O'Connor then hit Scott right to the boundary to square leg, and DaCosta standing just in the right place took a very nice catch—the total being 755 for 7. This was Scott's second maiden wicket, his average since he went in being 4 overs, 2 runs, 2 wickets.

Astill came in next.

Griffith came on at the top, and Haig got one to point off a good over. Haig put Scott for 4 to long on, and he turned him to leg for one. Haig got one to point off Griffith, and Astill one to mid leg. Haig put Scott to deep leg for 2, and again for the same number. Griffith bowled a good over to Astill for a maiden. Haig pulled Scott to leg for 3, and Astill stepped out to hit him to long off for 4, one which kept low, this very nearly got into the wicket. Astill got one to leg, and one to cover off Griffith, and Haig 3, Roach misfielding. Astill put one up in the slips off Griffith, but it did not go to hand. Haig drove Scott for one to cover, the only run off a good over. He then put Griffith for another to mid off. Scoring was very slow, the bowling being good, and both men playing carefully to pull the game round. Astill put Griffith just past point for one, and then stepped out to drive Scott for one past mid on. Haig played carefully to a very good length ball from Tommy, and then hit him for 4 to long on.

Frank Martin came on the field.

A CHANCE FOR ASTILL.

Gladstone replaced Griffith, and Astill pulled him square for 4, and then snicked him prettily to fine leg for another—the next ball he drove to Nunes' hand at mid off for a fairly easy catch, but the skipper failed to hold it. Astill had 24. Off the first ball of Scott's next over Haig hit to leg, and Griffith snapped the ball up from the ground—but the umpire decided it was not a catch. A single by Astill to mid on sent up 800, amid much applause. Both men got singles to mid leg. Haig put a full toss from Gladstone to long on for 4, and then got one to cover, Griffith misfielding. Astill got one to fine leg, and Haig drove through cover for one.

813 FOR 8.

Scott bowled a maiden to Haig, and Astill hit a full toss from Gladstone for 4 to long on, and then pulled him for a single. The next ball, a good length one, Haig played forward to, and was nicely caught in the slips by DaCosta—he had got 28, the total being 813. Wilfred Rhodes came in next. Astill stepped out to Scott and hit him for 4 to deep leg, and then turned him neatly to fine leg for another. Scott then bowled him with a ball which came very deep from leg—he had got 39—the total being 821. Voce came in last. Gladstone bowled a maiden to Rhodes. Voce got one to point off Scott, and Rhodes one to mid on. Voce then cut him for 2 to cover. Rhodes put Gladstone to mid leg for one, and Scott to cover for another. Voce had a near shave of being taken by Headley off Scott at short 2nd slip, and then cut him for 4 past point. Rhodes got a single to leg off Gladstone, and the bowler sent Voce a good one to just miss the wicket. Voce got a single to 3rd. He then put Scott for one to cover, and lunch came with the total at 834 for 9.

After lunch Griffith went on at the top, and beat Voce with a good ball. Voce cut to 2nd slip for one. Scott was on at the south, and Voce got one to cover, and Rhodes another. Voce then stepped out and drove him for one to long off. Voce late cut Griffith prettily for 4, and then turned him for a single. Voce drove Scott for one to long on, and Rhodes for 2 to the same place. Rhodes got one to mid leg, and Voce cut strongly to cover for a single. Voce got a single to 3rd off Griffith. Voce then hit out to one from Scott to touch it into DaCosta's hand at second slip and close the innings for 849—a great total.

WEST INDIES INNINGS.

R. K. Nunes opened the West Indies first innings with himself and C. A. Roach—the opening pair receiving a fine ovation from the crowd. The innings commenced at 2:25. Voce started at the top to Nunes and bowled a wide for his first ball. A very fast one passed Nunes off stump, and two balls later he gave a hard chance to Ames behind the wicket which he failed to hold. Off the last ball of the over he snicked through slips for 4. It was a very good over, and Karl was not at all comfortable.

Haig started at the south and Roach cut his fourth ball prettily to 3rd for a single. Nunes then turned him to fine leg for a couple. Roach cut Voce nicely to 3rd man for 2. Voce nearly beat him with a fast ball on the leg stump. Haig bowled a maiden to Nunes. Roach late cut Voce for a single—the only run in a very good over. Roach cut Haig for one to 2nd, and then got Voce for a lucky four past first slip, the next ball surviving an appeal for lbw. Roach cut Haig for one to 3rd, and Nunes got him through cover for 2 with his favourite shot, then turning him to leg for a lovely 4.

SOME FINE BOWLING.

He then got a single to mid off. Nunes got a lucky 4 through the slips off a rising ball from Voce, the ball going up but not to hand. Voce was bowling rather short and kicking a good deal. Nunes hit one of these up to leg off the last ball, but again it was lucky in not going to hand. Nunes snicked Haig through slips for 4—he then got him nicely away to 3rd for one. Both men were bowling very well, and Nunes, who was getting most of it had by no means settled down as yet. Rhodes at point fielded a fast cut from Nunes in good style. Nunes swung a rising one from Voce nicely to leg for one, the same shot he had missed before, timing it perfectly this time. Roach then turned him to fine leg for a single, another very pretty shot. Roach turned Haig to mid leg for one. Haig beat Nunes with one which came nicely from leg to just miss his off stump, and Nunes then turned him to square for one. Roach got a single to 3rd.

Astill came on for Voce and Roach got one to 3rd, Nunes turned him to fine leg for a pretty 4 to send up the first 50 after 40 minutes play.

Off the 4th ball of Haig's next over, a slightly slower one, Roach was clean in front of his wicket, and was given out lbw. by Hardstaff—but as far as could be seen, and gathered from everyone in a position to see, he played the ball quite distinctly before it hit his pad. He had made 15, the total being 53.

George Headley came in next, and got a single past mid on. Nunes got one to leg off Haig. A slight shower of rain was falling. Headley pulled Haig to deep leg to run 3, and Nunes got him past 2nd slip for a single. Astill bowled a good maiden to Nunes. Rhodes came on for Haig and bowled a maiden to Headley, flighting the ball a lot, Headley watching him carefully. Nunes cut Astill fine to 3rd for 2, Wyatt saving the boundary well. Astill beat him with a good ball. Rhodes bowled a maiden to Headley and tea came with the score at 67 for 1.

HEADLEY OUT FOR 10.

After tea Voce came on again at the top and Nunes put him to square leg for 2, and then in slips for a single. Headley cut him hard past point for 4, a very nice shot. Haig came on again at the south and Nunes snicked him for a single to first slip. Headley cut him square for one. Off the last ball of Voce's next over Headley tried to pull one which rose, and was easily caught by Haig. He had made 10, the total being 80 for 2.

Frank Martin came in next.

100 FOR 2.

Nunes got a lucky one through slips off Haig. Martin swung Haig strongly to square leg for 4 to open his score. Nunes got one to mid on off Voce. Martin drove Haig past cover for 2. Nunes got a lucky 4 through slips off a rising one from Voce, and then cut him nicely to 3rd for a single. Haig bowled a maiden to Nunes. Scoring was very slow, both playing carefully. Astill came on at the top for Voce, and bowled a maiden to Martin. Nunes swinging Haig for a good 4 to leg to send up 100 and then drove him for a single to mid off. Nunes cut Astill to 3rd for 2, Wyatt again saving the boundary well. Martin swung Haig to square leg for 4, and then put him prettily through slips for another. Astill bowled a maiden to Nunes.

Rhodes came on for Haig and bowled a maiden to Martin—so far he had bowled three overs and three maidens. Nunes pulled Astill to fine leg for a good four—he now had 60, and was batting in his usual confident style. He got a single to 3rd. Rhodes bowled another maiden to Martin.

RHODES' WONDERFUL LENGTH.

Martin swung a short one from Astill square for 4, and then got a single to cover. Rhodes bowled his fifth maiden in succession. Nunes got one to leg off Astill, and Martin one to point. Rhodes bowled his sixth maiden. Martin cut Astill for a single to point. Martin drove Rhodes for three to mid off—the first runs off him in seven overs—a remarkable record and a great tribute to his wonderful control of length. Nunes then got a single to square leg off him.

Nunes got one to 3rd off Astill, and next over put Rhodes to point for 2. Martin pulled a short one from Astill for 4.

NUNES OUT FOR 66.

Voce came on at the south for Rhodes—who had bowled 8 overs for six runs, and Nunes pulled a full toss to fine leg for 4—the third ball, a fast one, swung away and he touched it into the wicket-keeper's hands, Ames taking the catch to dismiss him for a very valuable 66—the total being 141 for 3. It was now 5 p.m. and the light being bad stumps were drawn for the day.

WEST INDIES 1ST. INNINGS.

R. K. Nunes c Ames b Voce	66
C. A. Roach lbw. b Haig	15
G. Headley c Haig b Voce	10
F. R. Martin not out	28
Extras	22
Total for 3 wickets	141

To bat: F. DeCaires, Passailaigue, Barrow, DaCosta, Scott, Griffith, Gladstone.

BOWLING ANALYSIS.

	O.	M.	R.	W
Voce	10	1	32	2
Haig	14	3	45	1
Astill	13	3	33	0
Rhodes	8	6	6	0

ENGLAND 1ST INNINGS.

G. Gunn st. Barrow b Martin	85
A. Sandham b Griffith	325
R. E. Wyatt c Barrow b DaCosta	58
E. P. Hendren c Passailaigue b Scott	61
L. Ames b Griffith	149
J. O'Connor c DaCosta b Scott	51
Hon. F. G. S. Calthorpe c Griffith b Scott	5
N. Haig c DaCosta b Gladstone	28
W. E. Astill b Scott	39
W. Rhodes not out	8
W. Voce c DaCosta b Scott	20
Extras	20
Total	849

BOWLING ANALYSIS.

	O.	M.	R.	W.
Griffith	58	6	155	2
DaCosta	21	—	51	1
Gladstone	42	5	139	1
Scott	80	13	266	5
Martin	45	6	128	1
Headley	5	—	22	—
Roach	5	—	22	—
Passailaigue	2	—	15	—

FAREWELL TO M. C. C. TEAM.

The farewell dinner by the Jamaica Cricket Association to the M.C.C. team will take place at the South Camp Road Hotel on Saturday night 12th inst. at 8 o'clock. Reservations can be made with the Secretary, Mr. D. P. Lacy, P/O box 122. Seats 15/ each, including drinks. The dance will come off, after the dinner, at Bournemouth Bath, and tickets can also be obtained from the Secretary at 7/6 each, including supper.

HARD LUCK—Our Telephoto picture shows C. A. Roach being given out by Hardstaff (the English Umpire) l.b.w. of the bowling of N. Haig. The decision caused a lot of comment as practically everyone was of the opinion that Roach played the ball before it hit his pads. He had made 15, and was batting stylishly.

Proposed Additions To Rules And Orders Of The Jockey Club

A special general meeting of the members of the Jockey Club of Jamaica will be held at their office, 10 Duke Street, on Saturday the 26th inst., at 11.20 a.m. for the purpose of considering, and if thought fit, passing and adopting certain alterations and additions to the rules and orders of the Jockey Club of Jamaica to take effect immediately on the passing thereof.

It is proposed to add after Rule 10 the following rule:

"10A. A committee of seven persons to be called "the Fixtures Committee" shall be elected by the members from among the members of the Club at the annual general meeting of members to be held in the month of April, 1930, and thereafter at every alternate annual general meeting. Such Committee shall be subject to the following regulations:

(i) No person shall be eligible for election thereto if he shall be financially interested in any manner in any racing association, Club, or racing company, or in the holding or carrying on or in the promotion of any race meetings in Jamaica.

(ii) The Committee may meet together at such times and may adjourn or otherwise regulate its meetings as it shall think fit. For all purposes five shall form a quorum and the Secretary of the Club or his deputy, if any, shall be ex-officio the Secretary of the Committee.

(iii) A Chairman of the Committee for each meeting shall be selected by the members present or a majority of them and such chairman shall have a casting vote in addition to his deliberate vote.

(iv) A member of the Committee shall be deemed to have vacated his office (a) if he dies, (b) if he becomes bankrupt or compound with his creditors, (c) if he delivers to the Secretary of the Jockey Club his resignation in writing, (d) if his appointment or continuance in office be disapproved by resolution passed by not less than four other members of the Committee, (e) if he is found to have had at the time of election or thereafter acquires any disqualifying financial interest as in sub-clause (i) of this rule mentioned.

(v) Any member of the Fixtures Committee shall be eligible to be an Executive Steward and vice versa if otherwise eligible.

(vi) Any member of the Fixtures Committee shall be eligible for reelection from time to time.

It is also proposed to add after rule 29 the following rule:

"29A. If any member of the Jockey Club of Jamaica (i) is or becomes a member of

(a) any racing club, association or company not under license of the Jockey Club of Jamaica, or

(b) any Club, association or company purporting to exercise control over racing in this island;

or (ii) is or becomes in any manner associated with or party or privy to any race meeting not conducted under License of the Jockey Club of Jamaica every such member shall ipso facto cease to be a member of the Jockey Club of Jamaica and shall forfeit all right to and claim upon the Club and its property.

Forthcoming Race Meeting At Knutsford

Our racing correspondent Old Sport writes: The weights for the Knutsford Park Easter races were published in Wednesday's Gleaner, and once again the racing public have expressed satisfaction at the manner in which Mr. A. C. Brandon, the official handicapper, has carried out the task of readjusting the weights.

The Knutsford Park promoters have decided to admit the public free on the race course proper, and I expect that the Savannah will be crowded. There are several features which will greatly add to the Knutsford Park fixture and that is the initial appearance of the five American horses which members of the Jockey Club of Jamaica will be racing at the meeting. The five new arrivals, Luakaha, Linda Archer, Nell, Trifling Trick and Hamaca will compete in the Easter Handicap on the first day and the Knutsford Park Handicap and the final Handicap on the second day. They will meet not only Robbie Burns, Capt. Henry McGrath's English colt who did very well in the Mother Country but also four of Jamaica's best thoroughbreds viz: By Jove, Tom Tit, Mithra and King's Messenger. These three races alone should attract thousands of turfites to Knutsford, and I predict that the attendance there on Easter Monday will beat all previous records. The fact is the public will be treated to racing such as they have never seen in Jamaica for scores of years; and the results will be so open that lucky investors are sure to get splendid dividends at the pool. Then again two American jockeys who have ridden with marked success in different parts of the United States will ride at the meeting, and it will be interesting to

SEE HOW THEY SHAPE.

against Pick, Grannum, Boddair and Hunt. It will be a case of class jockeys riding horses of class; and the public can therefore rest assured that they will see races which will be worthy of the Sport of Kings.

In days gone by it was no difficult task to find the winner of the two year old events at Knutsford Park, for the reason that there was always an outstanding two year old. To-day it is different. The youngsters in both the Knutsford Park Gold Vase and the Centurion Cup are a very classy lot and their breeding combine both speed and stamina and in both these races the racing public will be treated to fine finishes.

The purses which have been offered are on the whole, rather lucrative, but in addition two fine trophies have been added. There is the gold vase given by Mr. A. L. Keeling, the President of the Jockey Club of Jamaica and the Centurion Silver Cup, and speculation is rife as to which of the two year olds will win the trophies.

It is a little too early to comment on the prospects of the contenders in the handicap events but I will start within the next couple of days. In the meantime the thoroughbreds are undergoing steady and scientific training preparation, and it will be interesting to see how the candidates of Ramsing, Grannum and Neita—the three best trainers, in my opinion, in Jamaica—will shape at the coming Knutsford Park Easter meeting. So will a very large section of the racing public, and that is why I believe that those who know anything about horse racing will be found at Knutsford Park on Easter Monday and the Wednesday following.

BODY UNBURIED.

OLD HARBOUR, Saturday, (By Telegraph from Our Correspondent) —A man by the name of Louis March, who has been sick for a couple of months, died here on Thursday, and up to 4 o'clock this afternoon, the body had not been buried.

This causes much surprise, as it's the first case of the kind that has occurred in this community.

MASONIC

A regular meeting of the Royal Lodge, No. 207, District No. 1, will be held at the Masonic Temple, 80 Hanover Street, Kingston, on Monday, 7th April, commencing at 7:30 p.m. Visiting brethren will receive a cordial welcome.

struck a high boundary to long-off and was caught by Charles Clarence Passalique (as he was in contemporary accounts: today it is spelt Passailaigue) trying to do it again. An extraordinary catch: Passalique, who was evidently also a goalkeeper, sprinted towards the ball, flung himself on the ground and, arm outstretched, was able to seize it. As he rolled over, the crowd came on to the pitch to acclaim him.

That was 418 for 3.

Ames was soon busy, while Sandham took a couple to leg off Scott to reach 211. It gave him the highest score in the series, beating the 209 of Clifford Roach at Georgetown. Ames pulled Da Costa and they ran 3, bringing up the 450.

Roach replaced Griffith and Sandham spooned his first ball into the slips, nowhere near a hand. This was the closest he'd come to giving a chance all day. He cut a single and then someone came from the pavilion and solemnly delivered him a telegram. *The Gleaner's* reporter assumed it was to congratulate him on his 200 (and presumably could have come from England, which would explain the delay). It could hardly have been instructions from Calthorpe: what do you tell a batsman who is heading safely towards 250 in a timeless Test?

Ames was driving and pulling boundaries and quickly went to his 50 before he pulled Scott for a single to bring up the 500. Sandham was cutting and driving a path into the serious records. Immediately ahead lay Percy Holmes, the Yorkshire opener who would only play for England seven times and on the 1925–6 tour scored 244, the highest ever in Jamaica. (The matches on that tour were not regarded as Tests. The first recognised England v West Indies series was in 1928.) By an irony, Holmes had suffered just as Sandham had done, by being contemporary with Hobbs and Sutcliffe.

A single off Scott and Sandham passed Holmes.

George Headley, very much an occasional bowler, came on and Sandham 'prettily' cut him to third man for 3 and reached his 250. Ames, scoring faster and faster, drove Headley to bring up the 550 and, although he was beaten by a ball from Scott, hit a boundary on the leg side and smacked a full toss for another to make the score 563 at tea (Sandham 255, Ames 89).

After tea, Ames went safely to his century and then sent up the 600.

Sandham was now within reach of R.E. Foster's record Test innings, 287 at Sydney in 1903–4. Sandham cut Martin past point for 3 and got 4 overthrows, took a single to cover off Da Costa and then a 3 on the leg side, and that was 288. This time no telegram came but a drink was brought out instead.

Ames straight drove to bring up the 650 but Griffith, with a subtle change of pace, produced a slower ball that struck the middle and off stumps.

Jack O'Connor of Essex came in and, like Ames, bustled while Sandham cut Da Costa for a single to reach 299 and took a single in the covers from Griffith to have the 300. No Test batsman had ever been there before. The crowd thundered out their approval, while the scoreboard clicked to 673 for 4. That had become 700 for 4 at the close, Sandham 309. These days we'd have had live interviews, a press conference, photo calls but then players were rarely, if ever, quoted. Not many wrote their memoirs later on, and Sandham's feelings at reaching the triple century are in the silence of history too. We may assume with some confidence that no players kissed him, he did not kiss the ground and no high fives greeted him when he reached the pavilion; assume, also, that if he had been asked he'd have looked flustered and muttered something very modest.

Now *The Gleaner* wrote that Sandham's batting had been 'classic' and dissected its virtues, describing how his strokes were models of how they should be played, no matter whether defending or attacking, how he had favoured the cover drive and the cover boundary again on this second day as he had the first, and, although 'beautifully timed', late cuts had been threaded into the innings too. The reporter noted that Sandham lacked Hendren's repertoire and the power of Ames but what he did have was an ability to match the right stroke to every ball 'according to the just canons of batsmanship.' All this was founded upon a temperament so even that Sandham showed exactly the same confidence when he began an innings as when he started reaching milestones. In a telling judgement the reporter pointed out that tempting Sandham into indiscretion was as hard on 300 as it was when he'd made 50.

The reporter ruminated aloud again. *Will England make 1,000? Will England make more than 1,000?*

They didn't.

A large crowd, estimated at more than 10,000, came to see, however. They saw Sandham emerge looking fresh and fit and eager for a lot more, saw him work his way back into his innings – a turn to fine-leg for 3, a skied shot from Griffith for a couple into the covers, a single to cover and Headley, trying to run him out, conceding four overthrows.

Griffith began a new over and Sandham couldn't score off the first three. The fourth was Griffith's change of pace again and it was also virtually a yorker. Sandham got his bat down and managed to touch the ball but not enough to fend it off. He was out for 325, England 720 for 5. It had taken Sandham 10 hours and come off 640 deliveries, including a 7 and a 5 (the overthrows, remember, as well as 27 4s.)

England were all out for 849 and dismissed the West Indies for 286, but Calthorpe did not enforce the follow on. It proved a controversial decision, although, as Wyatt pointed out, if Calthorpe had enforced it and the weather had broken England might not have managed even a small score to win on a sticky wicket.

In the second innings, Sandham made 50 – itself unusual in that invariably a batsman making a triple century takes so long and puts his side in such a dominant position that he doesn't have a second innings. Consequently, Sandham's aggregate of 375 for the match stood as a record among the triple centurions until Graham Gooch (333,123) at Lord's in 1990.

There were two final ironies: rain fell, preventing play on the eighth and ninth days, and the England side had to catch the boat home. The match was left drawn[7] and Sandham never played in another Test match.

West Indies v England
Played at Kingston, 3, 4, 5, 7, 8, 9, 11, 12 April 1930

ENGLAND

G. Gunn	st Barrow b Martin	85	run out	47
A. Sandham	b Griffith	325	lbw b Griffith	50
R.E.S. Wyatt	c Barrow b Da Costa	58	c Passalique b Da Costa	10
E. Hendren	c Passalique b Scott	61	b Roach	55
L.E.G. Ames	b Griffith	149	c Nunes b Scott	27
J. O'Connor	c Da Costa b Scott	51	c Headley b Scott	3
F.S.G. Calthorpe	c Griffith b Scott	5	st Barrow b Scott	8
N. Haig	c Da Costa b Gladstone	32	c Passalique b Scott	34
W.E. Astill	b Scott	34	b Griffith	10
W. Rhodes	not out	8	not out	11
W. Voce	c Da Costa b Scott	20	not out	6
	Extras	21	Extras	11
		849		(9 dec) 272

	O	M	R	W		O	M	R	W
Griffith	58	6	155	2		21.1	5	52	2
Da Costa	21	0	81	1		6	2	14	1
Gladstone	42	5	139	1		8	0	50	0
Scott	80.2	13	266	5		25	0	108	4
Martin	45	6	128	1		9	1	12	0
Headley	5	0	23	0					
Roach	5	0	21	0		10	1	25	1
Passalique	2	0	15	0					

WEST INDIES

R.K. Nunes	c Ames b Voce	66	b Astill	92
C.A. Roach	lbw b Haig	15	c Gunn b Rhodes	22
G. Headley	c Haig b Voce	10	st Ames b Wyatt	223
F.R. Martin	lbw b Haig	33	c Sandham b Wyatt	24
F.I. de Caires	run out	21	b Haig	16
I. Barrow	b Astill	0		
C. Passalique	b Haig	44	not out	2
O.C. Scott	c and b Astill	8		
O. Da Costa	c Haig b Astill	39		
H.C. Griffith	c Hendren b Rhodes	7		
G. Gladstone	not out	12		
	Extras	31	Extras	29
		286		(5 wkts) 408

	O	M	R	W		O	M	R	W
Voce	22	3	81	2		29	3	94	0
Haig	30	10	73	3		26	15	49	1
Rhodes	20.5	12	17	1		24	13	22	1
Astill	33	12	73	3		46	13	108	1
Wyatt	4	0	11	0		24.3	7	58	2
O'Connor	2	2	0	0		11	3	32	0
Calthorpe						4	1	16	0

MATCH DRAWN

Notes

[1] *Three Straight Sticks,* Wyatt.

[2] According to his obituary in *Wisden* (1965 Almanac, Obituaries, page 971), Lieutenant-Colonel Ronald Thomas Stanyforth was a strong personality. On this West Indian tour he was injured after four matches 'and did not play again.' A replacement was even sent out from England. What seems to have happened in this second Jamaica match is that Stanyforth had recovered enough to have a try-out in the afternoon, replacing Ames – and presumably with no objection from the Jamaican captain. In the *Wisden* scorecard of the match, Ames appears but he does not.

[3] In the 1960s I was working on *The Journal* in Newcastle and interviewed an old Durham cricketer called Len Weight. He said that before World War Two he had been selected to play for a gentleman and players side (I can't remember who against). As he was waiting to bat in the players' dressing room a butler arrived bearing a silver plate with a folded piece of paper on it. He indicated that Weight should take the paper, which he did. He unfolded it and it read *Hit out, Weight!* And was signed by the (amateur) captain.

[4] *History of Cricket,* Altham and Swanton.

[5] *Beyond A Boundary,* James.

[6] *The Book of Cricket,* Batchelor.

[7] The 1938–9 MCC tour of South Africa shared this distinction. The Fifth Test, at Durban, was timeless but after 10 days, and with England just 42 runs short of victory, they had to leave to catch the ship home.

Australia in England, Leeds, July 1930

Donald George Bradman, born Cootamundra, New South Wales, 27 August 1908, died Adelaide, 25 February 2001.

Test career 1928–48: 52 Tests, 6,996 runs, 29 centuries, average 99.94.

It is very difficult now to recapture the full impact of Don Bradman for several reasons. The Australians came to England only every four years so there was a sense of anticipation that the jet age, spawning and enabling so many more Test playing countries to play so many more matches, has altered beyond recognition. Cricket was highly popular and county grounds were packed when the Australians played. Here was a chance to see your team try to humble the mighty and you'd have to wait another four years to see it again.

Before the era when a mass media, and particularly television, conjured celebrities effortlessly and endlessly, the famous were fewer and much more fascinating. They were also slightly mysterious because the era of intrusive journalism was decades away and lifestyle revelations all but unknown. Even on newsreel interviews, sportsmen were understandably uncomfortable and spoke in the most wooden way; and, unless you saw them in person, the newsreels were as near as you got. There was another factor: life was grim for much of Britain's working population. They were prisoners of endless terraced housing, low wages and what today would be regarded as a subsistence existence. Alcohol was one escape (in Newcastle, the celebrated Brown Ale was known as 'the journey out of Newcastle'), sport was another.

The celebrity from overseas, Australian cricketer, Hollywood star – so free of all this, and coming from such exotic, distant places – had a power of appeal out of all proportion to what he (or she) might actually be doing.

Then there was Bradman himself, neat, precise, and remorseless to a degree that had never been seen before. Decades later I spoke to an official at Headingley who had seen this innings. 'It were,' he said, 'like watching a bloody machine.' A harsh description, but it's easy to understand what he meant. In the efficiency of his stroke play, Bradman was machine-like.

The contradictions between Bradman and the idealised sporting Aussie hero have often been laid out. He was teetotal, and didn't smoke. He wasn't large and he knew how to look after himself, financially and otherwise. He was never one of the boys and, as it seems, never wanted to be. What he did do was make the Australian Test side extremely difficult to beat by the colossal amount of runs he made. In the 1930s there was a popular song written, 'he's our Don Bradman'.

Playing for Bowral as a boy, he made triple centuries, and for New South Wales he developed into an adult phenomenon. He'd come to England after making his debut in the 1928–9 series in Australia (and being dropped). He'd scored 340* for New South Wales against Victoria that season and the following season, before embarking for England, he'd scored the then highest first-class score of 452* against Queensland, also at Sydney.

There were questions about whether his technique could accommodate English conditions. These questions did not survive Bradman's first innings – 236 against Worcester – and from then on he plundered the land in a way that had never been seen before, a thousand runs in May and rippling double hundreds. Old county pros who'd seen a thing or two were flogged and flayed all over the park. There's an extraordinary insight into the mastery he felt he had already in England. During that Worcester innings he asked a bowler about one of the Leicestershire bowlers – the Australians were there next. He was already 'preparing himself mentally' for that.[1]

England won the First Test (Bradman 8 and 131), Australia the Second (Bradman 254 and 1) and they came to Leeds for the Third. In fact Bradman came from London, where he had spent a week on holiday, and joined his teammates at the Queen's Hotel where most of the England team were staying too. Herbert Sutcliffe was glimpsed driving through the city with his wife, hatless – worth a comment in those days. He looked 'bronzed and fit [...] more like a carefree holiday maker than one of England's great hopes,' wrote *The Yorkshire Post*, who clearly felt a cricketer driving a car was a news item, just as being hatless was. By the time Bradman had finished with them, none of the England team would be looking carefree.

On the eve and morning of the match, something like fever gripped Leeds.

The Australian captain, Bill Woodfull, won the toss – it was done at the edge of the pitch, with the England captain, Percy Chapman, stooping to pick up the coin and, when he saw he'd lost, smiling his cherubic smile. The Australians would bat on a chilly, windy morning with rain in the air. The ground was full and, as a backdrop, terraced houses stretched away in the trees, although this was middle-class Headingley and terracing didn't quite mean the same thing.

The England team came out in a group and moved through the dozen cameramen photographing them as they went towards the middle of the pitch. It was a favourite composition of the time and long after; a side slightly spread out and advancing. Woodfull opened with Archie Jackson, an elegant stylist who, some critics thought before the tour, would outscore Bradman.

Ominously, it was a flat wicket.

The crowd settled. Headingley resembled a bowl with uncovered stands packed by ranks and ranks of men in jackets, collars and ties. Almost all wore either hats or flat caps.

Headingley. Ah, Headingley. An Australian, Geoffrey Tebbutt, was covering the tour for the Australian Press Association and afterwards he wrote a book on it.[2] This book is unusual in that it deals with sensitive subjects, although in a careful way. He reviewed the English Test grounds and asked why Tests were played at Leeds at all. He described it as a 'desolate-looking ground' with a wicket whose durability had to be questioned. 'The uneven surface of the playing area with undulations like the waves of the sea, and the deplorable public facilities' should lead either to improvements or banishment.

In 1930, the age of supposed reserve and decorum, not many were telling it like it was.

After some eight minutes Maurice Tate, a gifted medium-pace bowler, had Jackson caught at short leg. It was, evidently, a feeble stroke.

Bradman came, wearing the famous baggy green cap, shirt sleeves rolled up to the elbows. Did he walk slowly to the wicket, giving his eyes time to adjust to the light as he so often did? No record survives. Did he absorb the field placings on that journey? He must have done. Did he feel invincible? Almost certainly.

He might have been bowled by his first ball from Tate. It pitched on middle and leg stumps and, as he groped towards it, the ball passed so close to his off-stump that Duckworth thought it must hit and almost roared out in celebration.

Then Bradman began his plunder. His footwork was as light as a tap dancer, his agility as fluid as a gymnast and his anticipation almost clairvoyant. He straight drove Tate to the boundary, clipped another to the leg side, steered another for a couple and scampered a single – 11 off the over.

We must presume that he had no premeditated strategy, and if he did he certainly, as far as I'm aware, never spoke or wrote about it. No doubt, in the time-honoured phrase, he treated each ball on its merits. The difference between him and all the others was in the definition of merit. Woodfull would move stolidly into the forward defensive position for a good length ball (he was known as 'Unbowlable'), but Bradman might have tap-danced to a different position altogether. Many years later Bill O'Reilly, one of the greatest Australian leg spinners, said publicly and plaintively that Bradman moved faster at the instant of the bowler releasing the ball than anybody else he had encountered. The game was being played in a new dimension: you bowled at him and the normal rules of line and length no longer applied. He made both into what he wanted them to be, and you were powerless to prevent him. The speed defeated you, the certainty of execution defeated you, the appetite to do it for a whole day and more wore you down – but it didn't wear him down, it fuelled his appetite.

Initially, nothing could contain him. Not Harold Larwood, who when he was fit was the fastest bowler in the world, who had been ill and could never summon his maximum pace, even with the wind behind him. Bradman drove him straight for 4 and, later, off-drove him to the boundary. At 31 George Geary, a fast-medium, replaced Larwood, but Bradman hooked a short ball for 4 and cut Tate delicately for another. Once Geary had found his length, he and Tate stemmed the flow, but when Dick Tyldesley, a rotund spinner, came on, Bradman went up the pitch and twice struck him on the full for straight boundaries.

He reached 40 out of 52 in less than even time and Woodfull, careful and patient, had the best view in the house.

Bradman went to his 50 in 49 minutes (out of 61). He was, as Pelham Warner pointed out, so fast on his feet that bowling a good length to him became almost impossible; so fast that he could position himself to hit the ball wherever he wanted.[3] There is a precious clip of film, the camera on Bradman as he waits, motionless. Duckworth, almost rotund, squats behind the stumps encased in broad pads and holding two dark leather gloves forward towards the stumps. The ball keeps a little low and Bradman stoops into it, pushes it away along the ground in a disinterested sort of way and wanders off with a look that seems to be saying 'you'll never get me out with those'.

Tebbutt records the 'tap-dancer' in action in a specific example of what he called 'Bradman's speed of foot, the activity of his mind and the resource that is repeatedly getting him out of trouble.'

He had gone up the wicket to attack Tyldesley but midway through the stroke discovered that the flight and length of the ball had deceived him. The ball was going past him, its spin curling it towards his off-stump. He hesitated fractionally. 'Then those little feet of his twinkled. Down he went on his right knee, and, stretched out like an acrobat, he deliberately tapped it back through the slips, and was off like a hare for the run!' A photographer caught this moment. Bradman had turned round completely and, that right knee acting as a pivot, was falling slowly, the bat already on the ground. The ball was three or four feet away, its trajectory taking it to the right of Hammond at slip.

Australia reached 100 after 80 minutes (Bradman 81, Woodfull 17). Briefly, Geary and Tyldesley managed to contain Bradman and he moved more slowly towards his 100. At 117 Larwood came back. Bradman clipped him for 4 past square leg and on-drove him for another to reach 102 out of 127 while he'd been in. Only Victor Trumper (Manchester, 1902) and Charles Macartney (Leeds, 1926) had scored a century before lunch. Bradman finished the session on 105 (16 fours). During this onslaught Bradman had only lifted the ball off the ground once. Woodfull was on 29.

After lunch, the England team moved in single file down the narrow alley that the spectators had left. The spectators were enjoying the magic of proximity. A single policeman stood on the lip of the pitch, supervising proceedings in a motionless, silent way. The photographers were out on the pitch again to capture the favoured image of the players coming towards them.

And Bradman emerged, capless now.

Larwood and Geary opened the bowling. In Geary's first over Bradman went on to the back foot and forced the ball to the cover boundary. That must have seemed like a warning. Bradman would hunt and harry the bowling all down a long afternoon. He took three boundaries from four Larwood overs, one a rasping off-drive. The other couple were evidently lucky, one going past Hammond's left hand at slip and the other past his right hand. These were not, however, chances. Larwood's spell lasted only four overs. He was, Hammond would remember, still visibly unwell and Hammond wasn't hearing the ball 'hiss' as Larwood delivered it.[4] Ordinarily, Larwood was as quick as that.

Australia added 45 in the first half an hour and now, with the score at 187, Hammond was bowling his medium-pace. At 194, and just after three o'clock, Hammond bowled Woodfull the Unbowlable for 50. He'd tried to play a forcing shot past mid-on but misjudged the length of the ball. Bradman was 142 and the partnership had been worth 192. If, at times, Woodfull had been as much a spectator as the crowd (albeit, as I've said, with a much better view of the slaughter) he had played the sort of innings a wise man would play, staying within his limitations and lending support.

Alan Kippax, a fabled stylist, came in and survived two appeals when he'd scored a single – an lbw appeal from Hammond, a catch behind the wicket off Larwood – and both times Duckworth raised his finger signifying *out!* The umpire did not agree. Otherwise, Duckworth was virtually unemployed because the ball hardly ever got past the bat and even Larwood couldn't get it above stump height.

During this long afternoon, Bradman played a game within a game, deliberately and regularly hitting the ball to where portly Tyldesley would have to run for it. Whether he did this simply to amuse himself or exhaust Tyldesley and thereby reduce his effectiveness as a bowler is unclear. It implies much more, however, that Bradman could take Test class bowling and not only dictate which stroke he would employ or which area he would send any particular ball but also how close to a chosen fielder.

It may be that during this same afternoon an amusing moment happened which

Bradman would remember. Tate had toured Australia in 1928–9 and had trapped Bradman lbw in the First Test and had him caught in the Fourth. Tate clearly felt that Bradman's style, using the cross-bat, would make him vulnerable on English wickets with their variable bounce. At some point Tate must have mentioned this to Duckworth because now Duckworth called to him: 'I thought you could get him out in England off that cross-bat shot, Maurice. When are you going to start?'

Bradman does not record what Tate retorted to this although he hints that Tate made noises about groundsmen preparing pitches for batsmen.

Kippax proceeded circumspectly and only reached double figures after 45 minutes. Meanwhile, Bradman moved from 150 to 200 in 40 minutes. Leyland, an occasional spinner, came on with the total at 254 but couldn't find a length. Bradman feasted: a couple of 2s, a couple of boundaries off full tosses and a single. That brought him to 199. In the next over he played an easy defensive shot. It was four o'clock. The next delivery, he adjusted his weight on to the back foot to a ball outside the off-stump and flicked it down towards third man. That was the 200. It had come out of 266 while he'd been at the wicket and taken him 3 hours 34 minutes.

A moment later he made his first genuine mistake, sending a ball from Tyldesley looping over Tate at mid-on. Tate was a heavy-footed man and *The Yorkshire Post* reporter felt that a more agile fielder might have made something of it. No matter, Bradman was not out and, as a matter of record, this was only the second ball he had lifted off the ground.

At tea he'd reached 220 (Kippax 33) out of a total of 305. The plunder since lunch had been 115 runs in 2 hours and 12 minutes.

After tea, unremitting and still eager, the appetite still being fuelled, he maintained the urgency of tempo, first moving past his own record score of 254 in the previous Test at Lord's, then advancing on Foster's 287. When he'd reached 273, however, he gave a real chance to Duckworth off Geary, who, exultant, shouted an appeal – but Duckworth didn't have the ball.

As the 400 came up Bradman was on 280. Larwood and Tate took the new ball. It may have been then, in a story from cricket folklore, that Chapman instructed Tate to 'try and keep this chap Bradman quiet' and Tate retorted 'I'll do better than that, I'll bowl the beggar out!' This tells us a great deal about Tate (John Arlott estimates that his bowling performance this day – five for 124 – was one of his greatest 'sustained spells'[5]). It must also tell us something else, that the modern idea of closing a game down scarcely existed and this was one of the reasons why Bradman was able to score so fast (Australia averaged 75 runs an hour during the day). Even he could not have sustained that if the field had been drawn back and he'd been given a comfortable single every time he faced the bowler.

To illustrate this point, Percy Fender, an arch strategist and psychologist of the game, wrote that when any batsman is nearing 200 'there is always a better chance for the opposition to get him out if they make it as difficult as possible for him to reach the mark'.[6] Fender thought it a grave error to bring Leyland, a very occasional bowler in Test cricket, on when Bradman was 186.

Fender added, and this is important for the context of Bradman's innings, 'otherwise

I thought that all that could have been done to stop the scoring was done, and though the fielders had very few chances of excelling themselves, they did save a few runs, but were *seldom so placed* [author's italics] that they had any real chance of catching the ball on its way to the boundary'.

The Test matches on the previous tour in 1926 had been of three days. Now that had been extended to four, but the whole impetus must have still been, on both sides, to go for a result rather than have draw after draw, and perhaps the spirit of the times decreed that a tactical withdrawal to a defensive field equated to moral defeat.

To put it another way, Bradman's final total of 334 would take 6 hours and 23 minutes, Brian Lara's 375 in Antigua in 1994 would take 12 hours and 46 minutes which, by another haunting historical coincidence, was exactly twice as long. In that time, Bradman would have reached 668...

That is one context, but there is another. That evening in 1930 at Headingley, the crowd, sensing that Foster's record would be broken any moment now, fell silent. Perhaps they were simply lost in awe. West Indies were not then regarded as a front-line Test playing country and consequently Sandham's record wasn't quite a 'real' one. Foster's certainly was and, set in the golden age of cricket before World War One, it had stood for a couple of generations. In the starkest terms, Foster set the record five years before Bradman was born and, between that Sydney day in 1903 and now, there had been 10 series between England and Australia. Only three men had reached 200 (Jack Ryder of Australia, 201* at Adelaide in 1925, Hammond 251 at Sydney and 200 at Melbourne on the 1928–9 tour, Bradman's 254 at Lord's.) The spectator had not been satiated by orgies of run-getting. Individual hundreds were very noteworthy achievements and double hundreds a source of wonder as well as examples of extreme rarity. The neat young man without a cap wasn't going to break one record among many but move decisively past *the* record and whatever he finished on might stand for many generations.

To recapture what this meant to ordinary folk – the ones in the flat caps coming, no doubt, from the sharp-edged industrial towns of Yorkshire – who were there to witness it is as elusive as recapturing the full impact of Bradman.

He on-drove Tate to the boundary to draw level with Foster and quickly milked a single to leg to beat him. The ground erupted. The cheering echoed and echoed. Bradman, bat aloft, saluted all sections of the ground and all sections saluted him back.

Bradman had got there an hour and 45 minutes quicker than Foster...

That was six o'clock. Ten minutes later Kippax went, caught by Chapman at backward point. Kippax and Bradman had added 229 for this third wicket in 2 hours and 43 minutes (Bradman 151 of them). The stand was an Australian record. Stan McCabe, two years younger than Bradman, came in. Soon after, Bradman moved to 300 with a single. Some time after that, according to Vic Richardson[7] – due in next – McCabe complained to Bradman that if they kept running short singles he'd be completely exhausted. Bradman, of course, had been in all day and running short singles all day too. He finished the day by driving Tate to the offside boundary.

He was 309 not out.

He had shattered all manner of records and he had devastated the English team's bowling. He'd remember some statistician working out that the England bowling tactic had been changed 25 times during the day. Chapman must have felt he had to approach the task by constant rotation so that somewhere, sometime, somehow one of the bowlers would get lucky. They didn't.

Bradman had shown the crowd what the future would look like. As someone said, other cricketers had inhibitions Bradman never knew. As he came from the field that evening he looked impossibly fresh and anything seemed possible. A monumental performance had occurred and cricket would have to adjust to accommodate it. Pelham Warner reflected that when he wrote plaintively that 'we must, if possible, evolve a new type of bowler and develop fresh ideas on strategy and tactics to curb his almost uncanny skill'.[8]

Tebbutt noted that Bradman had excited so much enthusiasm that, as he was coming off, the police came on to protect him from an exuberant invasion. Tebbutt also noted that as Bradman neared the pavilion he looked as fresh as when he'd gone forth that morning to start the whole thing.

Somewhere in the crowd a 14-year-old Yorkshire lad was watching intently. He was called Leonard Hutton.

When Bradman reached the dressing room he said to Woodfull: 'That wasn't a bad bit of practice. I'll be able to have a go at them tomorrow.'[9]

He wasn't boasting and he certainly wasn't being ironic. He was telling the truth as he saw it.

Next day the ground was full again long before the start of play. As Bradman prepared to leave the dressing room to resume his innings, he was handed a telegram which said *YOUR HOME ON FIRE, YOUR GIRL WANTS YOU*.[10] It was unsigned and, assuming the incident happened as Bradman later recounted it, a disgraceful attempt to distract him. He did not allow it to.

The crowd gave him a roar of approval when he appeared. The crowd hemmed him, slapping him on the back as he passed down the narrow alley towards the pitch. McCabe got only a slap or two. The policemen fore and aft of these two batsmen could do nothing except steer them out on to the pitch.

A sunny day at last. Bradman would soon note that the wicket was much faster now, Larwood and Tate quite different bowlers. Larwood opened the bowling and McCabe set about him while Bradman continued. At one moment he glanced Tate effortlessly square of the wicket for what looked a safe 2 but he – and McCabe – were so nimble that they ran 3, and with no danger of a run out.

Of all the triple centuries we shall meet in this book, you could argue that some batsmen clawed their way up the mountain to the magical summit; others burrowed – and bored – their way there; yet others found those conjunctions of circumstances, which were suddenly, and uniquely, favourable for it. Only three, perhaps, seemed genuinely to have no limitations on what they could do, as if human constrictions did not apply: Bradman, Garfield Sobers and Brian Lara. It is no coincidence that Bradman and Lara are, as we have seen, the only men to do it twice, while Sobers was quite capable of opening the bowling and then plying spin afterwards as well as scoring a triple century.

The rest of the triple centurions were very, very good – but mortals.

At 486, Larwood bowled McCabe leg stump (Bradman thought the delivery unplayable) and five runs later caught Richardson off Tate. Bradman finally went, caught at the wicket for 334, the total 508 for 6. As he turned away, 'there was one long roar, men and women standing up and waving hats and umbrellas and handkerchiefs'.[11]

In blunt (almost brutal) statistics he had been at the wicket for 6 hours and 23 minutes, and hit 46 boundaries all round the wicket. The distribution of them was so broad that no field could have been realistically set to contain him.

The man himself felt the 254 at Lord's had been a better innings and, even accepting that he'd put the 334 together at a faster rate *and* got that 100 before lunch, he was fully aware that there had been imperfections in some of his strokes.[12] This is the kind of thing people say because no man likes to claim he has achieved perfection (and surely none ever has), but if you were operating at Bradman's level you judged yourself by the standards of perfection and measured how close you got to it. Not many human beings do that.

Another aspect that must be discussed is Bradman's relationship with the team. An Australian businessman sent him a £1,000 cheque (a big sum) as a token of admiration. Bradman quietly accepted it after Woodfull assured him it was not a joke but, even unconsciously, it made the gap between him and the rest of the team wider, which implied that a gap existed already. He was a man apart and not, they felt, one of them. Tebbutt claimed that he spent the evening of the 334 in his hotel room alone listening to gramophone records. The team thought he might buy them dinner out of the £1,000 but he declined.

They were inescapably trapped in an inter dependence which would last for a further 18 years. Bradman needed them because cricket is a team game, but they needed him because he made Australia – and them – exceedingly difficult to defeat.

The Test, incidentally, was washed out by rain.

Notes

[1]   *Bradman and the Bodyline Series*, Docker.

[2]   *With the 1930 Australians*, Tebbutt.

[3]   *The Fight for the Ashes in 1930*, Warner.

[4]   *Cricket my Destiny*, Hammond.

[5]   *Cricketing Lives: Maurice Tate*, Arlott.

[6]   *The Tests of 1930*, Fender.

[7]   *The Vic Richardson Story*, Richardson.

[8]   Warner, op. cit.

[9]   Richardson, op. cit.

[10]   *My Cricketing Life*, Bradman. In those days, telegrams were routinely delivered straight to the person they were addressed to with, presumably, no filtering process by team management along the way. So any cricket lover who marked a telegram Don Bradman, and gave the location where he was, would be sure it would go to him. I don't want to make too much of this, and I don't want to be misty-eyed, but in general Britain was a polite place where people did *not* even think of sending telegrams like that, never mind actually sending them.

[11]   Warner op. cit. And before we leave it there, I once mentioned to Alf Greenley, cricket correspondent of *The Journal* in Newcastle, that I'd just met someone who'd seen the innings. Leeds was the nearest Test ground to the north-east of England and the Test match there every year something of a pilgrimage. 'Ah, yes,' Greenley said in his own imcomparable way. 'The number of people who saw it gets bigger every year...'

[12]   *Farewell to Cricket*, Bradman.

England v Australia
Played at Leeds, 11, 12, 14, 15 July 1930

AUSTRALIA

W.M. Woodfull	b Hammond	50
A. Jackson	c Larwood b Tate	1
D.G. Bradman	c Duckworth b Tate	334
A.F. Kippax	c Chapman b Tate	77
S. McCabe	b Larwood	30
V.Y. Richardson	c Larwood b Tate	1
E.L. à Beckett	c Chapman b Geary	29
W.A. Oldfield	c Hobbs b Tate	2
C.V. Grimmett	c Duckworth b Tyldesley	24
T.W. Wall	b Tyldesley	3
P.M. Hornibrook	not out	1
	b 5, l-b 8, w 1	14
		566

	O	M	R	W
Larwood	33	3	139	1
Tate	39	9	124	5
Geary	35	10	95	1
Tyldesley	33	5	104	2
Hammond	17	3	46	1
Leyland	11	0	44	0

ENGLAND

J.B. Hobbs	c à Beckett b Grimmett	29	run out		13
H. Sutcliffe	c Hornibrook b Grimmett	32	not out		28
W.R. Hammond	c Oldfield b McCabe	113	c Oldfield b Grimmett		35
K.S. Duleepsinhji	b Hornibrook	35	c Grimmett b Hornibrook		10
M. Leyland	c Kippax b Wall	44	not out		1
G. Geary	run out	0			
G. Duckworth	c Oldfield b à Beckett	33			
A.P.F. Chapman	b Grimmett	45			
M.W. Tate	c Jackson b Grimmett	22			
H. Larwood	not out	10			
R. Tyldesley	c Hornibrook b Grimmett	6			
	b 9, l-b 10, n-b 3	22	l-b		8
		391	(3 wkts)		95

	O	M	R	W		O	M	R	W
Wall	40	12	70	1		10	3	20	0
à Beckett	28	8	47	1		11	4	19	0
Grimmett	56.2	16	135	5		17	3	33	1
Hornibrook	41	7	94	1		11.5	5	14	1
McCabe	10	4	23	1		2	1	1	0

MATCH DRAWN

New record. The old record had stood for 4 months.

England in New Zealand, Auckland, March 1933

Walter Reginald Hammond, born Dover, Kent, 19 June 1903, died Durban, 2 July 1965.

Test career 1927–8 to 1946–7: 85 Tests, 7,249 runs, 22 centuries, average 58.45.

A cricket tour meant a cricket tour, not a flying visit. The MCC party left St Pancras Station, London, on 17 September 1932 and returned the following April via the Pacific and North America. In between they played 25 matches, lost one and recovered the Ashes, but at a fearful cost. This was the 'Bodyline' tour, which has spawned – and continues to spawn – a literature of its own.

After the five Tests in Australia the team sailed on to New Zealand in what *Wisden* (1934 Almanac page 630) described as a 'valuable missionary move'. A side had been before, in 1929–30, that same winter that the MCC sent a side to the West Indies and Sandham made his 325. Two tours meant, by definition, that neither side was the strongest, something compounded by the fact that several senior players didn't go on either, as we have seen.

This time, New Zealand was going to get the full effect.

The First Test at Christchurch was drawn after a dust storm struck, although there had been time for Hammond to score 227.

Hammond made writers of the time reach for vivid adjectives because he batted imperiously. One of those writers said he didn't drive the ball, he dismissed it from his presence. A strong, almost stocky man, he played clean, decisive and very powerful strokes. On his day, he butchered good bowling and across a couple of decades scored more than 30,000 runs for Gloucestershire (and took more than 700 wickets in his career, as well as being a superb slip fielder). There is a revealing Neville Cardus anecdote. He remembered Hammond scoring another century, coming in and saying without any sense of bravado 'it's just too easy'. He was, rather, stating a fact.

Of him, Pelham Warner said: 'Everything he does is graceful, with a tremendous sense of power. There is majesty about his batting, he makes the most difficult catches look easy, and his bowling action is perfect in rhythm, swing and delivery.'

The Auckland Star ran a column on how to identify the England players ('Mannerisms and Distinguishing Features'). They said about him that he was 'massive and blunt' and certainly didn't waste words. 'To pick out Walter Hammond you must glance at his right trouser pocket. Several inches of a handkerchief of dark blue silk constantly flutter there whether he is batting or fielding. He never pushes that handkerchief into his pocket. Why? He does not know himself.' Fielders, especially in the covers, did not need handkerchiefs to pick Hammond out. He'd send drives that would make their hands tingle and sting, if they got near the ball.

The Second Test in New Zealand started five days after the First. New Zealand won the toss and batted but Bill Bowes, doughty Yorkshire opening bowler, struck twice in his first over and the innings never recovered. Charles Dempster (but always known as C.S.) made a gallant 83 but it was all over shortly before three o'clock in the afternoon.

This was in the nature of a scene-setter, no matter that Hammond wrote that it was the best innings he had seen Dempster play.[1] Hammond admired how Dempster hadn't scored his runs passively but had gone out to get them and done so all over the pitch. The innings, Hammond concluded, would have been a credit to anyone, anytime.

England opened with Sutcliffe and Wyatt, who put on 56 before Sutcliffe was caught at cover. Hammond strode to the wicket, as he habitually did: a 'man 'o war with all sails unfurled'. He'd say that the ball looked big to him immediately, and would grow even bigger. It was one of those days when, wherever he looked, Hammond could see gaps in the field, although he was careful not to blame the fielders and paid a compliment to their 'dogged endurance'.

Douglas Freeman, a leg spinner, was then an 18-year-old schoolboy (although 6ft 3in) and he would remember that as he bowled to Hammond he noticed Wyatt was leaving his crease to back up very early indeed.[2] Wyatt, incidentally, was captaining England.

Freeman said 'excuse me, Mr. Wyatt, but are you leaving your crease before I have bowled?'

Wyatt evidently apologised but continued to do it. For many years afterwards, Freeman wondered what would have happened if he'd whipped the bails off with Wyatt out of his ground. He gauged that there would have been a hell of an outcry. (Wyatt makes no mention of this in his autobiography, *Three Straight Sticks.*)

Hammond, *The Auckland Star* reported, 'gave the impression of restraint, which he relaxed only at intervals for a square cut, pull or leg glance to the boundary'. At 5.12pm, when he had made 41 (in 56 minutes), he appealed against the light because the setting sun was shining full into the batsmen's eyes from the scoreboard end. Wyatt was 56 (in 112 minutes) and England 127 for one. The spectators were disappointed because they'd anticipated some lively run-getting from these giants of the game when they'd settled after the first half an hour.

If the spectators went on the second day they were not, let us say, to be disappointed.

This was a good wicket and an easy New Zealand attack. Freeman had to complete his over when play resumed. Hammond off-drove him to the boundary and 7 came off the over. Clearly, it established the tone and tempo.

Frederick Badcock, medium-pace, beat Hammond in his second over with a ball which also went over the wicket. John Dunning, off-breaks, then bowled Wyatt, who offered no shot. The ball hit the off stump and England were 139. Eddie Paynter, the Lancashire left-hander, joined Hammond and glanced Dunning for 3. Hammond went to his 50 in 76 minutes with a square cut for 2 off Dunning.

Paynter was not overshadowed (well, maybe) and for a time Badcock managed to keep Hammond under some sort of control: 12 overs for only 14 runs. The two batsmen were taking singles where they could until Hammond worked Freeman to leg for a couple to make the total 199 an hour into the day's play.

Dunning took the new ball and Hammond responded by driving him for 4. Soon after, the crowd began barracking because they felt the batsmen were being too cautious. Hammond responded to that by glancing Badcock for a couple from successive balls to move from 97 to 101. It had taken him 134 minutes.

Barracking? Hammond cut loose. He straight drove Dunning for 6, and Gordon 'Dad' Weir – New Zealand's number three batsman – came on to bowl medium-pace. Hammond square cut him to the boundary and on-drove him next over for another before he was almost bowled by a rank shooter. Hammond was putting his power into the strokes now and a cover drive off Dunning sang its way to the boundary. The partnership added 100 in 75 minutes (Hammond now 124, Paynter 27) and, when Hammond late cut Newman, England were up to 250. It had taken 210 minutes.

Barracking? There are no reports of any now.

At 134 Hammond gave his only real chance but it proved too difficult for Dempster to take. The ball was struck so hard that not only did Dempster badly hurt his hand trying to catch it, but it thundered through for 6.

The New Zealand captain, Milford 'Curly' Page, came on for the last over before lunch and Hammond hammered him to leg for 4; and that was his 150, in 2 hours and 52 minutes.

The ground had 5,000 people in it by the time play resumed after lunch – presumably word of Hammond's innings had spread into the town – and while he took a couple of singles Paynter played on to Dunning: 288 for 3.

Paynter would remember that, after the Christchurch Test when England made 560 for 8 declared, 'we again proceeded to pulverise the New Zealand bowlers. The 'we' includes every MCC batsman who went to the wicket, with the reservation that play was being strictly dictated from one end only, by Wally Hammond. For example, during my stand of 190 runs with him, my contribution was 36 runs, such was the power of his play.'[3]

Leslie Ames came in.

The 350 came up at 2.45pm, with Hammond on 190. He got to his 200 after 4 hours and 1 minute, and he cut completely loose. He went from that 200 to 250 in 27 minutes – but this was not slogging, not at all. *Wisden* (1934 Almanac) reported that Hammond placed his strokes 'with astonishing accuracy' regardless of where the fielders were placed.

He went from 250 to 300 in 20 minutes, including three successive drives for 6 off Newman, although just before the triple century he hit one ball with such ferocity that he broke his bat. With something approaching understatement, Hammond would remember that 'it is a little difficult to start with a new bat when a record is being approached'.[4]

The 300 had taken 4 hours and 48 minutes.

The new bat soon felt as comfortable as the old one had done.

Hammond would claim to have suffered 'stage fright' as he moved through 320 to 325 and 330. That brought him to the very edge of Bradman's record and he drew level: 334. 'No use hesitating at that stage – and off the very next ball I yelled 'Yes!' and we sneaked a wickedly swift single.'[5]

Badcock, whom Hammond praised for keeping his head while all about him were losing theirs, then bowled a ball which struck Hammond's new bat on the splice and he was caught at mid-off – but it was a no-ball. Hammond says he 'mopped his brow' because the excitement was getting too much for him. Hmmm…

He took another single which, psychologically, somehow made the new record safe for him.

He felt tired.

He had hit 10 6s and 34 4s – 196 in boundaries alone.

The Auckland Star noted that Hammond's playing of his famous cover-drive was 'superb, with a perfect combination of the three essentials, correct footwork, body swing and timing'. The newspaper also pointed out that England prolonged their innings to let him get past Bradman's 334. 'Such is the insatiable search for records with a cheerful disregard for the calibre of an opposing side' – meaning, I assume, that Wyatt, captaining England, felt he could give Hammond all the time he needed and still bowl New Zealand out again. It was a three-day Test, remember.

Wyatt declared with the total 548 for 7.

Hammond's 336 not out had lasted a mere 5 hours and 18 minutes: Bradman had taken 6 hours and 23 minutes, but that was of course against a strong England attack and not the same thing at all. *The Auckland Star* was candid in reporting that clearly and visibly the New Zealand attack hadn't been strong enough and 'sadly' lacked variety. The paper concluded that New Zealand was 'rather weak' at the moment and it was all very well bowling *faiue* which was 'plain up and down.' This might or might not get batsmen out, but when you were confronted with a Sutcliffe or a Hammond something more subtle was required.

That was the true context of the innings and as a consequence it was regarded as being of secondary importance to what Bradman had done, although in numerical terms it was the new record.

There's a stark illustration of this. Hammond's record would endure until 1938 when Hutton advanced slowly and remorselessly on it at The Oval. At the close of play on the third day of that Oval Test he'd made 300. He would write (in *Cricket is my Life*): 'It was then that I listened to my teammates, my friends and the newspaper men who had been reminding me of the chance that was being offered me of beating Don Bradman's record score of 334. I needed only 35 to reach the highest ever compiled in a Test match anywhere.'

THE AUCKLAND STAR, SATURDAY, APRIL 1, 1933.

Clearly, Hutton did not know that Hammond had the record score, and he needed 37 to beat it. Forgive him. Sportspeople are often careless about the statistics of the past but it's something more subtle even than that. Until 1950, when West Indies came, saw and conquered England, there were only three main Test playing countries, England, Australia and South Africa. What they did mattered. What they did against the others was... well, missionary work. The fact remains, however, that Hammond held the record, not Bradman, and the record was established by who had made the most runs, not how or against whom. Records are very simple things, you either break them or you don't.

The Second Test at Christchurch was washed into a draw, although Hammond recovered from his tiredness to open the bowling in the New Zealand second innings and, as it seems, tried leg theory. Since he bowled at a pleasant medium pace, nobody died of fright or anything else.

His aggregate for the two Tests was 563 for once out, giving him an average, of course, of 563. That, too, fell into the context of the same missionary work.

There was, truth be told, a rivalry between Hammond and Bradman in the sense that England needed someone of similar stature and appetite. Hammond demonstrated he had that in the 1928–9 tour of Australia when he'd made 251 at Sydney, 200 at Melbourne, 177 at Adelaide for an aggregate of 905 runs at an average of 113. The aggregate was a series record and the average was the first beyond 100. These were not just unprecedented figures but genuinely monumental in their time, a source of wonder as well as admiration. This was also Hammond's debut against Australia.

Who could honestly say that Boy Bradman, who had made a promising debut himself (468 runs, average 66, although as we've seen he'd been dropped after the First Test) would brush aside everything Hammond had done except the 336?

It is true: Bodyline in 1932–3 wrenched Bradman back to more normal human proportions, if you can put it like that, but he remained the object of fascination and unlimited possibilities. If Hammond fell slightly short of that so has every other batsman there has ever been.

Anyway, after the Bodyline Hammond was thoroughly happy in New Zealand. While he was there he enjoyed some swordfishing and would take some trouble to describe how terrifying swordfish were, impaling their victims with precision and ferocity.

The bowlers would have understood.

Notes

[1]   *Cricket My Destiny,* Hammond.

[2]   *Wisden* 1995 Almanac, obituaries page 1384.

[3]   *Cricket all the Way,* Paynter.

[4]   Hammond, op. cit.

[5]   Ibid.

New Zealand v England
Played at Auckland, 31 March, 1,2 3, April 1933

NEW ZEALAND

J.E. Mills	b Bowes	0	not out	11
D. Whitelaw	b Bowes	12	not out	5
G.L.Weir	b Bowes	0		
C.S. Dempster	not out	83		
J.L. Kerr	lbw b Voce	10		
M.L. Page	st Duckworth b Mitchell	20		
F.T. Badcock	b Bowes	1		
K.C. James	b Bowes	0		
J.A. Dunning	b Bowes	12		
J. Newman	b Voce	5		
D.L. Freemand	run out	1		
	b 9, l-b 4, n-b 1	14		
		158	(0 wkts)	16

	O	M	R	W		O	M	R	W
Allen	5	2	11	0		3	1	4	0
Bowes	19	5	34	6		2	0	4	0
Mitchell	18	1	49	1					
Voce	9.5	3	20	2		1.3	0	2	0
Brown	2	0	19	0					
Hammond	3	0	11	0		2	0	6	0

ENGLAND

H. Sutcliffe	c Weir b Freeman	24
R.E.S. Wyatt	b Dunning	60
W.R. Hammond	not out	336
E. Paynter	b Dunning	36
L.E.G. Ames	b Badcock	26
G.O. Allen	b Badcock	12
F.R. Brown	c Page b Weir	13
W. Voce	b Weir	16
G. Duckworth	not out	6
	b 7, l-b 6, w 1, n-b 5	19
	(7 dec)	548

Did not bat: W.E. Bowes, T.B. Mitchell.

	O	M	R	W
Badcock	59	16	126	2
Dunning	43	5	156	2
Freeman	20	1	91	1
Newman	17	2	87	0
Page	6	2	30	0
Weir	11	2	39	2

MATCH DRAWN

New world record by 2 runs. The old record had stood for 2 years 8 months.

Australia in England, Leeds, July 1934

Donald George Bradman
He became the first batsman in Test match history to score
two triple centuries – and he did it on the same ground. By
an historical freak Brian Lara, the only other batsman to
score two triple centuries (then continuing to a quadruple),
also did it on the same ground, Antigua.

Giants strode the land then, and not just Bradman. There was Bill Ponsford, the only man to score 400 in an innings twice: 437 for Victoria against Queensland in 1927–8 and 429 against Tasmania in 1922–3. He had the appetite of Bradman. There was the rock-like Woodfull, still called Unbowlable. There was nimble little McCabe, a batsman who could flay Test attacks. There was the wily leg-break bowler Clarrie Grimmett, the fiery leg-break bowler Bill O'Reilly and the neat, unobtrusive wicketkeeper Bert Oldfield. The British public had waited four long years to see the Australians again.

The context of the 1934 tour is an important one because it was the first series after the 1932–3 Bodyline tour and in a sense a time of healing, although the prime movers in the Bodyline controversy, captain Douglas Jardine and pace bowler Larwood, wouldn't play Test cricket again. (Jardine had played three times against the 1933 Indian tourists; Larwood not at all).

Bradman had been held to a Test average of 56 but now in England he resumed as if Bodyline had been a mere interruption: 206 immediately at Worcester, 65 at Leicester but then he lost form and it wasn't until the eighth match, Middlesex, that he found it again with 160. He made 29 and 25 in the First Test at Nottingham, which Australia won by 238 runs. Hedley Verity, deadly Yorkshire left-arm spin bowler on helpful wickets, caught the Australians on a wet one at Lord's, catching and bowling Bradman for 36 and having him caught behind for 13 as England won by an innings. Manchester was drawn (Bradman 30).

It brought him back to Leeds.

He does not seem to have been a superstitious man and that was as well. He'd remember that the Australians had a hotel at Harrogate and a fleet of Rolls-Royces to ferry them to and from Headingley, a pleasant drive away. They were about to set off for the Test when a woman supporter 'rushed up to the car in which I was, and as she attemped to give me a handful of 'lucky wishbones' the car moved off. It was only the extreme presence of mind of the driver that saved us from having to take her 'ashes' back to Australia'.[1]

England won the toss, batted and were all out for 200. Bowes, however, readjusted the balance of the match by taking three wickets before the close. Bowes was quick.[2] Ponsford was not out.

Next day, the sun shining, the large crowd cheered when the England team appeared. Ponsford came out with Bradman – some judges, like Jack Hobbs, thought it might have been better to send out McCabe, in prime form, with Ponsford.

Bradman felt, and thought Ponsford felt, a tangible sense of expectancy from the crowd, who were hungry for wickets. Bradman and Ponsford would resist that, of course. A journalist friend had already told Bradman that if he dared risk hitting a four in the first quarter of an hour he'd put him across his knee and give him a good smacking.

Bowes still had two balls of his over to finish, Bradman on strike. Bradman would remember the crowd fell absolutely silent as he took guard. The first ball was straight, fractionally short, and Bradman, already on the back foot, pulled it back past the bowler for 4. The second ball was also short and Bradman, again already on the back foot, pulled wide of mid-on for 4. Who would dare put him across their knee and smack him for that? Nobody anywhere.

J.M. Kilburn, an experienced and shrewd judge, wrote in *The Yorkshire Post* that from these two strokes alone you could construct an authentic 'impression of the man and his mood'. Neither stroke had carried any risk and, although he had had no time to guage the pace of the wicket or play himself in, both had been exquisitely timed. In fact, Kilburn added, if the distance to the boundary had been doubled that would have made no difference.

Kilburn elaborated. He felt that the notion of Bowes being a good bowler (which he certainly was) did not enter Bradman's thinking and this was proved because, in the following over, Bradman cut him to the boundary past point and took a couple on the leg side just as he liked, but, even more revealingly, Bowes managed to bowl a maiden at Bradman and, even more than that, actually made Bradman play at a couple that did not hit the middle of his bat. Nobody, Kilburn concluded, had any expectation that Bradman would be out for them or, for the forseeable future, anything else.

T.B. Mitchell of Derbyshire had opened the bowling at the other end but was soon replaced by Verity, whose absolute control of length produced seven successive maidens.

Bowes ventured a bouncer or two at Ponsford.

At 12.15pm Australia reached 100 when Ponsford made a delicate leg-glide off Verity, although Verity had troubled Ponsford a time or two. Bowes bowled one superb over, which had Bradman struggling to find his timing: two balls struck the under edge of his bat. Bowes bounced him too. One didn't rise as much as Bradman had anticipated and he hooked high over it, the ball just missing the top of the stumps. Another bouncer, however, Bradman did hook to the boundary.

At 118, Mitchell replaced Hammond and Hopwood of Lancashire (slow left-arm) replaced Verity. Bradman pulled Hopwood's first ball for 4, placed the next for a single and had his 50 in a minute longer than an hour and a half. Ponsford had taken just over two hours. The 100 partnership came shortly before one o'clock. Mitchell bowled a ball outside the leg stump and Bradman swept it to the boundary.

Bowes came back as lunch approached and bounced Ponsford and Bradman again. Ponsford retreated to get out of the way, Bradman retreated to try and hit the ball. It was what he'd done in the Bodyline series.

Bradman hooked one towards Hopwood at deep square leg so hard that you could barely see the ball, never mind follow its trajectory, but you could hear it whack against Hopwood's hapless hand on its way to the boundary. Opinion was divided as to whether this was anything but a technical chance. The ball had been struck as ferociously as that.

At lunch Australia had reached 168 for 3 (Ponsford 72, Bradman 76). The gates were closed shortly after, with 38,000 inside.

It was a long afternoon. Hobbs, up there in the Press Box near Kilburn, noted that 'there was something utterly inevitable about this wonderful stand by Ponsford and Bradman. Under its irksome spell the crowd became restive, chattered, fiddled about and showed a noticeable urge to go away'.[3] We may question that because when Bradman was at flood tide, and you could only savour it every four years, what you didn't do was go away. You didn't miss a ball.

Bradman marginally outscored Ponsford as the afternoon developed. The 200 was

THE YORKSHIRE POST, MONDAY, JULY 23, 1934 — 9

DEX AND SUMMARY

15, 16, 17, 18

HOME

sford and Bradman occupied
t all the time available in the
d day of the fourth Test at
ngley with a partnership yield-
88, and so established a new
for Test cricket by beating the
t together by Hobbs and Rhodes
bourne in February, 1912. Page 9

red Rhodes pays tribute to
an's great display of batsman
n the Fourth Test Match. Page 9

ralian Test tourists visited
oo House yesterday. Page 10

youths who had been canoeing
don, and bathers at Bridlington
oncaster, were drowned during
ek-end. Page 9

g a thunderstorm a man was
by lightning on the beach at
n. Page 9

persons were slightly injured
passenger train collided with
fers at Scarborough station. Page 9

Stanley Baldwin referred in a
on Saturday to the statement
e in Parliament regarding the
of the Air Force. Page 7

Government had no war-
ing intention, and no one
Britain would dream of saying
declared Lord Hailsham,
at St. Helens. Page 7

British Medical Association, in
nce at Bournemouth, rejected
uncil's recommendation that
ion should be given to
d chiropodists. Page 3

BRADMAN'S PEERLESS DISPLAY

RECORD TEST STAND WITH PONSFORD YIELDS 388

ENGLAND FACING DEFEAT

VERITY GETS THE ONLY WICKET

Test history was made by Ponsford and Bradman at Headingley on Saturday with a record partnership of 388, beating the 323 put together by Hobbs and Rhodes at Melbourne in February, 1912.

BRADMAN'S score of 271 not out was gained by a consummate display of batsmanship in which every stroke in the game was exploited.

England have so far been outplayed in all departments of the game in this fourth match of the series, and defeat seems almost inevitable.

The gates were closed at Headingley soon after one o'clock, when the ground held a record crowd of 38,000.

Fair weather is forecast for to-day, with an average temperature and a moderate north-west wind.

Wilfred Rhodes, who gives his impressions of the game in an adjoining column, declares the wicket is still in first-rate condition, with hundreds of runs in it.

RECORD-BREAKING DAY

By J. M. KILBURN, Our Cricket Representative

HEADINGLEY, Saturday

AT 11 o'clock this morning a man walked from the pavilion at Headingley: a man clad in flannels and with a green cap pulled down to shade his bright eyes. He carried with him a beautiful white bat and the only trace of aggression about him was the spring in his step. Yet that bat was a terrible weapon which dealt destruction all round it, and at 6.30 this evening Don Bradman ran for shelter, close-guarded by policemen; the long day's battle was over and he stood undefeated, the champion of champions.

Through the hours he stood defiant, with his enemies helpless around him, and in the course of the day he killed England's hopes of victory and spread destruction in the ranks of her bowlers. The story of Saturday is the story of Bradman, and that is doing no injustice to Ponsford, for who could refuse to bat well and stay there with Bradman as partner?

As the minutes went by and the boundaries flowed faster, record after record came rocking and tumbling and ream upon ream of statistics must be altered, but for those who were watching there was—Bradman. From the moment of his entry to the last stroke he made he was dominant, confident, utterly supreme.

...helped the googly to the square leg boundary, and with Bradman sweeping him away Mitchell must have pondered deeply on the difference between turf at Chesterfield and Leeds. Poor Mitchell; he is so eager to bowl, almost running back to his mark, and his fingers caress the ball oh, so lovingly, that had Bradman had any heart at all he must surely have made just one or two mis-hits for encouragement.

Bowes fielded so well this morning that the semi-humorous clapping which usually greets his efforts gave way to genuinely appreciative applause.

There is really no reason why it should ever be otherwise, for there is little justification for believing that Bowes is at his worst in the field. Anyway, he picked up smartly and saved more than one boundary when Bradman played the ball to mid-on.

This little paragraph on Bowes merely denotes (as they say of the lowering of the curtain in the theatre) the passing of time, and by now both batsmen were in the sixties and the score had passed the 150 mark.

Missed Chances?

All signs of a possible separation had vanished, and even two missed chances never gave a thrill of expectancy. I use missed chances more or less as a technical term, for had either been held we should have witnessed something approaching a miracle, and the batsmen would have been justified in bewailing their fate.

Bradman hooked a short ball from Bowes so hard to deep square leg that the eye

RHODES ON THE TEST

TRIBUTE TO BRADMAN

"Best Scoring Batsman I Have Seen"

ALL THE SHOTS

Headingley Wicket Still First-Rate

By WILFRED RHODES

HEADINGLEY, Saturday

THE scoring machine—that is Bradman—got to work again to-day and our bowlers had to pay tribute, as we all knew they would have to do, as soon as Bradman decided that the time had come for him to move seriously along the run-getting road.

He never hurried—never dashed, as cricketers say—yet at the end of a day on which he was at the wicket for five minutes less than six and a half hours he had 271 runs to his name. He scored over a hundred runs in the last hundred minutes, and just as there was no indication of quick-scoring in his general outlook, so, when he left the field, there was no suggestion that he was tired after the strain of standing at the wicket for so long.

Frankly, I do not know which is the most remarkable feature about this very remarkable young man, who is, all the way round, the best scoring batsman I have seen.

He has all the shots; he can apparently use them at will: he has wonderful strength in his wrists and forearms, and his timing is so perfect that one knows the quickest of eyesight is allied with lightning footwork and an astonishing judgment of the length of a ball; and, with all this, he has the confidence he has a right to have in his power, and a determination that enables him to do almost as he pleases.

I have heard a story that when he was playing his record Australia v. England Test innings at Headingley on the last tour—a record that he may easily beat on Monday morning—he was asked at lunch-time how he felt. His reply was characteristic: "Good for the day."

NEW TEST RECORDS

In their stand on Saturday Bradman and Ponsford broke the following Test Match Records:—

Partnership for any wicket. Previous figure was 323, set up for the first wicket by Hobbs and Rhodes at Melbourne, 1911-12 tour.

Fourth-wicket stand of 243 put up by Bradman and the late Archie Jackson at the Oval in 1930.

This was Bradman's eighth Test century. Only Hobbs, with 12, and Sutcliffe 8, have made as many hundreds in Tests between England and Australia.

FRENCH PARTY CRISIS

HOPE OF SAVING THE CABINET

TWO MINISTERS MAY RESIGN

PREMIER COMING TO PARIS

PARIS, Sunday

THERE appear to be brighter hopes for the solution of the Cabinet crisis following the visit of Senator Cheron, the Vice-Premier and Minister of Justice, to M. Doumergue, the Premier, at Tournefeuille yesterday.

M. Cheron said after his visit that M. Doumergue will preside at the Cabinet meeting in Paris on Tuesday. It is generally hoped now that the Prime Minister will be able to heal the breach between the two Ministers without Portfolio and former Premiers, MM. Tardieu and Herriot, and to avert the dissolution of Parliament.

The trouble arose over M. Tardieu accusing M. Chautemps, a member of the Radical-Socialist party, of being directly involved in the Stavisky scandal. M. Herriot, as the chief representative of that party in the Cabinet, felt that his party had been attacked and consequently that the party truce was gravely affected.

M. Doumergue the Only Hope

"M. Doumergue alone," writes the "Petit Journal," "can solve the crisis. If any of his colleagues were to doubt this they would be making a grave mistake."

Many of the newspapers occupy themselves with the question of future relations of M. Tardieu between the Radical-Socialist Ministers. In some quarters a suggestion of a Cabinet reshuffle involving the disappearance of the two Ministers without Portfolio receives serious consideration.

The "Œuvre" says: "Among both the Right and Left sympathisers exists a general feeling that M. Tardieu must go. There is in any case a growing suspicion in Cabinet circles that if M. Doumergue called on him for a "new sacrifice" he might possibly refuse.

"It is suggested that M. Herriot would thereupon ask permission to resume his liberty of action. Thus the political balance would remain the party truce would continue, and it would be possible to carry on with current affairs until October."

Socialist Call for Election

A demand for a dissolution of Parliament and a general election which would result

THE POUND ABROAD

The following table shows the value of the pound abroad on Saturday, as compared with Friday's values:—

	Friday s. d.	Saturday s. d.
New York	20 8½	20 8½
Montreal	20 5½	20 5½
Paris	12 3½	12 3½
Brussels	12 4½	12 4½
Holland	12 3½	12 3½
Milan	12 8½	12 8½
Zurich	12 3½	12 3½
Spain	29 3	29 3½

FIVE HURT IN YORKSHIRE RAIL MISHAP

TRAIN COLLIDES WITH BUFFERS

STATION ACCIDENT AT SCARBOROUGH

From Our Correspondent

SCARBOROUGH, Sunday

SEVERAL holiday makers were slightly injured in a train mishap at the Scarborough station to-day. The Sunday train from Middlesbrough was being reversed alongside a new platform which has just been put into commission, and which is considerably shorter than that used formerly.

The train struck the buffers at the end of the platform so violently that people who were standing in the carriages, ready to descend, were thrown off their feet.

Although the carriages were severely jarred, no glass was broken, and they all kept the rails. The buffers of the carriage next to the engine were broken.

The Injured

The train was fairly full, but only the guard, Walter Preston (53), of 21, Quay Street, Middlesbrough, and four passengers were injured. They were taken to hospital in taxi-cabs, and Preston was detained for observation. He has an injury to his right thigh. The others, after treatment, were allowed to go home. They are:—

John Durant (54), of 43, Falmouth Street, Middlesbrough; shock and cut over right eye.

Margaret Capstick (49), of 10, Ada Street, Darlington; shock and broken teeth;

Ernest Carter (28), of 2d, Albion Street, Darlington; cut over right eye and shock.

William Harrison (54), of 29, Primrose Hill, Skinningrove; shock and possible head injuries.

Although the doctor advised Harrison to remain in hospital for observation, he decided to go home.

PETAIN AND THE NEXT WAR

"It Will Break Like a Thunderbolt"

ST. MALO (Brittany), Sunday

"The next war will break like a thunderbolt," declared Marshal Petain, the Minister of War, addressing the Congress of Officers of Reserve here to-day.

"You who form the frontal elements of our defence will have a few hours at most to take up your posts and put in motion the delicate technical tasks which fall to you," he continued.

The Minister of War emphasised that increased rapidity of mobilisation of every branch of the services for the next war would demand greater specialisation on the part of the reserves than in 1914. He then recalled that he recently proposed a Bill

13 DEAD IN WEEK-END ACCIDENTS

Lightning Kills Man on Beach

LONDON STORM

Bathing and Canoe Tragedies

THERE were thunderstorms in several areas yesterday, and a man was killed by lightning at Paignton.

Rain, however, was local, and Yorkshire escaped with showers, chiefly in Wharfedale.

The weather in London yesterday was a little hotter than on Saturday and after midday those who had gone out prepared for possible thunderstorms would gladly have exchanged their umbrellas for parasols. Last night, however, a terrific thunderstorm burst over the south-west district. At Twickenham, water rose in the roadway so rapidly that in a few minutes it reached the axles of motor cars.

In other areas fine weather made bathing and boating popular, but the week-end was marred by several tragedies.

The number of deaths in road and other accidents this week-end is 13, including several northern victims.

"BOILING BASIN" TRAGEDY

Doncaster Bather Drowned

Walker Tapsall (21), who lived in a caravan in a field off Bentley Road, Doncaster, was drowned in the Old River Don, near Marshgate, Doncaster, yesterday afternoon. He went with several youths to bathe in what is known as the "boiling basin." It is stated that he was a non-swimmer and that when he waded out he was overcome by the strong current and his friends were unable to get him out. The West Riding Police dragged for some time and recovered the body last night.

Hull Victim

Louis Percy, fish merchant, of Belgrove Drive, Boothferry Road, Hull, was drowned at Bridlington yesterday, when bathing on the south side between Wilsthorpe and Auburn despite heroic rescue efforts by civilians and police. He had come over for the day with his son, Gerard (13), who was bathing with him, when Mr Percy appeared to get into difficulties. His son with others, shouted for help, and three youths launched a boat and rowed out to him, while other bathers and another man, who was fully clothed, rushed into the sea. William S. Okey, of Beilby Street, Hull, managed to get him to the boat, where he was dragged on board and brought to shore. He was put on the sands, and P.C.s C. Brooks and G. T. Dain applied artificial respiration for an hour and a half before Mr. Percy was removed to hospital. Oxygen was administered, but he died shortly after admission.

East Coast Rescues

reached in 3 hours and 15 minutes, and Bradman went to 100 with a single at 2.58pm (in 3 hours 8 minutes), Ponsford then on 84. Wyatt was 'trying everything he knew' to keep control of the scoring rate and he set the field with particular care. Wyatt relied on Verity, Hopwood, Bowes and Hammond and only gave Mitchell three overs because the Derbyshire bowler's length had proved inconsistent to the point where he felt he couldn't risk him. Anything less than a good length and Bradman would feast and gorge on it.

The wicket, too, was docile and even Bowes couldn't make the ball zip or nip from it.

Ponsford got to his 100 at 3.20pm in 4 hours and 16 minutes, Bradman then on 114. When the total reached 283 they'd gone past the Australian fourth wicket record, set by Bradman himself and Archie Jackson at The Oval in 1930. When Ponsford moved past 128 he'd beaten his own highest Test score, and at this point he was outscoring Bradman. It didn't stay like that. At tea the total was 329 (Bradman 169, Ponsford 137) and 212 had been added in the 2 hours and 12 minutes of afternoon play.

After tea, Ponsford hooked Mitchell to the boundary, which took the partnership past the 323 of Hobbs and Rhodes in 1911–12 (although that was for the first wicket:

it was so enduringly famous that getting past it all this time later was worthy of note). That stroke gave Ponsford his 150 and by now the bowling had been completely blunted. Both batsmen scored at will. Bradman scampered a single at 5.15pm to reach 200 in 5 hours and 5 minutes, Ponsford then on 155. Bradman had hit 30 boundaries.

Wyatt had to resort to Mitchell but again he couldn't find a length and although Hammond, a much under-rated medium-pace bowler, could always be relied on to find a length he could find nothing in the wicket. Ponsford, coming forward to Verity, did give one chance to Wyatt at silly mid-off. Wyatt flung himself full length at the ball, grasped it in his hand but the ball rolled out.

Bradman cut Verity to the boundary to take Australia to 400 in 6 hours and 16 minutes, and the crowd cheered lustily as Wyatt made another heroic attempt to catch Ponsford off Verity. The ball was coming at him like a missile, he laid his hands on it and knocked it up, twisted to try and reach it again and almost made it. Ponsford was 178, Bradman 218. The new ball was due but Wyatt sensed that it would come faster off the bat, run faster across the outfield and would increase the scoring rate further still. He didn't take it until the next day.

Soon after, at 5.51pm and with Australia 427, Verity bowled a slow ball that pitched outside the off stump. Ponsford gratefully hooked it to the long-on boundary and, while Verity stood waiting for it to be returned to him, everyone noticed that Ponsford had dislodged a bail by touching the leg stump with his foot. He had made 181 in 6 hours and 27 minutes, with 19 4s, and he'd put on 388. The full extent of his and Bradman's mastery is revealed in a further statistic: in one minute more than an hour since tea, they had scored 98.

McCabe joined Bradman and they enjoyed themselves. Bowes might have bowled Bradman, who was trying to hook him, but Bradman retaliated by hitting Verity for 6 at 238 and Hopwood for 6 at 262. At the close Australia were 494 for 4, Bradman 271, McCabe a sprightly 18.

On the third day Australia's tactics were clear. They'd score quick runs to take the match far beyond England then let their bowlers loose. On a more personal level, what might Bradman do? Time pressed, however, because of this four-day Test and they were now moving into the third day.

Bradman and McCabe did not attack immediately. Bowes opened the bowling down wind with the old ball, Hammond bowled one ball with it and then the new one was taken. In Bowes's second over he might have had Bradman bowled off his foot – the ball passed perilously close to the off stump. Bradman sent the 500 up by cover-driving Hammond to the boundary and McCabe hooked Hammond for 4 with ominous ease. Soon after, Bradman tried to off-drive Bowes but sent the ball to Verity at gully. Verity put an easy catch down and the vast crowd fell utterly silent. Bradman was then on 280.

Bowes was getting life from the pitch at last and twice he worried McCabe, then bowled him. The crowd roared, an absolute contrast to the silence of the dropped catch and an outpouring of relief. McCabe and Bradman had been increasing the tempo and, if both of them had broken free simultaneously, Wyatt risked a complete loss of control.

Len Darling came in, Bowes bowled bouncers at him and he cracked them away as if they delighted him. Hammond wasn't getting life from the pitch and Bradman repeatedly sent him to the boundary. At 11.45am Bradman went to 300 by snicking Bowes to the leg side boundary. Five minutes after that Bowes bowled him and there are varying accounts of that. One source suggests it was a 'fine break-back' of a delivery from Bowes. Another (Hobbs) says Bradman seemed to 'be playing an easy, careless shot, and I thought he was not sorry to go'. Fender wrote that Bradman played 'a defensive shot' at a ball, which he anticipated would bounce but it didn't.

His 304 had lasted 7 hours and 10 minutes and contained 2 6s and 43 4s.

All that remained was the end-game of the Australian innings and the England attempt to bat out time on the fourth day. They were helped by a thunderstorm of such ferocity that Fender felt 'never before in this country have I seen it rain as it did for the four and a half minutes that the storm lasted. In less than a minute the whole ground was under water'.[5]

Notes

[1] *My Cricketing Life,* Bradman.

[2] A first-hand story about the pace of Bowes. A master at my school had long been a member of the MCC and was also an opening bat for a Minor County. As a member he could go along to Lord's and use the nets while members of the ground staff bowled at him. Bowes was there but evidently injured and so only ran two or three paces to deliver the ball – but he was still sharp enough off the pitch to hit the master a time or two in the ribs and thump the pads repeatedly. Incidentally, the master had spent a part of his career working in education in Nigeria but took early retirement so he could return to England to see Bradman in 1948, the last chance he'd get. I mention this because chances to see Bradman were so strictly rationed by the four-year touring cycle. Hence the sense of anticipation and celebrity, which is, by definition, quite different today.

[3] *The Fight for The Ashes 1934,* Hobbs.

[4] *Kissing the Rod,* Fender.

[5] Ibid.

England v Australia
Played at Leeds, 20, 21, 23, 24 July 1934

ENGLAND

Batsman	Dismissal	Runs	Dismissal (2nd)	Runs (2nd)
C.F. Walters	c & b Chipperfield	44	b O'Reilly	45
W. Keeton	c Oldfield b O'Reilly	25	b Grimmett	12
W.R. Hammond	b Wall	37	run out	20
E. Hendren	b Chipperfield	29	lbw O'Reilly	42
R.E.S. Wyatt	st Oldfield b Grimmett	19	b Grimmett	44
M. Leyland	lbw, b O'Reilly	16	not out	49
L.E.G. Ames	c Oldfield b Grimmett	9	c Brown b Grimmett	8
J.L. Hopwood	lbw, b O'Reilly	8	not out	2
H. Verity	not out	2		
T.B. Mitchell	st Oldfield b Grimmett	9		
W.E. Bowes	c Ponsford b Grimmett	0		
	l-b 2	2	b 1, l-b 6	7
		200	(6 wkts)	229

	O	M	R	W		O	M	R	W
Wall	18	1	57	1		14	5	36	0
McCabe	4	2	3	0		5	4	5	0
O.Reilly	35	16	46	3		51	25	88	2
Grimmett	30.4	11	57	4		56.5	24	72	3
Chipperfield	18	6	35	2		9	2	21	0

AUSTRALIA

Batsman	Dismissal	Runs
W.A. Brown	b Bowes	15
W.H. Ponsford	hit wkt. b Verity	181
W.A. Oldfield	c Ames b Bowes	0
W.M. Woodfull	b Bowes	0
D.G. Bradman	b Bowes	304
S.J. McCabe	b Bowes	27
L.S. Darling	b Bowes	12
A.G. Chipperfield	c Wyatt b Verity	1
C.V. Grimmett	run out	15
W.J. O'Reilly	not out	11
T.W. Wall	lbw b Verity	1
	b 8 , l-b 9	17
		584

	O	M	R	W
Bowes	50	13	142	6
Hammond	29	5	82	0
Mitchell	23	1	117	0
Verity	46.5	15	113	3
Hopwood	30	7	93	0
Leyland	5	0	20	0

MATCH DRAWN
Failed by 33 runs to beat the record.

England v Australia, The Oval, August, 1938

*Sir Leonard Hutton, born Fulneck, near Pudsey, Yorkshire,
23 June 1916, died 6 September, 1990,
Kingston-upon-Thames.*

*Test career 1937 to 1954–5: 79 Tests, 6,971 runs,
19 centuries, average 56.67.*

He had a hewn, strong face and a pronounced Yorkshire accent. He did not look, even in his youth, like a natural athlete. Sometimes when he was batting his movements could seem slightly jerky and stiff, but he had the technique of a master, and on this he built batsmanship of a rare vintage. It was good enough to enable him to subdue one generation of Australian bowlers and make himself the most prized wicket to the next generation.

He'd first played for Yorkshire in 1934, when he was 17, and in the 1930s Yorkshire cricket was a self-contained and self-perpetuating world: youngsters were coached hard and expected to play hard, they were brought up within the club's folklore and would be woven into it themselves. They were taught to recognise the game's fundamentals and apply them. This approach reached its logical climax at The Oval in 1938 when, as we shall see, Yorkshire virtually defeated Australia on its own and by a powerful margin.

Interestingly, this general dominance bred hostility because players in those county sides that Yorkshire thrashed in the 1930s would be the coaches of the 1950s, and they didn't like Yorkshire at all. That's another story, except that it does illustrate the culture that produced, shaped and hardened Hutton. More than that, cricket folklore suggests that Hutton found it harder to make runs against the Australians when he came to know, and like, some of them.

He made his Test debut against New Zealand in 1937, and a year later scored exactly 100 on his debut against Australia at Nottingham. That was drawn and so was Lord's. The Manchester Test was drowned, washed out without a ball bowled, but the Australians won at Leeds and so to decide the series the Fifth Test, starting on a Saturday, would be played to a finish. More than this, the fabled Oval groundsman Bosser Martin had set out to create the perfect wicket. One of the umpires, Frank Chester, likened it to silk.

The toss assumed pivotal importance. Win it and you could dine out for days. Lose it and you'd wait days for scraps.

Bradman, in a suit and hat, called wrong. Hammond, captaining England, said he'd bat and some moments later he was reminding Hutton and the other opener, Bill Edrich, that he expected them to be there at tea. Len Hutton had met his conjunction of circumstances.

If Martin had made his wicket a conduit to 1,000, Hammond fully intended that England would reach it. England had long suffered under Bradman's lash, a generation of Englishmen had fielded out those enormous and interminable Australian totals, and, if the game was now about enormity, Hammond was more than prepared to inflict that. He would show Bradman and his team no mercy because that was how Bradman and his team played. There must have also been a sense that if England got as far as the 1,000 and, on such a wicket, Bradman had unlimited time, he might put together an innings so enormous it would dwarf all the rest of Test history. Absurdly, Hammond might need the 1,000.

Pugnacious Edrich, an all-rounder of great promise, was, at Test level, suffering prolonged agonies trying to establish himself. He'd scored a mere 55 runs in the three Tests of the summer. Now he faced a weakened Australian pace attack. Their genuine pace bowler, Ernie McCormick, was injured, although – anticipating a long, gruelling ordeal whoever won the toss – they may have been unwilling to risk him. The opening bowlers, Mervyn Waite and McCabe, were both all-rounders like Edrich and were useful with the ball.

In the dressing room, Edrich said, 'ready, Len?'

'Ready.'[1]

Somehow the beginning was as flat as the pitch. At 11.30am, when play began, The Oval was no more than half full, itself enough to soften any sense of anticipation. Neville Cardus called it 'almost a congregation'.[2]

Hutton and Edrich would proceed cautiously because, whatever their own inclinations, Hammond wanted that. Hutton took strike and played out a maiden from Waite then Edrich took a single from McCabe. At the end of that over, as McCabe took his sweater from umpire Chester, he said 'Frank, they'll get a thousand'.[3]

To Hutton came the conjunction that, even across a long career, might never come again: shirtfront wicket, weak attack except for spin and a timeless Test. He did not score a run until the fourth over and did not score a 4 until the eighth, when he cut McCabe late. In half an hour he and Edrich had made 20, neither crawl nor gallop, but soon after the Australians brought their spinners on and the real battle began. O'Reilly remains in historical terms one of the leading exponents of that elusive art, while the left-armer L.O.B. Fleetwood-Smith remains an enigmatic figure but quite capable of cutting deep into any batting side. Bradman pushed up two short legs as O'Reilly wheeled in, arms flailing in a windmill motion, to attack.

Hutton thrashed at O'Reilly's first ball and it went into the air for a couple of runs. If Hammond had been tempted to shout 'what the hell are...?' it would have been stifled mid-sentence, a no-ball. O'Reilly reacted with fire and fizzed a fast ball at Hutton who, anticipating what was coming, glanced it for 4. Anticipated? During his century at Nottingham Hutton had noticed O'Reilly always reacted like that.

At 12.16pm, Edrich misjudged the length of a ball from O'Reilly and was leg before wicket. That let in the stocky figure of Yorkshire's Maurice Leyland. Evidently there had been some debate about who would bat at number three because the crowd craned towards the pavilion expecting it to be Joe Hardstaff of Nottinghamshire. Hutton was pleased to see Leyland instead, whom he knew so well, with whom he ran so well between the wickets and with whom he had the same sort of earthy temperament and humour.

Yorkshire were about to strangle Australia, slowly. Leyland immediately reassured Hutton by telling him he was doing well and instructed him to keep going. Then Leyland drove a single. He was on his way. He intended it to be a long way. Hutton meanwhile pulled an O'Reilly googly for 4.

O'Reilly bowled a no-ball to Leyland and, Irish temperament rising again, produced a fast one. It reared just as Leyland ducked and almost flicked the peak of his cap. If it had knocked the cap on to the wicket...

At lunch England had reached 89 for 1 (Hutton 39, Leyland 35).

In the second over after lunch, and with the score 91, Hutton stepped down the wicket to drive Fleetwood-Smith through the covers. The ball swung and, when it bounced, its spin left Hutton stranded, but it beat wicketkeeper Barnett too and their stumping chance was gone. It was to be a horribly expensive mistake by Barnett and one he would have to spend the next two days contemplating. Hutton didn't stray into such dangerous places again and didn't allow himself to be lured into them either. He and Leyland settled again, although Leyland was bowled by a no-ball from O'Reilly. Evidently this amused Leyland, while O'Reilly's reaction is not recorded and perhaps does not need to be.

Leyland moved to his 50 in 94 minutes and Hutton to his an over later, in 2 hours 24 minutes.

As the afternoon unfolded, Bradman rotated his bowlers as best he could and, by force of circumstance, set defensive fields. There were only rare moments of hope for the Australians: when Leyland was 63 he might have been stumped off O'Reilly, and when he was 68 he edged a ball for Fleetwood-Smith but it didn't go to hand, it snaked away for a couple of runs. Waite was bowling off-breaks now, and once Leyland might have played on to him.

At 178, Sid Barnes, the Australian opening batsman, came on to ply his leg breaks. He had not bowled at all on the tour before, itself an eloquent statement. The new ball could not be taken until 200 and Bradman was working a path towards that, husbanding his resources as best he could.

Evidently Hutton was in some pain because the finger he had broken a month before (against Middlesex) began to swell. It did not show in his batting. When he was 86, however, he edged a Fleetwood-Smith full toss near first slip. The reporters in the Press Box dutifully recorded these potential chances, however slight, because, one senses, there was so little else to record. Fleetwood-Smith, bowling from the pavilion end, was occasionally inaccurate and Hutton helped himself to a boundary. Leyland did too.

At 3.47pm Hutton took a single on the leg side to reach his century, made in 3 hours and 32 minutes (Leyland 87). The single brought up the 200 and Bradman took the new ball. It slowed Leyland, who needed another 36 minutes to reach his century, off-driving Fleetwood-Smith for four. That was 4.23pm, and Leyland had been batting for 3 hours and 22 minutes.

Rain fell and tea was taken with England at 242 for one (Hutton 111, Leyland 104).

The shower, which had been heavy, might have enlivened the pitch. When play resumed, Waite made one ball lift past Leyland's cap and O'Reilly zipped one against Hutton's knuckles. That apart, Hutton was batting with balance and poise, turning Fleetwood-Smith into the on-side a couple of times in an over, all wrist-work. Leyland, 'less studious than Hutton, attended to the humanities; his drives were related to the man himself'.[4]

At 139, Leyland might have been run out, which seems to some reporters the most likely way he would be dismissed, and to others the only way. He stroked Waite briskly towards extra-cover where 'Jack' Badcock – an opening bat, whose name was actually Clayvel Lindsay Badcock – saw everything all in the moment, swooped and flung the ball towards the bowler's end: Leyland was chugging towards that as hard as he could. Waite cannoned into the wicket before he could catch the ball.

Barnes made Leyland play and miss but, that apart, the batsmen moved safely down the final session towards the close without undue alarms against O'Reilly and Fleetwood-Smith. Leyland felt that after so many years he had finally mastered O'Reilly, told Hutton so and was quite content to monopolise him.

At the close they had put on 318, five runs away from the 323 record for any England wicket against Australia (Hobbs and Rhodes, Melbourne, 1912). England were 347 for 1 (Hutton 160 in five minutes under 6 hours – the time lost to the shower – and Leyland 156 in 5 hours and 9 minutes). Hutton went back to the team's hotel, the Great Central Hotel over Marylebone station. He sat in the lounge drinking orange juice, while Hedley Verity talked through the day's play. He was tired and slept for 10 hours.

On the Sunday, a day off, Verity took Hutton to lunch at a friend's at Bognor Regis and then they played some beach cricket. Nobody recognised them. Perhaps Verity reasoned that it was important to occupy Hutton rather than letting him brood in the team hotel; perhaps because English Sundays were so dead in those days, the chance of a journey to Bognor, a little socialising and some fun on the beach was very welcome indeed.

On the Monday interest in the match increased. By eight o'clock some 1,500 people were queuing outside The Oval and, as the day went on, the ground filled completely. Rain delayed the start until 11.55am, although by then Hutton had been in the nets playing carefully down the line to Verity and, with each ball, playing himself in again. The Test, when it did resume, was only a continuation of that.

Now the sun shone and Fleetwood-Smith opened the bowling to Leyland. Bradman applied immediate pressure, with two short-legs, Jack Fingleton and Bill Brown, coming in close.[5] Fingleton had his 'cap pulled down over his eyebrows, he glared uncompromisingly at Hutton from the forward short-leg position'.[6]

Leyland took a couple of runs then a single from O'Reilly and the partnership equalled Hobbs and Rhodes. Hutton drove the first ball of Fleetwood-Smith's next over, a full toss, to the boundary past mid-off and they were past Hobbs and Rhodes with infinity beckoning.

After that, Fleetwood-Smith settled to line and length, Hutton repeatedly getting on to the front foot to defend against him. Both batsmen had reached 174 when Fleetwood-Smith beat Leyland with a rasping chinaman, which bounded just over the stumps. Shortly before 1pm, Leyland drove a boundary to bring up the 400 but seven minutes later – and both batsmen on 187, incidentally – Hutton stroked O'Reilly into the covers and they cantered the safest of singles. Lindsay Hassett misfielded and they set off for what appeared to be the safest of second runs. Hassett anticipated that, and at the same time Bradman, lurking around deep mid-on, sensed sudden vulnerability. As Hassett swooped on the ball, Bradman sprinted to the bowler's end. Leyland, heading towards that now distant port, tried to accelerate but it was too late. Hassett's throw went neatly to Bradman, and Leyland was run out by several yards.

411 for 2.

Leyland had batted for 6 hours and 24 minutes, hitting 17 4s.

Hammond the imperious came in. It may be that, having suffered Bradman for a full decade, he felt that here at last was a chance to make a merciless response: to confront

Bradman the monumental with a monument even Bradman could not scale. Hammond makes no mention of this in his autobiography[7], a book in keeping with the decorum of the age in which it was written: heavy in understatement and conveying feelings in a remote, reserved and obvious manner.

Bradman would wait until after lunch before taking the second new ball. Instead, he set Fleetwood-Smith against Hammond, this same Hammond who, as a deliberate and savage tactic, had butchered Fleetwood-Smith at Melbourne in 1932 when the MCC played Victoria. Fleetwood-Smith had been announced as a mystery bowler and was seen as a threat in the Tests. Hammond hammered him to the point where he did not take part in that series, did not go to England in 1934 and had to wait until 1936–7 to make his debut against England.

A double-bluff by Bradman in not taking the new ball immediately? Hardly. On this long day, O'Reilly and Fleetwood-Smith represented his only hope, and, of the two, Fleetwood-Smith seems to have been bowling better until Hammond really got at him. For a moment or two, it looked like Melbourne again. Hammond straight drove him to the boundary and pulled him there, taking in all 12 off the over. In the next over he pulled him to the boundary again. As they went in for lunch Hammond was already 20, England 434 for 2 and Hutton 191: he had added only 31 in the whole morning session.

After lunch Waite and McCabe had the new ball and used it well. Hutton played and missed at Waite a couple of times, and Hammond drove at him and missed a couple of times. This was deceptive because Hammond and Hutton were proceeding cautiously despite the affluence of the scoreboard and, as a consequence, the match no longer bore a semblance of normality. England, nearing 450, could now have rammed home their advantage by beating the Australian bowling all over The Oval, and if either batsman was out there were specialist batsmen waiting, Paynter, Compton, Hardstaff – due in at number seven. It does not seem to have entered Hammond's calculations. He was still dealing in monuments and, as if to emphasise that, he and Hutton put on 43 in the first hour after lunch. It wasn't even a respectable scoring rate with the total what it was, and clearly Hammond didn't give a damn about that.

At 2.33pm, and with the score at 447, Hutton moved to his 200 with a late cut. It had taken him 7 hours and 48 minutes, making his the slowest double hundred in all England versus Australia Test matches. If Hammond said anything it must have been 'well done, now keep on... and on'.

Occasionally Hutton off-drove to the boundary with 'as perfect a drive as any connoisseur could wish to see', Cardus wrote, adding that he was mystified as to why the batsmen hit boundaries off *this* ball but not *that* when the two were so similar.[8] Presumably, the Cardus logic was that you hit them all to the boundary or none of them.

Fingleton suddenly went down with a torn muscle in his leg and his teammates carried him as far as the boundary where they deposited him, leaving him to hop up the steps into the pavilion.

The 500 came in 8 hours and 45 minutes, but Fleetwood-Smith was turning the ball. He deceived Hutton once (the ball hit the side of the bat) and Hammond twice – all three genuine feats at this stage on this wicket. Hammond went to his 50 in 1 hour and 50 minutes, but at 4.15pm Fleetwood-Smith had him lbw. England were 546 (Hutton 257).

Paynter would remember that Hammond's dismissal 'meant that after nearly two days of waiting I could finally make my way to the wicket to join Len Hutton. My arrival at the wicket made no difference to Hutton; he did not allow a change of partner to affect the depth of his concentration. In a mammoth partnership of one run [Paynter's heavy-handed attempt at irony] I was never able to bring my concentration into play'.[9] He was lbw to O'Reilly, playing for a googly and getting a leg break. Paynter described Hutton's concentration as 'fanatical'.

Compton came in with strict instructions to stay until tea and managed that, Hutton 263 and the light deteriorating. Play resumed at 5pm and in Waite's first over Compton was yorked. At 555 for 5, and with the unquantifiable element of Bradman, the match had been brought back into some sort of balance. After so much self-denial by Hutton, Leyland and himself, Hammond still lacked the monument he had intended to build. Only four years before Australia had made 701 at this same Oval in well under two days and won by 562, 7 more than England now had.

Hardstaff and Hutton corrected that. At 5.39pm Hutton took a single off Fleetwood-Smith to beat R.E. Foster's 287 and that single also brought up the 600.

At 6.17pm Hutton late-cut O'Reilly for a single to reach 300 off 718 deliveries. He had hit 27 4s. An appeal against the light was upheld and play ended with England 634 for 5 (Hutton on 300, Hardstaff 40).

Bradman's great record from Leeds in 1930, which of course Hutton had watched, lay within reach. The morrow could only be a desperate anticlimax or high drama of genuinely historical proportions. No position between those two poles was possible, and the nearer Hutton got, the greater the drama.[10]

Hutton returned to the Great Central feeling exhausted and slightly overwhelmed. He 'collapsed into a chair in the lounge'[11] where Verity gave him a glass of stout mixed with port to revive and fortify him, no matter that Hutton was a teetotaller. He didn't sleep well, however, even though his body was so tired. Walking down to breakfast he felt stiff and even light exercising didn't bring his suppleness back.

He still felt this stiffness when he walked to the wicket with Hardstaff at 11.30am. He wore a cap and, when he was just clear of the pavilion, began to tug his batting gloves on. He turned his head and spoke briefly to Hardstaff as they strode forward. Hutton looked a young man of very serious intent.

The ground was full.

Bradman opened with O'Reilly and Fleetwood-Smith because they'd nag, probe and question. The medium-pacers might proffer loose stuff, let Hutton get moving along again. The morning would be a complete mental examination of a man, and Bradman was making sure that began immediately.

From the Vauxhall end, O'Reilly bowled a maiden to Hardstaff. Hutton faced Fleetwood-Smith and steered a single to the leg side. This was given thunderous applause. Hardstaff took a couple and a single before Fleetwood-Smith produced a fine over to Hutton, striking him on the pads twice. What effect did that have on Hutton amid all the mind games? Fleetwood-Smith remained a dangerous bowler, capable of conjuring the nightmare ball from nowhere.

Hardstaff glanced Fleetwood-Smith for 3 and cut O'Reilly to the boundary to reach his 50 in 1 hour and 32 minutes. Hutton had advanced by 5, all singles, but now he drove Fleetwood-Smith to the boundary. When he'd scored a couple more, Fleetwood-Smith beat and almost bowled him. Then, at 315, O'Reilly turned a leg break enough to tickle the edge of the bat and loop to first slip, but O'Reilly had no slips.

Bradman took the new ball, Waite from the Vauxhall end and McCabe from the pavilion end. Hutton leg-glanced Waite for a couple, late-cut him to the boundary and in an hour had moved laboriously to 321.

After only three overs of the new ball, O'Reilly was back, replacing McCabe. He pitched one up and Hutton steered it into the covers.

322.

Waite bowled a ball outside the off stump and Hutton late-cut it to the boundary. This brought the 700 up, made in 12 hours and 10 minutes.

326.

Bradman applied psychological pressure, bringing eight men up around the bat. Only Hassett, in the covers, was in anything approaching a defensive position. Bradman applied more psychological pressure, by bringing back Fleetwood-Smith to replace Waite from the Vauxhall end. Fleetwood-Smith did not normally bowl from this end and it may be that Bradman calculated that the backdrop of the crowd wouldn't help Hutton see the ball. Hutton only picked up the first from Fleetwood-Smith when it was already on its journey to him.[12] It spun, it bounced, it thumped into Hutton's pad and he'd played back. The Australians howled a great communal appeal.

Not out, said umpire Chester, the bounce was taking it over the top.

Hutton kept the next two balls out but the fourth beat him, thumping into his pads again, but he'd nicked it, and umpire Chester had heard that.

Not out.

Fleetwood-Smith bowled a long hop and Hutton despatched it instinctively.

330.

He cut Fleetwood-Smith for a single.

331.

It took him down the other end to face O'Reilly. At this most delicate and sensitive moment, drinks were ready to be brought out but E.W. Swanton, then working for the *Evening Standard,* managed to shoo the waiter away.[13]

Bradman fiddled with the field, stationing Brown and himself at silly mid-off. O'Reilly tried one of his faster balls, like an old soldier who won't surrender sensing the young soldier facing him, exhausted, on the lip of immortality. O'Reilly overstepped.

No ball.

Hutton, seeing immortality presented to him free, lunged at the ball to send it far away. He missed it completely.

Before the over's end he took a single on the leg side, a business stroke, an accumulation stroke.

332.

That brought him down to face Fleetwood-Smith, and he was feeling more comfortable against him now, seeing the ball clearly as it came from the Vauxhall End. He didn't score off the first four balls of the over. He was of his time: a motionless stance, the knees bent a little. Only his bat moved, once, in the automatic mannerism of raising it, tapping it back down as he waited for the fifth ball. It was, as he saw immediately, a long-hop chinaman that was going to pitch in line with, or just outside, the off stump. Hutton's initial movement was on to the back foot, the bat already high as if it had been a scimitar. He brought it down just like a scimitar too, a clean cleaving of the air. He cut the ball into the deep somewhere down towards third man and set off in a scamper for the other end. He needn't have bothered. It flew to the boundary. He completed the first run, turned and, after he'd taken two or three strides, saw that it was a boundary.

336.

He slowed to a walk and before he had reached the middle of the wicket Bradman was shaking his hand and patting him on the back.

It was 12.47pm.

Hutton had been at the crease for 12 hours and 19 minutes, itself a monument inside the monument that Hammond had decreed.

Now Hardstaff was shaking his hand, then wicketkeeper Ben Barnett who also patted him on the back, then all the Australians except O'Reilly who took the opportunity to lie down but rose briskly when (Swanton permitting) the drinks appeared.

Someone with a cornet played *For He's A Jolly Good Fellow* and the crowd joined in, creating a great swell of noise, although as Cardus, also the *Manchester Guardian's* music critic, noted the voices and the cornet 'did not keep together.' He meant this as a gentle aside, he insisted, not 'a piece of pedantic musical criticism'.

At 12.55pm Hutton passed Hammond's 336 and at lunch (1.30pm) he had pressed on to 361 (Hardstaff 96). After lunch, Hardstaff wasted no time getting to his century (Hutton 362). At 2.30pm exhaustion finally claimed Hutton. He spooned a ball from O'Reilly to Hassett in the covers and, after 13 hours and 17 minutes, the great innings was over. He cantered off and removed his cap as he went, holding it in his left hand. He had the bat in his right, raised it and waved it to the crowd who were on their feet and then he was gone up the steps and into the shadows of the pavilion.

England were then 770 for 6 and already enough records had been set to keep a statistician busy through the winter. The most important of those, the highest score in any Test match, would remain inviolate for two decades, and 364 remains, as I write these words, the highest innings in the England versus Australia series. In that sense, what Leonard Hutton did between 11.30am on Saturday 20 August 1938 and 2.30pm on the Tuesday remains very much alive.

Hutton spoke to the camera, perhaps on a balcony high up in the pavilion. He was bare-headed and the breeze tugged at a tousel of hair that hung down his forehead. The collar of his white shirt was upturned and the breeze tugged at that too. He said in a strong Yorkshire accent: 'Today has been, I think, one of the happiest days of my cricketing career. I managed to beat Don's great record and I must say I felt very pleased when I had achieved it.' It was the sort of polite, understated thing people said then.[14]

The rest was, as in the nature of these things, an anticlimax. Eventually Bradman put himself on to bowl, fell into a bowler's rut and had to be carried off with a damaged ankle. He, like Fingleton, would not be able to bat. England declared at tea on 903 for 7, although evidently groundsman Martin was keenly disappointed that Hammond had not gone for the 1,000. Clearly the people working The Oval scoreboards did not share this mathematical disappointment because there was only room for three figures. Nobody had even imagined a total of 1,000 in England before.

Australia put up minimal resistance and were no doubt glad when it was over and done with. They took the Ashes home, of course, because they'd come holding them and won at Leeds, the only finish before The Oval.

Yorkshire had had an extraordinary match. Their four batsmen (Hutton, Leyland, wicketkeeper Arthur Wood and Verity) scored a total of 612 runs, their bowlers (Bowes, Verity and Leyland) had taken 10 wickets and Wood had taken three catches. There used to be a dictum, *when Yorkshire cricket is strong, England cricket is strong*. It was true then and it might well be true today too.

Nobody could know, of course, on the evening of 24 August 1938 that Hutton's 364 would actually grow as time passed. It became an Everest of a thing, the highest summit and always there, looming from the distance, unclimbed. It is true, Everest was finally conquered in 1953, but no man would score a triple century in a Test match again until 1958 and by then only two of the young men in the England team at The Oval were still playing first-class cricket, Edrich and Compton, and they were only just playing.

You can put this another way. The next man after Hutton to score a triple century was four in 1938, the man to score the one after that was two.

Notes

1   *Ten Great Innings*, Barker.
2   *The Essential Neville Cardus*, Cardus.
3   *Cricket's Dawn That Died*, Valentine.
4   Cardus, op. cit.
5   Fingleton, Brown and Badcock were all openers but in the Tests Badcock had been batting down the order. When Fingleton was injured at The Oval and couldn't bat, Badcock did open.
6   Barker, op. cit.
7   *Cricket My Destiny*, Hammond.
8   Cardus, op. cit.
9   *Cricket All The Way*, Paynter.
10   *Punch* magazine carried a cartoon, c. the 1960s, of a man on a desert island being rescued. He calls out to the rescuers 'Did Hutton break the record?!?!'
11   Barker, op. cit.
12   Denis Compton was cricket correspondent for the *Sunday Express*, London, through the 1970s and I was a humble sub-editor. Compton played for the paper's cricket team, which

England v Australia
Played at The Oval, 20, 22, 23, 24 August 1938

ENGLAND

L. Hutton	c Hassett b O'Reilly	364
W.J. Edrich	c Hassett b O'Reilly	12
M. Leyland	run out	187
W.R. Hammond	lbw b Fleetwood-Smith	59
E. Paynter	lbw b O'Reilly	0
D. Compton	b Waite	1
J. Hardstaff	not out	169
A. Wood	c & b Barnes	53
H. Verity	not out	8
	b 22, 1-b 19, w 1, n-8	50
	(7 wkts, dec)	903

Did not bat: K. Farnes, W.E. Bowes

	O	M	R	W
Waite	72	16	150	1
McCabe	38	8	85	0
O'Reilly	85	26	178	3
Fleetwood-Smith	87	11	298	1
Barnes	38	3	84	1
Hassett	13	2	52	0
Bradman	3	2	6	0

AUSTRALIA

C.L. Badcock	c Hardstaff b Bowes	0	b Bowes	9
W.A. Brown	c Hammond b Leyland	69	c Edrich b Barnes	15
S.J. McCabe	c Edrich b Farnes	14	c Wood b Farnes	2
A.L. Hassett	c Compton b Edrich	42	lbw b Bowes	10
S. Barnes	b Bowes	41	lbw b Verity	33
B.A. Barnett	c Wood b Bowes	2	b Farnes	46
M.G. Waite	b Bowes	8	c Edrich b Verity	0
W.J. O'Reilly	c Wood b Bowes	0	not out	7
L.O.B. Fleetwood-Smith	not out	16	c Leyland b Farnes	0
D.G. Bradman	absent hurt	0	absent hurt	0
J.H. Fingleton	absent hurt	0	absent hurt	0
	b 4, 1-b 2, n-b 3	9	b	1
	Total	201		123

	O	M	R	W		O	M	R	W
Farnes	13	2	54	1		12.1	1	63	4
Bowes	19	3	49	5		10	3	25	2
Edrich	10	2	55	1					
Verity	5	1	15	0		7	3	15	2
Leyland	3.1	0	11	1		5	0	19	0
Hammond	2	0	8	0					

ENGLAND WON BY AN INNINGS AND 579

New world record by 28 runs. Old record had stood for 5 years 5 months.

is how I came to be waiting at the non-striker's end as he made his way to the wicket (having arrived late and without a full set of kit) with our score at about 16 for 5 against the demons of the *Sunday Times*. They had a lively medium-pacer who moved the ball both ways, hence our pitiful score. First ball, Compton – a portly man in his fifties – stepped up the wicket and smacked the ball right past my left ear and against the sightscreen, thump. The medium-pacer was off after a couple of overs. Afterwards I asked Compton about that first ball. 'See the ball out of the bowler's hand, know where it's going to pitch, hit it! You cannot play the game if you cannot see the ball out of the hand.' Hence Hutton's potential nightmare against Fleetwood-Smith.

[13]   Valentine, op. cit.

[14]   Interestingly, when England had regained the Ashes at The Oval in 1953, Hutton, on the balcony, was asked to say a few words to the crowd gathered below. By now his voice had lost virtually all trace of the Yorkshire accent – elocution lessons? – and he sounded frankly upper middle-class. It may be Hutton felt he had to speak like that as England captain, another sign of the times, just as BBC newsreaders all spoke Oxford English.

Pakistan in West Indies, Bridgetown, January, 1958

Hanif Mohammad, born Junagadh, Gujarat, India, 21 December 1934.

Test career 1952–69: 55 Tests, 3,915 runs, 12 centuries, average 43.98.

Pakistan had not visited the West Indies before and the anticipation was that both sides were stronger batting than bowling, which led to a further anticipation that on the batting-friendly West Indian pitches this strength would produce a lot of runs.

Pakistan played a couple of warm-up matches (against the Windward Islands and Barbados Colts) before it got serious against Barbados at Bridgetown. That was drawn, although the tourists saw what a left-handed batsman called Garfield Sobers could do (in the Barbados first innings he was 183 not out). There had never been much doubt about Sobers's ability since he made his debut against England in 1953–4. The debate was rather about the few parts of cricket he could not do. Lithe, lean, seemingly double-jointed and with the insinctive balance and poise of a great athlete, he could bat anywhere and take an attack apart, could open the bowling and revert, as required, to spin and, fielding close, was more like a bird of prey than a mere catcher of the ball.[1]

The interesting aspect of this is that, after standing for so long, Hutton's record was about to be threatened and then broken within five weeks. The ironical aspect is that Sobers, so richly endowed, would not be the first. Instead, it would be done by a neat, compact, organised chap who stood no more than 5ft 6in and didn't weigh very much at all.

The First Test was also at Bridgetown and West Indies looked strong, although Frank Worrell, their captain, was studying in England and didn't play. West Indies batted first and made 579 for 9 declared, and in reply Pakistan could only reach 106. They followed on 473 behind and the little opener who'd made 17 in the first innings took strike again. He was called Hanif Mohammad.

The Hindu of India gives the background with a lovely eloquence when it points out that some 16 families are reputed to have control of Pakistan's economy, 'a textbook case of exploitative oligopoly. But that might seem like egalitarian socialism when compared with the state of Pakistan cricket'.[2] Here the controlling interest wasn't 16 but for a long time merely two, and of diametrically opposed backgrounds. The first, the Mohammad family, was 'plebeian, as befitting their base, the trading port of Karachi'. The second, the Khans, were 'feudal, and lived in the town of kings, soldiers, and poets: Lahore. In fact a lyrical sociologist (were there such an animal) could use the story of these two families to write a larger social history of the nation. Punjab versus Sindh, land versus commerce, indigenous Pakistani versus imported Mohajir.'

The fact that they were diametrically opposed was reflected in the players themselves, how they dressed, how they behaved, their cricket and 'how they viewed the enemy'.

Hanif was one of five brothers: Wazir the eldest, then Hanif, Mustaq and Sadiq all played international cricket, only the second born, Raees, did not. They were born in India and their father had been a club cricketer so it did run in the family. When they moved to Pakistan Hanif was 12.[3] He'd say a major formulating influence was playing long innings by lamplight in the street in Junagadh. In Karachi, young Hanif was coached by Jaoomal Naoomal, who had played for India at Lord's in 1932. According to *The Hindu,* Naoomal saw Hanif's potential and, delightfully, told the local umpires never to give him out lbw. That would enable him to gain confidence and prepare himself for the lengthy rigours of Test cricket. In short, he would learn that most valuable thing, concentration.

Now, in January 1958, he and the other opener, Imtiaz Ahmed, began Pakistan's long haul towards trying to save the match from following on that 473 behind. Jaoomal Naoomal's preparation might have been for exactly this.

Almost immediately Imtiaz was in trouble. He edged an outswinger from Roy Gilchrist but Gerry Alexander, the wicketkeeper, could do no more than touch it with his right glove as it went to the boundary, this Gilchrist being a ferociously fast and headstrong opening bowler.[4] Hanif did not begin like a man preparing to bat for many hours. He square cut Gilchrist and next over, late-cutting him, sent the ball over the slips. And he late-cut Eric Atkinson, a fast-medium, swing bowler who had just taken over from his brother Denis. Imtiaz, however, was setting the pace, and when the left-arm spinner Alf Valentine came into the attack he off-drove him to the boundary to bring up the 50 in 45 minutes. At tea Pakistan had reached 79 (Imtiaz 41, Hanif 30).

When they came back out both batsmen seemed comfortable and Imtiaz drove Gilchrist through the covers for 4 to bring up his 50 and on-drove him to the boundary to bring up the 100 in only 79 minutes. Alexander rotated his bowlers, including Sobers, but Imtiaz and Hanif moved sweetly on. Sobers bowled a seven-over spell for 11 runs and a couple of maidens.

Hanif got to his 50 by on-driving Collie Smith, an occasional bowler but gifted batsman, and it had taken him 3 minutes over 2 hours. It contained five 4s. However, when Pakistan were past 150 Imtiaz fell lbw to Gilchrist, he'd been trying to force a ball off his pads. His 91 had taken 2 hours and 17 minutes.

Alim-ud-Din joined Hanif and by close they had added 10, Hanif 61 not out. For the man known as 'The Little Master' it was the perfect foundation. More than that, he had time, plenty of time, three whole days (the Test matches this tour were over six days).

The next day Hanif applied the concentration he had learnt when umpires wouldn't give him out. He and Alim-ud-Din put on 23 in the opening 30 minutes and the crowd already understood that Pakistan were capable of extreme attrition in order to save the match. They were still 288 behind and clearly couldn't hope for anything else. The wicket remained essentially benevolent and the West Indian batting might make any target seem paltry.

As the *Barbados Advocate* noted, while the score crawled towards 200, 'it was abundantly apparent that the batsmen were concentrating more on making minutes than runs, and justifiably so in the circumstances'. Alim-ud-Din had cast himself in a supporting role to Hanif.

An hour into this fourth day Pakistan had added a mere 34 and the 200 took 3 hours and 37 minutes, no mean striking rate itself but representing a remorseless slowing from the adventures of Imtiaz the day before. Hanif stole a single immediately and that was his thousandth in Tests. Eric Atkinson came on and Hanif treated the swing warily but eventually turned him into the covers to reach his century. It had taken 3 hours and 34 minutes and contained no more than six 4s. The *Advocate,* perhaps wielding gentle understatement, described the innings as 'painstaking'. There was, perhaps, a sense of timelessness about it, just as there had been about Hutton's, two decades and a world war before. Bradman had made his runs at a crackling pace, Hammond had eventually butchered a weak New Zealand attack, but Hutton and Hanif played another type of cricket, more measured and born of prudence: cricket from another era, another mentality.

Gilchrist might have had Hanif straight after lunch. Hanif lost concentration for an instant of peril, snicked an outswinger, but it flew past first slip. Gilchrist, remember, was fast. Hanif reasserted himself by straight-driving Gilchrist to the boundary.

Alim-ud-Din eventually played forward to a Sobers spinner and was caught at the wicket. The innings had lasted 2 hours and 45 minutes but contained only one 4. Pakistan were now 264 for 2.

Saeed Ahmed came in and a substitute fielder, Holder, 'funked' a catch at a point when Valentine was bowling. Holder caught it on the bounce rather than advance and try to catch it. The theme and shape of the innings did not change. Saeed now cast himself in a supporting role to Hanif, scoring only 10 in his first hour at the crease. At tea Pakistan had reached 295 for 2 (Hanif 139).

Into the final session, Hanif square drove Sobers with a stroke of such murderous power that it burst through Eric Atkinson at extra cover. Hanif moved past his previous highest Test score (142 against India in 1954) and brought up his 150 with an elegant drive off Clyde Walcott, a very occasional bowler.

At this point, the *Advocate* demands to be quoted. 'The West Indian players, now two full days in the field, began to show signs of becoming weary. They seized every interval taken for refreshments to relax on the ground and when just before five o'clock play was stopped because of a nearby car reflecting the sun in the batsman's eyes, their weariness was more pronounced as the majority of them flopped to the ground.'

Hanif was grinding them on and on, and there was a precise illustration of that because when the score had reached 234 it stayed there and neither batsman appeared unduly concerned or was prepared to be hustled into getting off it. This lasted for seven overs, until, finally, Saeed steered Denis Atkinson past third slip for a single. In the next over Saeed drove a boundary and had made 25 in just over 2 hours. He had been grinding on and on too.

Gilchrist came on shortly before the close and bounced Hanif, who just managed to duck under it, not troubled in the slightest. At the close he was 161, Saeed 26 and Pakistan 339 for 2, still 134 behind. A collapse might still have opened the match to the West Indies again. Hanif, of course, didn't intend to allow anything like that to happen. Quite the contrary. On day five he would take guard and do it all again.

Alexander took the new ball after a handful of overs of spin from Sobers and Collie Smith. From that new ball, Pakistan reached 350 in 7 hours and 55 minutes, Hanif and Saeed very deliberately re-establishing their concentration and rhythm, although it was not without anxiety. Hanif snicked Eric Atkinson between wicketkeeper and slip and Saeed got two successive bouncers from Gilchrist and waved the bat dangerously at the second.

By now Hanif was on 175, Saeed was reaching towards his 50 and the century partnership had come up after 3 hours and 16 minutes. The first hour of play had produced 40 and Hanif was now making Pakistan safe, minute by minute, run by run. Saeed took on Sobers, off-drove him to the boundary twice and the 400 came up. That was 73 behind.

At lunch Hanif was within sight of a double hundred (186) and Saeed was safely past his 50. After it, Hanif smacked an over-pitched ball from Valentine to the long-on boundary, but then Saeed tried to drive Collie Smith off the back foot, nicked the ball and Alexander, who had seemed particularly tired as his wicket-keeping was almost ragged, made no mistake. Pakistan were 418 for 3 and Wazir, Hanif's elder brother of course, came out to join him. Hanif welcomed him by playing an exquisite cover drive to the boundary at 199. He had been at the crease for nearly 9 hours.

That done, he and Wazir continued the grind. The score froze again at 448, this time for some 20 minutes, before Hanif took a single off Sobers. A run later Pakistan had reached 450, within touching distance of making West Indies bat again. It had taken 10 hours and 42 minutes to get there. At tea Hanif was 216, made in the 11 hours and 5 minutes that the Pakistani innings had lasted – so far.

As they came out of the pavilion and on to the field side-by-side (shoulder-to-shoulder might be more apt), the contrast between the brothers became unmissable. Wazir was five years older, thick set and smiling broadly under his cap. Hanif was boyish and capless but had a white neckerchief round his throat, neatly notted. He looked very fresh.

He survived an lbw appeal from Valentine soon after the resumption, and when Wazir chipped Valentine for a single Pakistan were level. Alexander took the new ball and Hanif edged Gilchrist through the slips for 4 to reach 250 in 12 hours and 1 minute, with 21 4s. He had barely lifted a ball all the way through and although he did now, sending one from Eric Atkinson to the on-side boundary, he took care to make sure it was a no ball.

It brought up the 500.

The *Advocate* noted that 'a strange experiment that reflected the limited scope of the West Indies bowling was that in which Sobers was brought on to bowl fast'. It must have seemed strange, as if a pace bowler had been created from a spinner without warning. The versatility of Sobers was still emerging.

At the close of this fifth day Hanif had 270, Wazir 31 and Pakistan were 525 for 3. Clearly Hutton's record would be vulnerable on the sixth day, which Hanif could legitimately bat right through to draw the match. That was all Pakistan had been trying to do of course. The *Advocate*, saying that Hanif would obviously be going for the record, noted that Hutton had batted for 13 hours and 20 minutes and Hanif had already batted for 12 hours and 35 minutes. In the matter of longevity, Hanif could get past Hutton too.

On the same page of the *Advocate*, a horoscope by Estrellita announced that if it was your birthday it did not mean 'risky chance-taking. Good judgement will be all important.' It wasn't Hanif's birthday (that had been the month before) and he certainly didn't need a star-gazer to tell him about avoiding chances and exercising good judgement.

Hanif began the final day from the non-strikers' end, Wazir facing Gilchrist who had a loud lbw appeal refused off the fourth ball. Hanif set the day in motion with a single off Eric Atkinson before Atkinson moved one off the seam and had Wazir caught behind. Wazir had restrained himself to an almost inhuman degree, taking 3 hours and 33 minutes to chip and claw his 35 with only a solitary boundary.

Wallis Mathias came in and Hanif ground on. When he reached 293 he had gone past Hutton in terms of that longevity and at lunch he was 297 out of 566 for 4. He moved past 300 soon after the resumption with a neat turn to leg off Sobers and, a moment or two after that, he went past Bradman's 304.

Mathias was lbw to Eric Atkinson at 598 and the captain, Hafeez Kardar, came in. When the 600 was reached in 15 hours and 17 minutes the match was dying. Pakistan did not intend to accelerate and give West Indies an uncomfortable hour or two. No, they'd make absolutely sure of the draw and any declaration would be made only when the match was truly dead.

At tea the score had crawled on to 623, Hanif 334 not out – past Sandham and within 2 runs of Hammond. It must have been a long interval for Hanif because the great prize lay so tantalising close, and, more than that, Hanif might reasonably have expected that if he did get past Hutton whatever new record he set would stand for another couple of generations, as Hutton's had done.

There's a haunting line in the poetry of T.S. Eliot about the way the world ends, not with a bang but a whimper.

Hanif came back out again and took guard. He scored three so that, at 337, only Everest loomed ahead – and then, just when nobody expected it, his concentration failed him. He played too late at a ball from Denis Atkinson and was caught at the wicket by Alexander, standing up. He had given only one chance before when on 14 he'd cut Gilchrist over the slips, days ago.

His 337, out of 626, had taken 16 hours 13 minutes and contained 24 4s. Throughout, there had been no hint of trying to hit 6s with the risks that that would involve.

The *Advocate* wrote of his 'masterly display of concentration, skill and application' and felt the innings would be remembered as one of the most 'painstaking innings' ever played at Kensington.

Pakistan declared at 657 for 8, leaving West Indies half an hour to score 185. As if to prove that Sobers wasn't the only versatile cricketer in the match, Hanif bowled fast, then slow right arm, then slow left arm in the knock-about at the end. Hanif would do this again and at a most interesting moment, but not here and not yet.

As I write these words, his innings is easily the longest in Test history and, in terms of the first-class game, second only to the 1,051 minutes that Rajiv Nayyar took to score 271 for Himachal Pradesh against Jammu and Kashmir at Chamba, India in season 1999–2000. The nearest to Hanif is Gary Kirsten, who took 14 hours and 38 minutes to make 275 against England at Durban in 1999–2000, and after that there's a gentlemen called Jayasuriya we shall be meeting later in the book. A lot of cricket has been played in a lot of places down all these years, but Hutton's innings at The Oval remains fifth longest.

Notes

[1] In the distant days when there was little or no first-class cricket on a Sunday, various celebrity sides went round the country and one such, featuring Frank Worrell and Sobers, came to Gateshead to play a team of locals. Worrell and Sobers were batting together and a mis-call left Sobers heading hopelessly towards the bowler's end and a run out. In mid-stride he accelerated and *elongated* himself, the elongation eating the ground, and made it comfortably. He seemed, truly, to have no physical limits.

[2] *The Hindu Magazine,* 31 March 2002.
http://www.hindu.com/thehindu/mag/2002/02/31/stories/2002033100300300.htm

[3] Britain's Indian Empire ended on 15 August 1948, and from it two independent countries, India and Pakistan, were born. It was a violent time of religious and racial hatreds, and families did move from one to the other.

[4] The first Test I ever saw was England v the West Indies at Headingley in 1957. I was sitting side on, Gilchrist bowling to Tom Graveney with wicketkeeper Alexander standing a long way behind the stumps. Gilchrist ran up to bowl and gave a tremendous leap as he did so. He bowled a yorker that plucked one of Graveney's stumps out of the ground and sent it cartwheeling crazily all the way back to Alexander, who caught it. At no stage had I been able to see the ball. Perhaps Tom Graveney didn't either.

West Indies v Pakistan
Played at Bridgetown, 17, 18, 20, 21, 22, 23 January 1958

WEST INDIES

C. Hunte	c Imtiaz b Fazal	142	not out	11
R. Kanhai	c Mathias b Fazal	27	not out	17
G. Sobers	c Mathias b Malmood	52		
E.D. Weekes	c Imtiaz b Malmood	197		
C.L. Walcott	c Mathias b Kardar	43		
O.G. Smith	c Mathias b Alim	78		
D. Atkinson	b Mahmood	4		
E. Atkinson	b Fazal	0		
F.C.M. Alexander	b Mahmood	9		
A.L. Valentine	not out	5		
	b 9, l-b 4, w 3, n-b 6	22		
	(9 dec)	579	(no wkt)	28

Did not bat: R. Gilchrist.

	O	M	R	W		O	M	R	W
Fazal	61	12	145	3		2	1	3	0
Mahmood	41.2	5	153	4					
Kardar	32	5	107	1		3	1	13	0
Haseeb	22	0	84	0					
Nasimul	14	1	51	0					
Alim	2	0	17	1					
Hanif						3	1	10	0
Saeed						2	2	0	0
Wazir						1	0	2	0

PARKISTAN

Hanif Mohammad	b E. Atkinson	17	c Alexander b D. Atkinson	337
Imtiaz Almed	lbw b Gilchrist	20	lbw b Gilchrist	91
Alim–ud-Din	c Weekes b Gilchrist	3	c Alexander b Sobers	37
Saeed Ahmed	st Alexander b Smith	13	c Alexander b Smith	65
Wazir Mohammad	lbw b Valentine	4	c Alexander b E. Atkinson	35
Wallis Mathias	c Alexander b Smith	17	lbw b E. Atkinson	17
A.H. Kardar	c D Atkinson b Smith	4	not out	23
Fazal Mahmood	b Gilchrist	4	b Valentine	19
Nasimul Ghani	run out	11	b Valentine	0
Mahmood Hussain	b Gilchrist	3	not out	0
Haseeb Ahsan	not out	1	b 19, l-b 7, n-b 7	23
	b 4, l-b 5	9		
		106	(8 dec)	657

	O	M	R	W		O	M	R	W
Gilchrist	15	4	32	4		41	5	121	1
E. Atkinson	8	0	27	1		49	5	136	2
Smith	13	4	23	3		61	30	93	1
Valentine	6.2	1	15	1		39	8	109	2
D. Atkinson						62	35	61	1
Sobers						57	25	94	1
Walcott						10	5	10	0

MATCH DRAWN
Failed to beat the record by 28 runs

West Indies v Pakistan, Kingston, February, 1958

Garfield (Gary, then Garry) St Aubrun Sobers, born Bay Land, St Michael Parish, Barbados, 28 July 1936.

Test career 1957–73: 93 Tests, 8,032 runs, 26 centuries, average 57.78.

West Indies won the Second Test at Port of Spain two weeks after Hanif's 337, and this time he scored 'only' 30 and 81. He failed in the Third Test at Kingston, Jamaica, caught behind off Gilchrist for 3. Pakistan made 328 and in reply West Indies lost Kanhai at 87. The *Daily Gleaner* felt that Kanhai shouldn't have been opening anyway, and described him as coming back to the pavilion a 'dejected and disgusted little man'. When, the newspaper asked plaintively, would the selectors give 'this gifted batsman a real chance to establish himself as the truly fine strokeplayer that he potentially is?'

Conrad Hunte, a natural opener, had been batting well and now Sobers joined him. He was a lean man, almost slight, sleeves rolled up, no armguards, and wearing a cap. The crowd of 10,000 waited: Sobers was uninhibited, exciting and a beautiful player of all bowling. He took a single immediately and soon enough he was driving and hooking left-arm spinner Nasimul Ghani for boundaries, while Hunte moved to his second Test century just before the close. West Indies were 147 (Hunte 100, Sobers 20) – 181 behind.

Pakistan were already in deep trouble as they approached the following day. The wicket looked a beauty and the weather was lovely. Ghani had a fractured right thumb and was not expected to play again on the tour, while Kardar had a finger injury that ought to have prevented him from bowling for three weeks. Mahmood Hussain, who'd opened the bowling as West Indies' innings began, pulled a muscle and was out for the rest of the tour too.

Essentially, Pakistan had two stock bowlers left, paceman Fazal Mahmood and Khan Mohammad. This was not the way to confront 21-year-old Garfield Sobers. He punished Khan with three boundaries in an over, a glide, an obvious snick and a square cut. He might have been staking the wicket out as his territory and might have been setting out his terms of occupation of it. If Hanif had the siege mentality, Sobers was a conquistador. Soon enough Sobers had Pakistan in all manner of trouble. The *Daily Gleaner* wrote of 'panic' so intense that even the throws to the wicket from the fielders were wild. Trapped in the midst of this, Kardar felt he had to gamble – with himself. He'd bowl – whatever the doctors had said. Because his injured finger had had a plaster put on it he had to ask the batsmen if they were happy for him to bowl and they were. The conquistador was happy to face any bowling, always had been and always would be.

Hunte was in impish form, cutting Fazal for a single to make the partnership worth 100 in 1 hour and 34 minutes and then stealing a swift-run single off Kardar to hoist the 200. Drinks were taken after three quarters of an hour, and 63 had been added.

Kardar, clearly reduced to further desperation, gambled again, putting on Wallis Mathias, a batsman who had not previously bowled a ball on the tour, and Sobers on-drove him twice to the boundary. After 1 hour 83 had been added and Pakistan were facing a long-drawn agony. Because of the plaster, Kardar couldn't hope to spin the ball and was reduced to floating it up. Sobers helped himself. Fazal managed a maiden to Hunte and it was greeted with profound applause.

The run rate slowed as lunch approached, although West Indies were 243 for 1 (Hunte 139, Sobers 76). The crowd had grown from 6,000 when play began to around 14,000 and after lunch they were about to get very excited indeed. Pakistan took the new ball. It had been available some half an hour before lunch, but they hadn't taken in then because, no doubt, the scoring had slowed. Now Hunte rampaged: a couple of on-drives to the boundary and a 6 over fine leg from Khan's third over with this new ball, 15 runs in all. Hunte went past 150 as Sobers reached into the 90s. On 93, Sobers went on to the back foot against Khan and smacked him through the covers making the stand worth 200. He prodded a Kardar leg-break, or an attempt at a leg-break, to square leg and set off for a dangerous single, turned back and might have been run out, but the return (panic?!) was so wide that they took an overthrow. This was Sobers's first Test century and it was greeted by applause so prolonged and deep that the *Daily Gleaner* reporter found himself amazed. Nowhere else in the world, the reporter said, could you get applause like that.

Of this, Sobers would write that the century had boosted him nicely but, once completed, he resumed his concentration.[1] He'd remember a lot of people subsequently, and understandably, probing him for his feelings and he'd tell them he didn't feel any different. He saw himself as one batsman among many in the team and if he was making runs well so was Hunte. He was, he concludes, not raising his own innings over the overall welfare of the team, rather he was happy the team was doing so well.

He had been at the wicket for 3 hours and 28 minutes and hit 10 4s. This, interestingly, was only 6 minutes faster than Hanif at Bridgetown.

Straight after, Sobers edged Kardar and it almost carried to first slip but he pulled Fazal to the square leg boundary with characteristic flourish to bring up the 300 in 5 hours and 15 minutes. Sobers went on to the back foot again and pushed Kardar into the covers for a single that took him and Hunte past the West Indian second wicket record of 228, set in 1930 by George Headley and Karl Nunes.

It was a hot afternoon, and just before three o'clock Hunte hooked Kardar to take West Indies level with the Pakistani first innings total. Off the first ball of the next over, he took a single to push West Indies ahead. Drinks came on, to the relief of the Pakistanis, and the bearer of them also bore a message for the batsmen to keep pushing the score along. Neither Hunte nor Sobers needed to be told that, and now Sobers broke loose. He steered 'crisis' bowler Alim-ud-Din – this far in the tour he'd bowled only 24 overs – for a couple to third man, took five more off the over, drove Khan majestically to the boundary and turned his full attention to Alim-ud-Din, purveyor of 'teasers to an open field'. He attacked Khan, pulling and square cutting and punching him through the covers for boundaries. He was 150 in 4 hours and 19 minutes (18 4s). The last 50 had come in 51 torrid minutes.

Hunte, who hadn't been getting much of the strike, moved into the 190s, Sobers with 163. They beat the West Indian first-class record for the second wicket, 295 by Stollmeyer and Ken Trestrail against Jamaica in 1950, and shortly before tea the 400 came up in 6 hours 17 minutes (Hunte 196, Sobers 170).

After tea Hunte moved quickly to his double hundred and Hanif became Pakistan's eighth bowler before the new ball was taken at 445. When the total was 450, Sobers had reached 199 and he got to his double century with a cheeky single by pushing an outswinger from Khan towards Hanif at silly mid-off. Hanif threw to the non-strikers' end and hit the stumps, but Sobers was already home. The ball ricocheted away for four overthrows.

Fazal gambled a final time and tried to bowl fast but the stream of runs broadened to a torrent. Fazal and Khan were getting some tap, as the saying goes. The 400 partnership was reached with 10 minutes of the long day left – it had taken a mere 5 hours and 46 minutes – and at the close West Indies were 504 (Hunte 242, Sobers 228).

Sobers would write that the impact of where he was only struck him after the close of play, with so many people suddenly talking about records[2] (although of course they might equally well have done that about Hunte, who was, after all, closer). Sobers wished he didn't have to face a whole night waiting. As a youngster, he'd made a vow to himself that he wouldn't ever take the game 'to bed with me'. This night he found that difficult and didn't get to sleep until about four in the morning.

He needn't have worried. The next morning, the ground packed, eager and noisy, he strode to the wicket and felt the nocturnal pressures falling away from his mind. Better still, within a few minutes and a few strokes he was batting as if continuing from the day before uninterrupted.

Hunte took strike to Fazal, Khan at the other end, and immediately both batsmen were scampering singles. Therein lay the undoing. After 29 had been added Hunte pushed an inswinging delivery from Khan to a substitute fielder and set off for an

The Sunday Gleaner

Vol. XVIII No. 9.   KINGSTON, JAMAICA, W.I., MARCH 2, 1958.   Price: THREEPENCE

TWENTY PAGES

PLAY ENDS ABRUPTLY IN SABINA TEST AS HUTTON'S 364 IS BEATEN

SOBERS SETS RECORDS

Hits 365 n.o. against Pakistan; Hunte 260

W.I. 790 FOR 3 THEIR HIGHEST

By L. D. ROBERTS, Gleaner Sports Editor

PANDEMONIUM broke out at Sabina Park yesterday afternoon on the fourth day of the third Test match between the West Indies and Pakistan, after 21-year-old Barbadian Garfield Sobers had beaten Sir Leonard Hutton's Test record score of 364, by scoring 365 not out.

'Sign of progress everywhere'

Lord Hailes ends visit

Foreign Ministers parley sought by Russia

Queen Mother wins at races

150 drowned as boat overturns

Proposal seen concession

impossible run. He knew he was out and kept on running towards the pavilion without turning round to see the umpire's finger go up.

He had made 260 out of 533. With a partnership of 446, he and Sobers were a mere nine short of the world first-class record – set by R.B. Nimbalakar and K.V. Bhandakar in India in 1948–9 – and five short of the second wicket Test record, set by Ponsford and Bradman at The Oval in 1934.

Sobers is wonderfully vague at this point, writing that he believed Hunte thought they required one run to break the record, although he doesn't say which record. He'd record that, before this, 'we have a break, but I honestly cannot remember whether it was lunch or tea.' Of course, they were still in the first hour of the day's play.

Everton Weekes came in and stroked a ball to another substitute off Khan at mid-wicket. Sobers travelled at high speed to within reach of where the immobile Weekes stood but the rest was bagatelle. The substitute misjudged the situation and threw to the wicketkeeper's end where Weekes stood in perfect safety. The wicketkeeper, Imtiaz Ahmed, caught the ball but Sobers was fast on his feet, very fast. By the time Imtiaz had flung the ball to the bowler's end Sobers was already there.

He was 248 and drove Khan through the covers to move to 250 (in a minute over 7 hours). It is not fair to measure Hanif's innings against that of Sobers because the state of the matches was so different, but the fact remains that Hanif had taken 12 hours and 1 minute to score 250, exactly 5 hours longer. That's a day longer.

At lunch West Indies had made 592 for 2 (Sobers 265, Weekes 33). Word spread, as it was bound to do, 'Hutton might be vulnerable and soon.' The gates had to be closed with 20,000 inside.

Sobers was seeing the ball very early once he went on to the back foot and waited for it to come to him. Weekes, a pitbull terrier of a batsman, played a murderous square cut off Kardar's leg-break, and the afternoon so rich in promise was launched. The 600 came up in 9 hours and 18 minutes. Then Weekes slashed at an outswinger from Fazal and was caught ankle-high at slip by Hanif.

The West Indies were 602 for 3 and now the mighty Clyde Walcott was striding on to the wicket. Walcott was a comforting figure if he was on your side. For a decade this immensely powerful man had made heavy runs against top bowling. Sobers felt such comfort that, he'd write, his mind opened up to the possibility of records. He needed only one more to equal George Headley's 270, the highest Test score a West Indian had ever made. Shortly before two o'clock Sobers drove Kardar to the off-side for a single and he'd beaten it. The crowd gave him another world-beating explosion of applause.

The *Sunday Gleaner* reported that 'so dense was the crowd that trees in the ground were crowded and people also sat along walls and on top of the bleachers and sightscreens'.

Walcott struck a ball from Kardar out of the ground and it took 5 minutes to find the ball. Khan took the new ball and Sobers pulled him to the boundary then pushed Fazal for a single for his triple century. 'Maddening cheers' rang out, the *Sunday Gleaner* reported. The whole crowd was on their feet and the cheering went on like great wave-like echoes. The Pakistani players came up and congratulated Sobers and, at the end of the over, so did Walcott. That gesture set the crowd cheering again. Different times, of course: Sobers would no doubt have been mortified if Walcott had come to him immediately and hugged and kissed him, just as Walcott would have been mortified by doing it.[3]

Walcott: *Gerry Alexander is thinking of declaring.*

Sobers: *Well, that's that.*

Walcott: *Not to worry. Settle down, take it easy. I'll give you as much of the strike as possible. Don't worry about time – the runs will come.*[4]

Walcott drove Fazal to the cover boundary and West Indies were 682, their highest Test match total. Sobers then came at the runs rather than waiting for them to come to him. He launched a ferocious attack, spraying his shots all round the wicket, and the 100 partnership was hoisted in only an hour and a half. Sobers late-cut Fazal for a couple and that eased him past Sandham's 325, which was set, of course, on this same ground. Sobers was now in among the triple-century heavyweights and from here he could see Everest's peak, not looming but beckoning.

Walcott kept Sobers calm, which was important because Sobers felt detached from time and didn't feel the mounting tension as he stroked the ball about. As the tension mounted he'd express surprise that with so much 'human electricity' flowing the whole ground didn't 'catch fire'. Never mind that. It all turned on him not getting out and the ball was coming at him 'big as a breadfruit'.

At tea he'd gone past Bradman and drawn level with Hammond, West Indies 730 for 3 (Walcott 68). Of that tea interval, the ground in a tumult of anticipation, Hutton's record at his mercy and with, perhaps unstated, the profound prospect of a guy from a small colony beating the best the Mother Country had ever been able to do, Sobers's literary narrative was entirely silent.

Of more immediate concern was Hanif's 337 and when play resumed Sobers stole a couple of singles off Fazal to beat that, Hanif sprinting in from cover to shake him by the hand. Disaster might have followed. He ran a speculative 2 and only just got home. At 345 he was past Headley's 344 against Tennyson's touring team of 1932, also at Kingston, the highest first-class score made by a West Indian.

Walcott was giving him most of the strike, although once Walcott smote a ball from the exhausted Fazal over the sightscreen. Sobers reached 350 (in 7 minutes short of 10 hours) out of 762, Walcott on 77.

The tension increased. On 360 Sobers took a single from Fazal bringing Walcott down to face. He swept Fazal to the fine-leg boundary and completed a sharp single, returning the strike to Sobers, who turned a ball from Fazal behind square leg for a couple.

363.

At this point Hanif was given a bowl with his slows. He went over the wicket and bowled right-arm from the northern end. Walcott took a single from his second ball, returning the strike to Sobers. Now Hanif changed to round the wicket and bowled left-hand. Sobers pushed the ball to long-off.

364.

Walcott struck the next ball for 6; it was hard to break the habit of a lifetime even in circumstances like these.

Fazal bowled at Sobers – a wide. He couldn't reach it.

The second ball struck him on the pads and for an agonising instant everyone in the ground, including Sobers, must have wondered if he'd always have to share the summit with Hutton. A thousand anxious eyes scanned the umpire for movement. His finger stayed down.

Not out!

Fazal gave the umpire his best glare and, either in frustration or simply wanting the thing over, delivered the next ball without bothering about his run up. It was there for Sobers to push and he pushed it to cover and ran.

The ground erupted. The crowd swarmed on from all directions. They reached Sobers, grabbed hold of him and held him. They carried him about. Sobers thought the place had 'exploded' and he could hear Walcott shouting at them to stay off the wicket. Sobers couldn't even see the Pakistani players, they were lost in the swarm. Sobers heard cheering and some people singing. He felt curiously drawn in different directions: the difficulty in quantifying what he had just achieved and, simultaneously, a guilt that it had stopped the match.

He had been batting for 10 hours and 8 minutes, hitting 38 4s.

For some reason, Alexander ran out on to the field in the confusion to tell the Pakistanis he had declared. Presumably his gesture from the pavilion had gone completely unnoticed.

That provoked a particular West Indian controversy because some people in the crowd felt Sobers was eminently capable of going on to 400 and a declaration deprived him of that chance, although it was not a view Sobers shared. If, he felt, the captain judged a declaration necessary to try and win the match then that was fine. As it was he had moved Everest upwards.

That evening of 1 March 1958 it was a legitimate question whether anybody would ever make 400 in a Test match. Never is a long time but 400 is a long, long way in cricket terms. If you needed a conjunction of circumstances to score a triple century, and it had only been done six times before, what rarefied conjunction would you need for the quadruple? Nobody knew on the evening of 1 March 1958 that it would be another six full years before another batsman even got beyond 300 again, nor that the next West Indian to do it, Lawrence Rowe in 1974, would be the last anywhere for 16 years.

Perhaps the quadruple was destined to be a fabled thing, not so much Everest but the whole Himalayan range.

Meanwhile the Pakistanis pointed out that the crowd had been on the wicket and for them to have to bat on it was unfair if not illegal. Repairs took so long that play was not resumed and the day ended in a strange atmosphere.

Kardar paid fulsome tribute to Sobers: 'I have seen all the great left-handers and today Sobers surpassed them all. He is a very great player'. He would get greater and surveying the whole history of cricket the claim that he is the greatest all-rounder seems unanswerable.

Pakistan struggled to 288 when they did bat again leaving the West Indies winners by an innings and 174.

That, in part, may be the measure of Sobers's innings, but it meant something much more profound. As C.L.R. James wrote in *Beyond a Boundary,* 'what do they know who only cricket know? West Indians crowding to Tests bring with them the whole past history and future hopes of the islands. English people… have a conception of themselves breathed from birth. Drake and mighty Nelson, Shakespeare, Waterloo, the Charge of the Light Brigade, the few who did so much for so many… those constitute a national tradition. Underdeveloped countries have to go back centuries to rebuild one. We of the West Indies have none at all, none that we know of. To such people the three W's, Ram and Val wrecking English batting, help fill a huge gap in their consciousness and their needs. In one of the sheds on the Port of Spain wharf is a painted sign: 365 Garfield Sobers'.

That was what had really been happening.

Notes

[1] Sobers wrote his life story in 1966 (*Cricket Crusader,* Pelham Books) with the collaboration of R.A. Martin. I have used tiny fragments of what appeared about the innings and even those with a certain caution. For example, in Chapter 4 – titled World Record: 'We come to Kingston, Jamaica for the second Test. I am well and in form, and eager to make a good game of it. No more than that.' The initial problem is that he is talking about the Third Test, and if he can't remember in which Test he broke the world record, and Mr Martin evidently didn't look it up, what does that say about the accuracy of the rest?

[2] *Cricket Crusader.*

[3] Jim Laker has recounted how he once showed a film of his 19 wickets against Australia at Old Trafford in 1956 – such a short time before the Sobers innings – to an American audience and they were amazed by how restrained it all was afterwards. Laker took his pullover, slung it over his shoulder and walked off, the rest of the team walking off with him: the precise opposite of rah-rah-rah. Cricket was theatre but the players were players – not actors.

[4] *Cricket Crusader.*

West Indies v Pakistan
Played at Kingston, 26, 27, 28 February, 1, 2, 3 March 1958

PAKISTAN

Hanif Mohammad	c Alexander b Gilchrist	3	b Gilchrist	13
Imtiaz Ahmed	c Alexander b Gilchrist	122	lbw b Dewdney	0
Saeed Ahmed	c Weekes b Smith	52	c Gilchrist b Gibbs	44
Wallis Mathias	b Dewdney	77	c Alexander b Atkinson	19
Alim-ud-Din	c Alexander b Atkinson	15	b Gibbs	30
A.H. Kardar	c Sobers b Atkinson	15	lbw b Dewdney	57
Wazir Mohammad	c Walcott b Dewdney	2	lbw b Atkinson	106
Fazal Mahmood	c Alexander b Atkinson	6	c Alexander b Atkinson	0
Nasimul Ghani	b Atkinson	5	absent hurt	0
Mahmood Hussain	b Atkinson	20	absent hurt	0
Khan Mohammad	not out	3	not out	0
	b 2, l-b 5, n-b 1	8	b 16, l-b 3	19
		328		288

	O	M	R	W		O	M	R	W
Gilchrist	25	3	106	2		12	3	65	1
Dewdney	26	4	88	2		19.3	2	51	2
Atkinson	21	7	42	5		18	6	36	3
Gibbs	7	0	32	0		21	6	46	2
Smith	18	3	39	1		8	2	20	0
Sobers	5	1	13	0		15	4	41	0
Weekes	3	1	10	0					

WEST INDIES

C. Hunte	run out	260
R. Kanhai	c Imtiaz b Fazal	25
G. Sobers	not out	365
E.D. Weekes	c Hanif b Fazal	39
C.L. Walcott	not out	88
	b 1, l-b 8, w 4	13
	(3 dec)	790

Did not bat: O.G. Smith, E. Atkinson, L. Gibbs, F.C.M Alexander, T. Dewdney, R. Gilchrist.

	O	M	R	W
Mahmood	0.5	0	2	0
Fazal	85.2	20	247	2
Khan	54	5	259	0
Nasimul	14	3	39	0
Kardar	37	2	141	0
Mathias	4	0	20	0
Alim	4	0	34	0
Hanif	2	0	11	0
Saeed	6	0	24	0

WEST INDIES WON BY AN INNINGS AND 174

New world record by 1 run. The old record had stood for 20 years and 3 months.

Australia in England, Old Trafford, July 1964

Robert Baddeley Simpson, born Marrickville, Sydney, 3 February 1936.

Test career 1957–77: 63 Tests, 4,869 runs, 10 centuries, average 46.81.

The past is another country, and cricket in England in 1964 was being played in another country. The Gentleman v Players match had only been abandoned a couple of years before; a side called the Rothmans Cavaliers had proved that one-day cricket on a Sunday was what a lot of people wanted in 1963, although what that might mean was unclear. Apart from anything else, the Lord's Day Observance Society was a vocal lobby in making sure that virtually nothing happened on a Sunday at all.

Cricket was still being played within its traditional matrix of three-day county matches and five Tests of five days each. The county grounds were strange, haunted places where a few hundred of the faithful watched the endless ritual of the game being enacted to gentle, distant applause from these few. Test matches were being played defensively, itself a curiosity in what were known as the uninhibited, 'swinging' 1960s where young people were suddenly exploring what they thought were limitless horizons. That mood certainly hadn't reached cricket.

Certainly the urgency of one-day cricket was almost unimagined and so was the energy it would bring to the five-day game, to the point where, by the 1990s, runs were being scored at a tremendous rate and the grounds were full again. To take a random but appropriate example, the first day's play in the 2001 series between England and Australia at Birmingham produced 427 runs at an average of 5 an over. Inside four days (the time it took Australia to win by an innings) 30 wickets had fallen and 1,074 runs had been scored. More than that, bad weather cut the equivalent of two sessions from the four days and the fourth day consisted entirely of England moving from their overnight 48 for 1 to 164 all out.

Contrast it with that other country in 1964. The opening day of the First Test at Nottingham was skewed by rain and so was the Second Test at Lord's, both matches drawn. So I'll use the first day of the Third Test at Leeds. In 10 minutes short of a full day England scored 268 at 2.60 an over. Australia won inside four days, 23 wickets fell for 997 runs but it had taken virtually a whole day more to get them.

The game was dying of prudence, caution and siege mentality, in short the opposite of the 1960s. The Fourth Test at Old Trafford mirrored this exactly. The First and Second Tests were drawn, Australia won at Leeds by seven wickets and it meant that as holders of the Ashes, a draw at Old Trafford would be enough to retain them.

The Australian captain, Bobby Simpson, won the toss and that was clearly visible because, although he didn't make a 'melodramatic' gesture like throwing his hands in the air (nobody did that sort of thing any more than Walcott would be hugging and kissing Sobers), he had a 'springy walk back to the pavilion'.[1] The wicket was flat and laden with runs and now Simpson could bat on it first. He fully intended to bat England out of the game however long it took and whatever the consequences for the game. It would be like setting it in concrete.

Simpson opened with Bill Lawry, a dour, angular left-hander who took strike. John Price, a Middlesex pace bowler with a long arcing run, bowled to Lawry and an appeal for a catch at the wicket was refused off the last ball of the first over. Now Simpson, who had never made a Test century, faced Fred Rumsey of Somerset and the marathon had begun. Simpson and Lawry made a circumspect 17 in the first half an hour although, in a bizarre sequence, Lawry hooked Price over fine-leg for 6 and when

Warwickshire seamer Tom Cartwright came on Lawry hooked him for 6 too. The bizarre aspect was that, amid all this caution, Lawry's initial 6 was the first boundary of the innings.

Australia were 40 after the first hour (Lawry 29, Simpson 9) and the 50 took an hour and 14 minutes. Simpson brought that up by square cutting the first 4 of the day. It was, as someone noted, the last aggressive stroke off Cartwright for some time. That latter phrase must be seen as either irony or under-statement.

Fred Titmus, the small Middlesex off-spinner with a twinkling run-up and a right-arm to make the ball curl as well as spin, was on now. He and Cartwright were old hands, long fashioned by the disciplines of the county game, and both could bowl to a field and a length. At last Simpson drove Cartwright to the boundary and, using his feet, hit Titmus past mid-wicket to the boundary.

Cartwright looked the most likely bowler to take a wicket and Lawry had a couple of tricky overs against him, but at lunch Australia had reached 84, Lawry 45 and Simpson catching him, if you can put it like that, on 37. (Comparisons are dangerous, as I keep saying, but to pursue the 1964–2001 analogy, Australia won the toss and batted at The Oval and they scored only 66, although there had been time lost to rain.)

Lawry moved to his 50 in the second over after lunch, scored in 2 hours and 6 minutes, and the Australian 100 came up soon after. Lawry celebrated by hooking Rumsey for 6. It was a short ball, Lawry rocked back and, as it rose off the pitch, hit it over the fine leg boundary. In fact Lawry didn't hit a 4 – a peach of an off-drive from Price – until he'd reached 65. Simpson moved to 50 by cutting Price to the boundary and then turning him for a single. It had taken him 2 hours and 36 minutes.

The Gloucestershire spinner John Mortimore came on at 3.25pm when Australia were 147. 'An amusing point of difference was that Titmus rubbed the ball in the dust, and Mortimore rubbed it on himself to preserve the shine. Neither tactic worked'.[2] Mortimore looked steady rather than deadly and his first over cost a couple of runs, then Simpson drove Titmus to bring up the 150 in 3 hours and 17 minutes.

The crowd began a slow handclap. Australia crawled into and through the 160s and now the crowd was saluting the occasional runs with ironical cheering. Lawry was into the 90s and, as someone wrote, was particularly dour when he got there.

Lawry reached his 100 by off-driving Mortimore for 3 after 3 hours and 55 minutes (three 6s, five 4s). Denzil Batchelor, who has already been quoted a couple of times in this chapter, was an expressive and sometimes amusing writer on the game, and now he wrote that on this 'pluperfect wicket' with England's attack 'toiling but helpless' he could see no good reason why Lawry shouldn't add another 100 by lunchtime the following day and a third 100 by close of play.

At 4.15pm Simpson flicked Ted Dexter, an occasional medium-pace bowler, to fine leg and Australia were 181. That, amazingly, beat the country's record for the first wicket by Warren Bardsley and Syd Gregory at The Oval in 1909. The crowd cheered this genuinely. Tea was taken at the end of the over, Australia 183 (Lawry 101, Simpson 76). The 2001 comparison: 203 for 1.

After it, the scoring crawled again and the crowd slow handclapped again. Simpson finally moved into the 80s with an exquisite off-drive from Cartwright but – perhaps the proximity to his first Test 100 was affecting him – he became hesitant, nicking a Cartwright inswinger to fine leg. A leg bye brought up the 200 in 4 hours and 34 minutes. A run later Lawry pushed a ball from Mortimore between the bowler and mid-on and thought the ball had gone past Mortimore. He began to run but Mortimore reached the ball. Simpson saw this, turned and flung himself full length to get his bat into the crease. Lawry had run on and Mortimore lobbed the ball to the wicketkeeper, Jim Parks, to run him out easily.

Lawry's 106 had lasted 4 hours and 41 minutes, and – meagre, watchful, endlessly patient – he had given only one chance to Titmus off Dexter at 39.

Ian Redpath came in and Dexter took the new ball. Redpath looked immediately comfortable and ready to hustle the scoring along, while Simpson defended his way towards the century, if you see what I mean. Redpath had altered the tempo. At 223 he cut Price and Rumsey, in the slips, dropped it, and at 226 he might have been run out. A couple of balls later Simpson might have been run out too.

He finally reached his 100 at six o'clock, turning Price away for a single. He had made it out of 232, in five and a half hours (six 4s and, worth noting, 50 singles).

Redpath went at 233, lbw to Cartwright, and Norman O'Neill, an explosive and muscular batsman of rare talent, batted out the day, Simpson 109 not out. Australia were 253 for 2. The 2001 comparison, 324 for 2, and the final eight overs lost to bad light.

On the second day Simpson defended on while O'Neill played strokes. Even the calcification of the 1960s could not rob every man of his birthright. Even so, the pair put on only 20 in the first half hour, but when Titmus was brought into the attack O'Neill hammered him through the covers. Adding 45 took an hour and the 300 came up shortly after. That had taken more than 7 hours.

Denzil Bachelor found this evocative paragraph.

'We were grateful for the warm Manchester sunlight gilding the semi-circle of skyscrapers, factory chimneys, church spires and the trees stretching away to the Derbyshire and Cheshire borders. The flags hung limply in the softest of south-west zephyrs at the masthead: the banner of Australia; and that of England that the sun never set on in the days when Hobbs, MacLaren and Grace threw their shadows over this field, flanked by that of firms advertising Beccles and Honey Malt cakes.'[3]

Price came on for Cartwright, and O'Neill cut his second ball to the boundary, had an lbw appeal refused on the next ball and was yorked the ball after that for 47. He'd been in for 1 hour and 43 minutes and hit five 4s. In that time Simpson had made 34.

Burly Peter Burge emerged and took a single from his first ball, settled himself in and then off-drove Price massively to the cover boundary. Simpson did the same next over, off Titmus. His 150 took 7 hours and 45 minutes and he looked perfectly composed, perfectly within himself, perfectly capable of batting as long again.

By lunch Simpson had added 46 and Australia were 352 for three. The 2001 comparison: 440 for 2.

Burge seemed intent on announcing what he meant to do during the afternoon because he drove Price's first ball to the boundary. He tried three sweeps then Simpson spoke to him telling him to go carefully. The scoring rate sank back and the slow handclapping began again. Simpson took half an hour to score 7.

On 34 Burge drove Cartwright through the covers, straight drove him and then tried to swing him – half a slog – and Price caught him at short leg. In that time Simpson had made 27 and Australia were 382 for 4.

Bob Booth, an ascetic, slender, correct batsman, made his own statement by pulling Mortimore for 6. Then Simpson square cut Mortimore to the boundary to bring up the 400, but in the first hour after lunch Australia had scored only 45, and Simpson had scored only 17 of them. The 400 had taken 9 hours and 8 minutes. The match was drifting into a sequence of statistics, somehow numbing, and little else.

Australian journalist Percy Beames wrote that Simpson's 'average scoring rate for the first three hours of play was 20 runs an hour, which was carrying defence far beyond the point of sensibility'.[4]

Price took the new ball and that broke the tedium up, however briefly. Simpson square cut the first ball to the boundary then hooked another, and 11 came from the over. This unexpected sprint completed, Simpson reverted to his previous rhythm and froze on 190. He had to wait until just before four o'clock to poach a single from Price on the leg side to inch up to 192, giving him the highest Test innings ever played at Old Trafford (the previous best was Bill Edrich against South Africa, 1947). Batchelor wrote that the 'educated crowd applauded respectfully' because they'd realised that slow-handclapping had no effect whatsoever.

At tea Australia were 449 for 4 (Simpson 198, Booth 30). The 2001 comparison, 580 for 4.

In the second over after the resumption Simpson on-drove Titmus for a couple and that was his 200. It had taken 10 hours and 8 minutes. He was not encouraged to moderate his caution. Booth on-drove Mortimore to the boundary but Simpson played a tame maiden to Mortimore, drawing another round of slow handclapping. Simpson did, however, hit 2 boundaries in an over from Titmus.

Shortly after five o'clock the 100 partnership was reached (in 8 minutes under 2 hours), and Booth hauled Mortimore to leg to get to his 50. It was an aggressive stroke, something a reporter thought well worth mentioning. Over these two days aggression had always been worth noting.

The 500 took 10 hours 3 minutes (Simpson 220, Booth 58), but there was no suggestion of a declaration. Booth proceeded at his own cautious pace and he and Simpson looked entirely safe, although Booth nicked Price over the slips and Titmus found the edge of Simpson's bat; not much else until, when Simpson was 228, he might have been run out. Parks threw the ball to Titmus at the bowler's end but Simpson had just got in.

Before the close, in one bound Simpson set himself free. He stepped into Mortimore and straight drove him for 6. He was 265 at the close, Booth 82 and Australia 570 for 4. The 2001 comparison, 641 for 4 declared, England 80 for 1.

Surely Simpson would declare now? As E.M. Wellings, a trenchant critic, wrote, it 'seemed to be carrying caution too far'. Wellings pointed out that Simpson 'had already exhausted two thirds of the playing time. Moreover, the weather was threatening rain'.[5]

Wellings was missing the mood of the era. Rain would merely confirm what Simpson had set out to do.

He had now put together the highest Test innings of any Australian since the war, and still he was nowhere near finished. The sequence of statistics mounted on day three but something had changed. Simpson decided that the best tactic was to go for *quick* runs. (Evidently he had had a net before the start of play, and one of the English selectors, Doug Insole, bowled to him – although whether this had any relevance is unclear). Inside the first 20 minutes of play Simpson had gone past Ponsford's 266 at The Oval in 1934 and now he was trying to score off every ball. Dexter pulled the field back but that made no difference. Soon enough Simpson was past Bradman's 270 at Melbourne in 1936–7.

The 200 partnership came up and then the Australian 600 after 12 hours and 20 minutes. Then Booth went, caught and bowled by Price. It was, as someone said, as if Price could simply not believe this had happened in the real world, as if he was momentarily released from some kind of dreamworld.

In came Tom Veivers, jolly and by temperament unlikely to want to bat for three days, while, after 30 minutes, Simpson straight drove Mortimore to move past R.E. Foster's 287, which, in a certain way, had remained a landmark. The fourth new ball was taken at 616 and Simpson went to 300 by square cutting Price. Shortly after, at 12.15pm, he lashed at Price and was caught behind by Parks. That released the whole England team from the dreamworld that had seemed to have no end. They had had to wait 12 hours and 42 minutes for that end. Simpson had hit that one 6 off Mortimore and 23 4s. It was the longest ever innings played against England and it attracted fierce controversy.

Ted Dexter would write that Australia had been at the crease for virtually half of the match and 'once more the little urn had put the blight on a series'.[6] Dexter had made this point before, and it had attracted scorn. He made the point again here at Old Trafford, but kept his voice down while he was doing it. He felt sorry, he added, for those who had paid to watch.

The 'blight' was easily explained because winning or retaining the Ashes had grown into an absolute imperative and the well-being of a five Test series would not be allowed to influence that. At the time it seemed insoluble.

Certainly, as Percy Beames pointed out: 'Had Simpson set his sights on Bradman's record he may have surpassed it and gone on to better Len Hutton's feat.'[7] Denzil Batchelor, defending Simpson, wrote that no one gave the slow handclap to Hutton ... 'as some sporting patriot confessed: you can't knight Hutton and hang Simpson.'[8]

Wellings (typically) felt that Simpson had been fully justified in doing what he did because the onus was on England – needing victory if they were to regain the Ashes – to 'issue the challenge and set the pace [...] If they were minded to be negative in the field, Simpson was justified in declining to take risks to overcome the defensive tactics of his opponents, until he had placed his side in a safe position'.[9]

All these views were centred around a specific problem. If playing cricket like this was legitimate, who would come and watch it and which youngsters would want to play it? One of the lessons of history is that seemingly permanent structures and empires

SIMPSON, LAWRY IN RECORD TEST STAND

TEST SCOREBOARD

AUSTRALIA.
First Innings.

LAWRY, run out	106
SIMPSON, n.o.	109
REDPATH, lbw, b Cartwright	19
O'NEILL, n.o.	10
Sundries	9
Total for two wickets	253

FALL: 201, 233.

BOWLING:

	O.	M.	R.	W.
PRICE	19	3	58	0
RUMSEY	17	4	35	0
CARTWRIGHT	43	17	76	1
DEXTER	4	0	12	0
TITMUS	19	8	32	0
MORTIMORE	20	7	27	0

STUMPS.

Centuries to Both

From Percy Beames and A.A.P.

MANCHESTER, July 23. — Centuries to Bill Lawry and Bob Simpson in a record opening partnership of 201 gave Australia a magnificent start to the fourth Test at Old Trafford today.

Lawry, run out for 106, and Simpson 109 not out — the first century of his long Test career — stayed together until just after tea in a stand which may have made the Ashes safe for Australia.

At stumps the tourists were 2/253, with O'Neill, who came in shortly before stumps, 10 not out.

There were few fireworks in the Simpson-Lawry partnership.

They went in obviously determined to stay there until their side was well on the way to victory, and both refused to take the slightest risk in a long, dour struggle.

They took a lot of barracking as the score slowly mounted, but they still waited for the right ball to hit, and rarely gave the bowlers any hope of success.

Lawry was there for 235 minutes for his 100, and Simpson took 330 minutes.

Their 201 partnership eclipsed the previous record of 180, by Warren Bardsley and Sid Gregory, at the Oval in 1909.

Lawry's innings was a masterpiece of well-disciplined defence and unwavering concentration.

The only bowler who really worried him was Tom Cartwright, who managed to slide a few of his fast-medium seamers close to the edge of the left-hander's bat.

The rest of the England attack Lawry handled with comparative ease, waiting for the right ball to attack, and occasionally letting loose with his favorite hook.

He batted for 282 minutes for his runs, and although he hit only five 4's, he established some sort of a Test record by hooking two fine 6's in the first hour of play, and another later in the day.

Simpson was slower than Lawry but, if anything, was even safer than his partner.

He was a long time in the "nervous 90's," but despite his slowness no-one begrudged him his century when it finally came.

Simpson won the toss from Ted Dexter for the first time in this series this morning and elected to bat on a wicket tinged with green.

It looked the sort of pitch that would assist England's pace bowlers, but the certainty with which the Australians played them soon showed that the new ball was not having much effect, and that Simpson's decision had been the right one.

England used six bowlers during the day as Dexter desperately rang the changes in an attempt to force a break-through.

However, apart from Cartwright, the bowling could only be described as steady. Certainly, it was never particularly dangerous.

By mid-afternoon, with Australia's total soaring, England's bowlers and fieldsmen badly needed a "lift" from their captain.

But Dexter appeared to have run out of inspiration. He was just waiting for something to turn up.

England made Warwickshire batsman Mike Smith 12th man this morning, and went into the Test with its full complement of bowlers —three pace and two off-spinners.

Lawry and Simpson opened sedately against England's new pace bowlers Fred Rumsey and John Price, only 19 runs coming in the first half-hour.

The only early fright was brought about by the last ball of Price's first over. It lifted and moved away to the off, beating Lawry badly, but apart from that he seemed quite comfortable.

His timing was a little astray when he tried a hook in Rumsey's fourth over and the ball fell just clear of Boycott at fine leg, but he made amends when Price pitched one short in the next over.

Lawry moved quickly and a beautiful hook, very fine, was still high in the air as it sailed across the boundary.

Dexter immediately replaced Price with medium-pacer Tom Cartwright — only to see Lawry hook his second ball hard and high for another 6.

Simpson was more restrained, but was in no trouble. He seemed content to let Lawry do the scoring and after the first hour had made only eight of Australia's total of 38.

In another quick bowling change, off-spinner Fred Titmus came on at 0/42. His first over produced two runs, but Lawry played a careful maiden to his second.

Runs Came Slowly

The 50 came up after 74 minutes when Simpson drove the first 4 of the day off Cartwright, but it was the last aggressive stroke off him for some time.

Cartwright, operating at the other end to Titmus, had fallen into a length and both batsmen—but particularly Lawry — had to watch him carefully.

Finally Simpson took a 4 off him with a lovely drive, but in the same over Cartwright beat Lawry all the way with successive balls.

Simpson Scores

Simpson negotiated this tricky period much more effectively than Lawry, and gradually began to overhaul his partner.

Neat leg glances off Cartwright and Titmus, and a 4 off Titmus punched off his toes, took him to 37 as Lawry moved slowly from 39 to 45 in an Australian total of 0/84 at lunch.

Lawry's 50 came up in the second over after lunch — he had batted for 126 minutes for it — and Australia's century was posted 10 minutes later.

Soon after, Lawry got his third 6. Rumsey pitched one short, and as it reared, Lawry lay back and slammed it high over the fine leg fence.

But it was still anything but aggressive batting by the Australians. They were simply grinding out the runs when the right ball to hit came along, and were well behind in their race with the clock.

Lawry did not hit a 4 until he was 65, but when he did get his first, from a sweetly timed cover-drive off Price, he immediately repeated the shot for the same result.

He had drawn away from Simpson again, mainly because he was getting most of the strike. But Simpson had seen enough of it to cut Price for 4, turn him for one, and pass 50 after 146 minutes.

He had hit only three 4's, but if anything it had been a more convincing innings than Lawry's.

He was using his feet beautifully to the spinners, moving down the wicket to turn good-length balls to over-pitched ones.

Lawry, on the other hand, was still having his difficulties with Cartwright and Titmus, and several times was tempted to flash at balls outside the off stump.

Spinner John Mortimore, one of England's bowling replacements, for this Test, was not given his first over until Australia was 0/147.

Like England's other bowlers, he looked steady rather than dangerous, and two runs off his first over, followed by a Simpson drive for two off Titmus, made Australia 0/150 after 197 minutes.

Crowd Jeers

Slowly the score mounted —and the crowd was not happy about it. As Australia crawled through the 160's the crowd slow hand clapped and greeted runs with ironical cheers.

Passing through the 90's, Lawry was in his most dour mood, but finally a magnificent cover-drive to the fence off Mortimore gave him his century, after 234 minutes.

He had hit five 4's and three 6's.

Soon after, a single to Simpson took the total to 181, eclipsing the previous best opening stand for Australia, by Bardsley and Gregory at the Oval in 1909.

At tea, the total was 0/183, and after the interval, the grim battle for runs continued — to the tune of more jeering and slow hand-clapping from the crowd.

Run Out

It seemed Lawry and Simpson were there for the day, and then, at 201, Lawry was run out.

He pushed a ball back just wide of the pitch, and called for a suicidal run.

Simpson began to move, but when he saw the bowler, Mortimore, pick up the ball, he turned and hurled himself full length on the pitch to get his bat back into the crease.

Lawry had continued on, and Mortimore had only to lob the ball back to Parks to run him out.

Redpath joined Simpson, who was struggling laboriously towards his 100, and began confidently, stroking the ball well.

He had a "life" at 12, however, when he snicked Price into the slips and Rumsey dropped a sitter.

Simpson 100

Simpson was really in the horrors, but after a long, long wait, he pushed the single which gave him his first Test 100.

He had been there for 330 minutes, and had hit six 4's and 50 singles.

Apprentice for Persian Opera

By Tony Kennedy

Owner Mr. Keith Gregory has decided to take advantage of an apprentice's allowance for prepost favorite Persian Opera, and last night engaged Charlie Bartolo for the colt in the 2nd Derrimut Welter at Moonee Valley tomorrow.

Bartolo, rated one of the best young riders in Melbourne, will claim 7 lb. on Persian Opera, reducing the colt's weight to 9.2.

Mr. Gregory may not run Persian Opera if the track is too heavy, but plans at the moment are to start the colt.

With Bartolo's claim, Persian Opera comes in very well on 9.2 on an 8.0 minimum.

Persian Opera's last outing was in a similar race at Moonee Valley on June 27, when he finished second to Native Village in the 2nd Oak Park Handicap.

Smart South Australian High Income, an acceptor for the 2nd Derrimut will be scratched, and will run at Morphettville (S.A.) tomorrow.

End of Season

The eight-event programme at the Valley will wind up the 1963-64 racing season.

Trainer Angus Armanasco has easily won the Victorian Trainers' Premiership and Alan Burton has the jockeys' premiership well in his keeping.

From a riding point of view main interest will centre on the struggle between Harry White and Jim Courtney for the apprentices' premiership.

Both boys have ridden 20 winners.

White is apprenticed to Stan Murphy, and Courtney is with his father, Pat Courtney.

So far White has been engaged to ride Native Village and Katab, and there is a strong chance he will be on Announcer in the Sunset Handicap.

Courtney will ride St. Maurice, Pennant Star, Soldate and Norfolk Lad.

Zinga Lee

Brian Gilders has been engaged to ride Zinga Lee in the 1st Derrimut Welter.

Zinga Lee will be having his first start since Easter Monday, when he won the Sydney Cup at Randwick.

Apprentice Brian Gaw will be back in the saddle tomorrow after suspension, and has been booked for Westerly and Sir Cameron.

Sir Cameron, winner of the Grand National Steeple, is engaged in the 13-furlong Glen Orla Handicap.

Feature of the programme will be the jumping double—the Mia Mia Hurdle and A. V. Hiskins Steeple.

Form in both races will be a sound guide to the Australian Hurdle and Steeple double, at Caulfield on August 1 and 8.

No Wedding, Says Clay

MIAMI, July 23.

Heavyweight boxing champion Cassius Clay, smiling broadly and holding the hand of a girl in a yellow frock, denied rumors tonight that he was secretly married.

"Man, when I get married, the whole world is going to know it," said Clay, who was spotted walking around the terminal of the international airport here.

There have been rumors—one of them published in a local newspaper — that Clay had taken a wife.

"This is my girl, man, this isn't my wife. I haven't got a wife yet. I'm still looking," said Clay, who returned to Miami last week end.—A.A.P.

Boycott Threat on World Cup

CAIRO, July 23.

Member nations of the African Football Confederation will boycott the World Cup competition "unless the International Football Federation (F.I.F.A.) grants places for at least one African and one Asian country in the final stages," a confederation official said here last night.

RENT
FALCON
10!

DONS' SKIPPER FIT TO PLAY

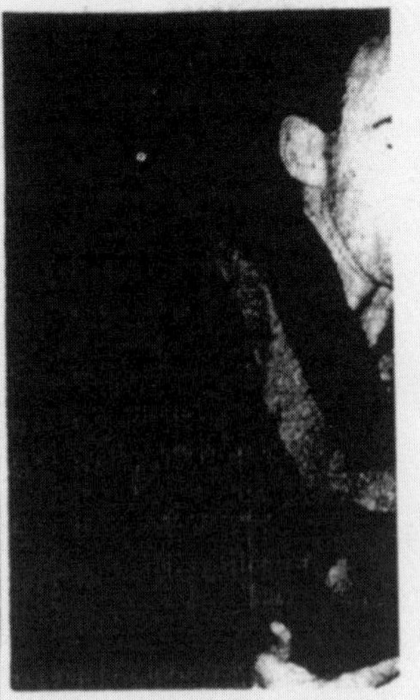

A BOOST TO ESSENDON'S morale was giver above, trained last night and was declared f match against North Melbourne. Clarke has injury.

Whitten for Against Colli

FOOTSCRAY captain-coach T after missing last week's ga thigh, has been named in Bulldogs against Collingwood to

Whitten started the season at the centre, but was switched to centre half-forward after two games.

However, Noel Fincher played particularly well at centre half-forward last week and, with Graeme Chalmers needed to rove tomorrow, the pivot position was opened for Whitten.

Chalmers will take over as No. 2 rover because George Bisset is out injured.

Bisset, who is troubled by a bruised knee, attempted to train last night, but the injury was too sore for him to attempt a serious fitness test.

Another fresh player in the Bulldog line-up this week is Don McKenzie, who was named on a half-forward flank.

With McKenzie in on a flank, Alan Hunter has been switched on to a wing as a replacement for Ian Bryant, who has been dr ped to 19th man.

There is only one cha in the COLLINGWO team. Paul Wadham g into the side in place of injured Trevor Steer.

Steer, who has a b blood vessel in a calf mus trained for 20 minutes l night, but was declared available.

Although he mov fairly, he was declar unavailable because of t injury.

Half-forward flanker Tuddenham, who had stitches in a cut forehe after last week's ga against Geelong, trai well last night to prove hi self fit for selection.

Two Rested

He will have the stitc removed from the cut morrow morning.

Ted Potter and K Turner were both rest

League Teams

CARLTON v. MELB

B.: Benetti, Buckley, Greenwood.
H.B.: Anderson, Collis, Varlamos.
C.: Stewart, Collins, Pleydell.
H.F.: Cox, Thiessen, Hall.
F.: Sankey, Lofts, Best.
Foll.: Nicholls, Silvagni.
Rov.: Nankervis.
Res.: Hoggett, J. Gill.
In: Benetti, Best, Thiessen.
Out: Crowe (inj.), Comben, Hoggett.

B.: Cromp
H.B.: Anc
C.: Dixon
H.F.: Ken
F.: Jacobs
Foll.: Bar
Rov.: Tow
Res.: Dav
In: Adam
Out: Wats

COLLINGWOOD v. FOO

B.: Reeves, Potter, Wadham.
H.B.: Hill, Mahon, Wright.
C.: Turner, Henderson, Hutchesson.
H.F.: Tuddenham, Urquhart, Chapman.
F.: Waters, Graham, Norman.
Foll.: Gabelich, K. Rose.
Rov.: Bone.
Res.: Fellowes, Irwin.
In: Wadham.
Out: Steer (inj.).

B.: Walke
H.B.: Jilla
C.: Smith,
H.F.: McK
F.: Marsh,
Foll.: Schu
Rov.: Hobl
Res.: Brya
In: Whitte
Out: Bisset

RICHMOND v. SOUTH M

B.: O. Madigan, Swift, Cameron.
H.B.: Selleck, Gahan, Grimmond.
C.: Brown, Barrot, Davenport.
H.F.: Northey, Busse, Dean.
F.: Warner, Jewell, Dimattina.
Foll.: Crowe, Hammond.
Rov.: Lawson.
Res.: Arnold, Hickman.
In: Busse, Cameron, Dimattina, Selleck.
Out: K. Smith (inj.), Guinane, Hickman, B. Smith.

B.: K. Par
H.B.: Rant
C.: G. Park
H.F.: Mage
F.: Matthe
Foll.: Reilly
Rov.: Skilt
Res.: Philli
In: Harrison
Out: Colvin

ST. KILDA v. HAWT

B.: Head, Synman, Mynott.
H.B.: Walsh, McHugh, Griffiths.
C.: Billing, Stewart, Read.
H.F.: Baldock, Cooper, Oakley.
F.: Wallis, Morton, Payne.
Foll.: Ditterich, Morrow.
Rov.: Smith.

B.: Parkin,
H.B.: McPh
C.: Youren
H.F.: Arthu
F.: Browne,
Foll.: Beck

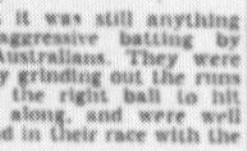

TAKE WILLIE TURNER:

Willie Turner is a maltman. He constantly

can go away very, very quickly and there were many (including this author) who began to fear for the future of the game. If it was no more than a turgid ritual at its highest level, it would become irrelevant to modern life very quickly and especially a modern life exploding with youth, sex, colour and vitality. You could feel the pulse of life in Carnaby Street, whether you liked Carnaby Street or not. You could feel no pulse at all in a batsman on a good wicket, in the prime of his life and in front of an eager crowd spending almost 13 hours in defence.

The remainder of the match maintained the theme, although Rumsey picked up a couple of wickets and Simpson finally declared on 656 for 8. England then made 611 so that there was only time in the Australian second innings for two overs. Simpson made 4.

As it happened, four years later I was sitting next to Jack Fingleton in the Press Box at Old Trafford and Simpson, then retired, came up to him. They talked quietly about something which seemed to be worrying Simpson. 'Tell them,' Fingleton said – whoever they were – 'that you're the fella who scored 300 here four years ago. That should do it.' Simpson smiled, and in just the way he hadn't permitted himself to do for those 13 long hours.

Notes

[1]   *The Test Matches of 1964*, Batchelor.
[2]   Ibid.
[3]   Ibid.
[4]   *The Age,* Melbourne.
[5]   *Simpson's Australians,* Wellings.
[6]   *Ted Dexter Declares*, Dexter.
[7]   *The Age,* Melbourne.
[8]   Batchelor, op. cit.
[9]   Wellings, op. cit.

Englands v Australia
Played at Old Trafford, 2, 3, 4, 6, 7 July 1964

AUSTRALIA

W.M. Lawry	run out	106	not out	0
R.B.Simpson	c Parks b Price	311	not out	4
I.R. Redpath	lbw b Cartwright	19		
N.C. O'Neill	b Price	47		
P.J. Burge	c Price b Cartwright	34		
B.C. Booth	c-b Price	98		
T.R.Veivers	c Edrich b Rumsey	22		
A.T.W. Grout	c Dexter b Rumsey	0		
G.D. McKenzie	not out	0		
	b 1, l-b 9, n-b 9	19		
	(8 dec) 656		(no wkt) 4	

Did not bat: N.J.N. Hawke, G.E. Corling.

	O	M	R	W		O	M	R	W
Rumsey	35.5	4	99	2	Barrington	1	0	4	0
Price	45	4	183	3	Titmus	1	1	0	0
Cartwright	77	32	118	2					
Titmus	44	14	100	0					
Dexter	4	0	12	0					
Mortimore	49	13	122	0					
Boycott	1	0	3	0					

ENGLAND

G. Boycott	b McKenzie	58
J.H. Edrich	c Redpath b McKenzie	6
E.R. Dexter	b Veivers	174
K.F. Barrington	lbw b McKenzie	256
P.H. Parfitt	c Grout b McKenzie	12
J.M. Parks	c Hawke b Veivers	60
F.J. Titmus	c Simpson b McKenzie	9
J.H. Mortimore	b Burge b McKenzie	12
T.W. Cartwright	b McKenzie	4
J.S.E. Price	b Veivers	1
F.E. Rumsey	not out	3
	b 5, l-b 11	16
		611

	O	M	R	W
McKenzie	60	15	153	7
Corling	46	11	96	0
Hawke	63	28	95	0
Simpson	19	4	59	0
Veivers	95.1	36	155	3
O'Neill	10	0	37	0

MATCH DRAWN

Failed by 55 runs to beat the record.

310*

England v New Zealand, Leeds, July 1965

John Hugh Edrich, born Blofield, Norfolk, 21 June 1937.

Test career 1963–76: 77 Tests, 5,138 runs, 12 centuries, average 43.54.

One time, long ago, I was lucky to be sharing a luncheon table with, among others, John Edrich at The Oval. Memory holds him as a square, chunky, strong fellow, a whisp of his native Norfolk in his speech and a broad, open smile. A current and controversial topic was the West Indian team's use of four fast bowlers in rotation. It was intimidating but, as Edrich explained, it was more than just that.[1] Because they were all fast they bowled very few balls per hour, and, in any given over, a certain number you couldn't reach, a certain number you couldn't get away for runs and, across an hour, this left very few opportunities for a batsman to actually score.

The inescapable equation of the four fast bowlers, he said, was that the batsman was, of necessity, scoring slowly and that brought all manner of pressures of its own, whereas he might have been scoring at a respectable rate if you looked at the ratio of balls you could actually score off.

Edrich understood these things because, as an opener, he had faced it often enough while he made runs and made himself into a difficult man to dismiss. You don't average 43 in Tests if you are anything else. Memory holds him there, too, the forearms of a blacksmith, suprisingly dainty on his feet when he needed to be but, above all, determined. And he loved to give a cricket ball a proper smack. He was born into it and he became the fifth member of his family to play county cricket (Bill Edrich was an uncle).

New Zealand had proved weak opponents when they toured England in 1958, and some of the Tests finished so quickly that exhibition matches were arranged. To prevent a repetition across five Tests they'd share the 1965 summer with South Africa. The New Zealanders would tour until July playing three Tests and the South Africans from the end of June to September also playing three Test matches.[2] As *Wisden* pointed out, (1966 Almanac, page 270) nothing like this had been tried since 1912 when England, Australia and South Africa played a triangular tournament, which had not been a success.

Now New Zealand encountered a wet English summer, poor wickets and, during the First Test at Birmingham (which England won by 9 wickets), weather so cold that hot coffee was brought on for batsmen and fielders. England won the Second Test by 7 wickets in somewhat better weather and so they had taken the series. Leeds and the Third Test remained.

Edrich had not played in the first two Tests and, in truth, since his debut in 1963 had not managed to establish himself as a permanent member of the side. A curiosity. Dexter and Geoff Boycott were both injured so that Ken Barrington, dropped for negativity after taking 7 and a quarter hours to make 137 in the First Test, could return to replace Dexter and Edrich could replace Boycott.

Pausing here and returning to the theme explored in the previous chapter about how cricket was living entirely outside the swinging 1960s, *Wisden* (1966 Almanac, page 282) castigated Barrington's performance at Birmingham ('tedious exhibition' stayed at 85 for 62 minutes 'adopting the most exaggerated two-eyed stance ever seen'), pointed out that only 107 people had paid to watch the final day, and welcomed Barrington's dropping for the Second Test because it meant action was finally being taken to make the game more entertaining.

Edrich sensed a different pressure. He was being given a final chance to prove he was a Test player, and he found 'nerves that had lain dormant all my life suddenly came alive'.[3]

England captain Mike Smith won the toss and batted. There were 5,000 spectators in the ground, a scattering and a smattering, and this at one of the traditional citadels of the game. Yes, cricket was dying. Where was the bustle, hum and buzz that Bradman had known? That's unfair, of course, because cricket's greatest draw cannot be compared with a pleasant and popular side of New Zealanders who were workman-like, but in another way it's not unfair at all because any Test at Headingley offering the rich promise of Barber, Edrich, Barrington, Cowdrey and Parfitt batting – not to mention their own Ray Illingworth – ought, if nothing else, to have brought the annual pilgrims from the Ridings to the citadel, and this was before the overt commercialisation of the game brought Test and touring sides to a whole medley of competitions all over the planet. In 1965, however, to any working man in Yorkshire this Third Test was more than the annual opportunity to see the best cricketers in the land in combat, it was the only opportunity.

People weren't coming any more, except in these small numbers.

Due to the measure of what John Edrich was about to do, many of those absent must have bitterly regretted it when they caught the evening news bulletin or opened page 14 of the following morning's *Yorkshire Post*. They'd missed a feast.

Both openers, Edrich and Bob Barber of Warwickshire, were left-handers. Barber took strike against Dick Motz – sharper than medium – from the Kirkstall Lane end and cut his fourth ball to the boundary. The wind was bitter but the outfield fast and the wicket true. It boded well because it would allow the batsmen to play their full range of strokes and, more than that, once the ball had been hit past a fielder it travelled to the boundary so fast that turning and chasing was futile.

Initially, however, Edrich could only play the opening over of Bruce Taylor, a 21-year-old right-armer, for a maiden. Barber clipped a couple off the next Motz over but Edrich still couldn't get Taylor away.

Barber was a bustling stroke-maker and now he struck Motz to the mid-wicket boundary, leg-glanced for a couple and steered a single to mid-off. That brought him to face Taylor and, off the last ball of the over, he got a thin edge to wicketkeeper John Ward. England were 13 for 1 and Barber had made all of them.

At 11.55am, Barrington strode to the wicket but Edrich was close to despair. The harder he tried, the more elusive his first run proved to be and he only got it after 25 minutes: a single from Motz. It was the most modest, tentative beginning for a man who was trying to set out his CV and get the job permanently.

After Edrich had his precious single he survived an appeal for lbw and retaliated by driving Motz to the boundary past mid-off. Perhaps it was then that, in his own words, 'something clicked'.

Dick Collinge, left arm, replaced Motz and Barrington, who had been in for 20 minutes and still not scored, stroked for a single. He was on his way and soon enough travelling like a 'bomb'.[4] This was in the nature of a sub-plot because dropping Barrington after Birmingham had placed him, at Leeds, in a potentially parlous condition.

Dare he score slowly again, even if the situation demanded it? If he did would the selectors dare drop him again? Barrington answered all that himself. He took boundaries off successive balls from Taylor, the first a cut, the second down to third man. Edrich drove Collinge to the off-side boundary and was feeling his way into his innings, gaining in assurance. Barrington bombed on. He struck Taylor to the boundary three times in an over, straight drive, square cut, pull and the 50 was up in slightly more than an hour.

The matrix of the day's play had been established. Barrington intended to plunder, Edrich to accelerate. They were, Edrich felt, a strange pair: Edrich 'for 12 months [...] not considered good enough to play for England,' and Barrington 'sacked' for the slow scoring.

Barrington plundered. He pulled Motz to the boundary, got a seven – 3 plus 4 overthrows – and might have been run out from a superb throw by Bev Congdon, the New Zealand opening bat. He might also have gone when he lashed Collinge near John Reid in the gully.

Edrich, accelerating, took boundaries from Motz and Collinge.

Edrich had been coaching and playing in South Africa the winter before and he'd developed a method against medium-pace bowling playing 'straight and hard.' When he got back he continued with the method, which he'd describe as a 'deliberate style of aggressive driving'.[5] As this innings against New Zealand deepened and developed he played the bowling with 'the full face of the bat'.

Barrington hesitated for a couple of overs on 49 before reaching his 50 with a rasping cover-drive off Motz, and that same stroke brought the 100 up. Barrington had needed only 15 scoring strokes to get there. At lunch England were 102 for 1 (Barrington 53, Edrich 35).

When play began again the crowd had grown to some 7,000.

Taylor opened and Edrich sent the ball scurrying through the covers to launch the afternoon; it would be an assault. This cover boundary off Taylor made the score 106, and of those 72 had come in boundaries, a continuing testament to the speed of the outfield as well as the nature of the batting. Barrington took up the running with a cover boundary from Collinge and soon after the 100 partnership was up in 1 hour and 47 minutes, Edrich 40. He made his first mistake now, edging Collinge into the slips where Taylor dropped it.

J.M. Kilburn in *The Yorkshire Post* wrote that in general, however, New Zealand lacked a bowler 'to trouble unduly' and there was 'no misunderstanding or policy or progress, no period of mis-timing to rouse temporary anxiety.' The afternoon would produce 157 runs scored 'without any impression of haste or hustle.'

Slow left-arm spinner Brian Yuile was on and Edrich square cut him to the boundary to reach 50, in 2 hours and 32 minutes, out of 145 (eight 4s). By now the pair were at full gallop. The 150 came up a couple of minutes later. An impression was forming – ephemeral, unprovable – that Edrich was playing like a man who, almost from nowhere, had been granted this chance to prove his great truths to all the doubters and was doing it.

It happens but not as often as you'd think.

OPEN THRILLER

CRICKET

THIS SPORTING LIFE
BY ALAN HUBBARD

est

A triumphant Thomson leaves the 18th green with Lema.

...r service to Austra-... in 11 years. He has ...the record number

...nship, notable for see-...4,000, Thomson, who ... 72 and 71 to earlier ...es.

...players — were Ryder ...Welshman Brian Huggett ...(...ford) with 73, 68, 76, 70. ...xt best on 288 was Roberto ...Vicenzo, 74, 69, 73, 72, the ...ntinian who finished third ...t. Andrews last year.

...of the picture faded all the ...d Americans including ...Lema, holder of the Gold ...which goes to the winner. ...a strange coincidence that ...first of Thomson's Open ...phs was also gained over ...oyal Birkdale links at South-

...ce that July day in 1954, ...as won at St. Andrews ...Hoylake (1956) and Royal ...m and St. Annes (1958). ...e that day too, Royal Birk-...has been re-designed and ...ened to 7,037 yards to be ...one of the toughest courses ...e world.

...r the last three days it has ...as mild as one can hope ...et nobody has really con-...d it.

...for an hour or so yesterday ...ng, Birkdale really shook ...teeth, and in wind-driven ...scores climbed and strange ... happened.

...n the wind eased, the sun ... out and everything ...ned to normal.

Blown away

DETAILS

285—P W Thomson (Australia) 74, 68, 72, 71.

287—C O'Connor (Royal Dublin) 69, 73, 74, 71; B Huggett (Romford) 73, 68, 76, 70

288—R de Vicenzo (Argentina) 74, 69, 73, 72.

289—K Nagle (Australia) 74, 70, 73, 72; A Lema (US) 68, 72, 75, 74; B J

WOMEN'S GOLF

First time win for

Edrich joins the greats

By A Special Correspondent

John Edrich, the left-handed Surrey opening batsman, blasted his way to a place among cricket's greats yesterday.

For, at Headingley, Edrich joined the select band of men who have scored 300 runs in a Test match, as he thrashed an unbeaten 310 off the New Zealand attack before skipper Mike Smith closed the England innings at 546 for four.

Career best for Jackson

Derbyshire batted out time on a day of uninspiring cricket at Colchester yesterday.

At the close of a rain-interrupted session they had taken their second innings total to 78 for four, after Brian Jackson had shot out Essex in their first innings for 174.

A torrential downpour just before the scheduled start delayed play for one hour, but Essex, needing 42 to overtake the visitors, decided to bat on. Despite the heavy wicket, the batsmen struggled against Richardson and Jackson, and took three overs to add to the overnight score.

The crawl continued, with only 16 painstaking runs scored in the hour's play before lunch. These runs cost Essex the wickets of overnight batsmen Knight and

Thus Edrich joined the immortals — only Hutton, Hammond and Sandham among Englishmen have scored more runs in a Test innings.

In the long history of Test cricket only seven men of any nationality had previously made triple centuries — Sobers, Hanif Mohammed, Hammond, Bradman, Sandham, Hutton and Simpson.

But one honour IS Edrich's. For no man, not even the insatiable Bradman, has scored more boundaries in a Test innings.

Lapse

Five sixes and 52 fours flowed from his bat in 532 minutes of uninhibited aggression.

At 287 he might have been out when he sliced a ball from Dick Collinge past Bruce Taylor's hands at slip.

But that lapse apart, there was nothing to suggest that he could not pass Hammond's record of 336 against New Zealand or any other record he wanted.

His treatment of the second-rate New Zealand slow bowling was brutal.

In one over, he hit the slow left-hander Brian Yuile for two fours and two sixes.

Yet it is impossible to detract from this innings on the grounds of the poverty of the bowling, for the New Zealand pace attack performed magnificently without any real incentive.

It is hard to imagine any fast

For the first time, Edrich caught up with Barrington, who was now proceeding carefully towards his century. Edrich did this by stepping down the wicket and driving Yuile into the football stand for 6. That was the stroke that took him to 93 and past Barrington, who picked up the pace and reached his century in under 3 hours when he struck his 18th boundary. Edrich picked up the pace too, and at moments he was clearly the dominant partner.

It was almost as if the batsmen were in competition with each other 'in bursts of scoring',[6] although Edrich would describe it in a slightly different way. He felt his innings was 'spasmodic' and consisted of periods when runs were scored slowly interlocking with chances which he'd take, making those strong forearms wielders of power. The spin was given the harshest treatment by Yuile and occasional bowler Vic Pollard who dealt in off-breaks. 'I really let my front-foot drives go.'[7]

At tea England were 259 (Edrich 129, Barrington 111).

To celebrate his 150 Edrich drove Pollard for 6 – Congdon at long-off caught it but stepped back over the boundary rope – and, to bring up the 300, Edrich on-drove

Pollard into a corner of the football stand. His off-driving was exquisite, too, in placement and execution.

Bad light (briefly) stopped play in the evening session and so did a little rain – at six o'clock with England on 357 – but when Edrich and Barrington got back to the crease they continued as before. New Zealand didn't even take the new ball, saving it for the morrow. At the close England were 366 for the loss of only Barber so long before, Edrich 194 (three 6s, 30 4s), Barrington 152 (24 4s).

J.M. Kilburn rounded it off nicely enough: 'The details of their scoring merely emphasise the splendour of their play. They made the occasion their own, not by grim accumulation, not by furrowed brow and halting step, but by accepting the bowling at its face value, and the duty of batting as a pleasure. They played splendid cricket.' Kilburn could scarcely have written that about Simpson at Old Trafford in 1964, but of course that innings had been within the constriction of the Ashes and against a much stronger England bowling attack.

Edrich was very tired that night and, of course, conditioned in his thinking by the state of the match and England's requirements. Although he had 194, it was certainly not a monumental score in historical terms. Bradman (of course) had been further than this eight times against England, twice against South Africa, once against India, and once against the West Indies. You don't measure yourself against Don Bradman whether you are John Edrich or anybody else, but if you were ascending through an individual innings Bradman gave you the altitude. Edrich was ascending, literally and figuratively, but he was still facing the pull of gravity. Bradman, it seems, never had, especially in 1930 and 1934 here at Headingley when the crowd was so large that they had to sit on the grass.

It may be that Edrich was entirely right to be pragmatic and, at only 194, was going to do what all sportspeople in their different ways always insist they are going to do: take it one ball at a time.[8] Edrich knew England wanted more runs and he would do his best to get them. It was as simple and direct as that.

On a cool, overcast day another 5,000 came. Motz opened the bowling with a maiden to Barrington then Edrich faced Collinge. During another maiden he had played and missed once. Motz then took the new ball and three times in the over forced Barrington to play and miss. The New Zealand bowlers were winning universal praise for their persistence and spirit. J.M. Kilburn felt they bowled 'as though the figures on the scoreboard were a nightmare dispersed in the dawn.' Barrington on-drove the last ball from Motz for a couple to set the scoreboard moving again, but Edrich played a further maiden from Collinge.

Barrington cracked a square cut off Motz like a gunshot and the trajectory took the ball past Reid in the gully: a moment of potential danger. England intended to make runs quickly once Edrich was back in his stride. Then Barrington touched a ball from Motz and was caught behind. His 163 had taken 5 hours and 39 minutes and contained 26 4s in a partnership of 369, a record against New Zealand. It beat the 218 by Hutton and Bill Edrich at The Oval in 1949 and, of course, stayed within the Edrich family. John Edrich was then 199 and after the new batsman, Colin Cowdrey, had steered Motz to the mid-on boundary, Edrich chipped a ball from Collinge down to third man, they ran the single and he had 200. He'd remember timing the ball better than he had ever done before and 'this was the innings of my career – not because it became the highest but because I was using every shot I knew and nearly all those shots were coming off. The longer the innings went the more relaxed I became. All my inhibitions were gone'.[9]

It may be that Edrich was referring to the afternoon because in the first hour of this morning session the New Zealand bowlers limited the scoring to 35, and limited Edrich to only 45 by lunch.

Motz forced Cowdrey to play and miss, and when Taylor came on he forced Edrich to play and miss too. With the England total at 407, Cowdrey played back to Taylor and was clean bowled. He had needed 44 minutes to score 13, a testament to the bowling.

Peter Parfitt of Middlesex was eminently capable of scoring fast but all eyes remained on Edrich. Three times in an over he drove Taylor to the boundary and went past his own highest first-class score, 216 against Nottinghamshire three years before.

Bill Bowes, writing in the *Yorkshire Evening Post,* pointed out that if you examined a diagram of Edrich's shots you'd see that, from the football stand end, most were towards the point boundary and fine leg to bowling from the football stand end, but from the Kirkstall Lane end a lot of shots had gone to third man. That, however, Bowes concluded, was 'by no means the whole story. Criss-cross lines showed off and on-drives also to the boundary.'

A shower brought play to an end near the lunch interval. England had scored 78 against the 101 of the day before, another testament to the bowling. When they came back out, Edrich 'clubbed' (his own word). The crowd, as the day before, had grown to an estimated 7,000 when word must have spread that Edrich now had the opportunity to rewrite one aspect of cricket history.

Taylor had to finish the over that the shower had interrupted and did that. Collinge bowled to Parfitt from the football stand end. Edrich played a false stroke against Taylor but the ball passed his leg stump and then Parfitt brought up the 450 with a drive for 3. Parfitt had made 32 in 97 minutes (two 4s), adding 109 with Edrich, before he tried to drive Collinge and was beaten for pace.

Edrich cut loose and struck Yuile for two 6s and two 4s in an over, although at 287 he survived a slip chance when he sliced a Collinge delivery past Taylor in the slips. Mike Smith, the new batsman, scratched around while Edrich advanced towards his 300 and got to within a boundary of it. There was, he'd remember, 'no time to meditate'. Motz ran in and Edrich sent a majestic, rippling off-drive through the cover field.

The direction of his career had been altered. He'd play another 50 Tests and at that level the career would extend into the mid-1970s.

He'd ascended.

Smith scratched on (his innings would comprise two singles), while Edrich struck a couple more boundaries and Smith declared. Edrich had been at the crease for 8 hours 52 minutes and his five 6s and 52 4s had given him at least one world record. Nobody in Test history had scored more runs in boundaries. He had shown a sureness of touch, which had suggested the 'possibility of dismissal can scarcely enter his considerations at the crease. His batting has a golden touch.'[10]

As a matter of context, the *Sheffield Telegraph* pointed out that 'it is impossible to detract from this innings on the ground of the poverty of the bowling. The New Zealand pace attack performed magnificently without any real incentive. It is hard to imagine any fast bowling combination in the world outside the West Indies who would have bowled better than Motz, Collinge and Taylor.' The weakness, almost the fatal weakness, had been spin.

Some people wondered, as Edrich also pointed out, whether the declaration might not have been delayed for, say, half an hour to give him time to attack Sobers's 365. It might, Edrich concluded, have been enough time. Edrich's creed, however, was quite different. His innings was a contribution to England winning the match and he was content with that. As he pointed out, England only just bowled New Zealand out a second time, after they'd followed on of course, before heavy rain fell and Headingley was drowned in it. By then Edrich had been on the field for the whole match. On 8 July, when he'd gone out to bat with Barber, he was fighting for a place. By 13 July he looked (and maybe even felt) like a positive veteran.

And the matter of giving a batsman the chance to beat the world record? This is always going to be uneasy territory for any captain who might simultaneously face a choice between depriving the individual of the one great chance of his life – Everest – and subordinating his side's chances of a win. Sometimes, like Edrich, a batsman putting a triple century together is a great liberator for a captain. Sometmes it must be a mixed blessing – or a damned nuisance.

Notes

1   For an informed discussion on the West Indian tactic of rotating four bowlers, see the Preface of *Bodyline Autopsy* by David Frith (Aurum, London, 2003, paperback edition).

2   Writing in the *Rothmans Test Cricket Almanac* brochure published before the tour Reg Hayter, long-time journalist and cricket lover who ran his own press agency, wrote that 'following a request from the successful and popular West Indies team of 1963 that they should tour England more frequently, the Imperial Cricket Conference asked MCC to examine the possibilities of two countries visiting the United Kingdom in the same season'.

3   *Runs In The Family*, Edrich.

4   *The Sheffield Telegraph.*

5   Edrich op. cit.

6   *The Yorkshire Post.*

7   Edrich op. cit.

8   Reportedly W.G. Grace himself was once asked how he'd bat if he had to bat a whole day to save a match. 'I'd play normally', he said, 'because after all I'll still only be playing one ball at a time'.

9   Edrich op. cit.

10   *The Yorkshire Post.*

England v New Zealand
Played at Leeds, 8, 9, 10, 12, 13 July 1965

ENGLAND

R.W. Barber	c Ward b Taylor	13
J.H. Edrich	not out	310
K.F. Barrington	c Ward b Motz	163
M.C. Cowdrey	b Taylor	13
P.H. Parfitt	c Collinge	32
M.J.K. Smith	not out	2
	b 4, l-b 8, n-b 1	13
	(4 dec)	546

Did not bat: J.M. Parks, R. Illingworth, F.J. Titmus, F.E. Rumsey, J.D.F. Larker.

	O	M	R	W
Motz	41	8	140	1
Taylor	40	8	140	2
Collinge	32	7	87	1
Yuile	17	5	80	0
Morgan	6	0	28	0
Pollard	11	2	46	0
Congdon	4	0	12	0

NEW ZEALAND

G.T. Dowling	c Parks b Larter	5	b Rumsey	41
B.E. Congdon	c Parks b Rumsey	13	b Rumsey	1
B.W. Sinclair	c Smith b Larter	13	lbw b Larter	29
J.R. Reid	lbw b Illingworth	54	c Barrington b Rumsey	5
R.W. Morgan	b Illingworth	1	b Titmus	21
V. Pollard	run out	33	c Cowdrey b Larter	53
B.W. Yuile	b Larter	46	c Cowdrey b Titmus	12
B.R. Taylor	c Parks b Illingworth	9	c and b Titmus	0
R.C. Motz	c Barber b Illingworth	3	c Barrington b Titmus	0
J.T. Ward	not out	0	not out	2
R.O. Collinge	b Larter	8	b Titmus	0
	b 5, l-b 1, w 2	8	n-b 2	2
		193		166

	O	M	R	W		O	M	R	W
Rumsey	26	6	59	1		15	5	49	3
Larter	28.1	6	66	4		22	10	54	2
Illingworth	28	14	42	4		7	0	28	0
Titmus	6	2	16	0		26	17	19	5
Barber	2	0	2	0		14	7	14	0

ENGLAND WON BY AN INNINGS AND 187

Failed by 56 runs to beat the record.

Australia v England, Melbourne, February, 1966

Robert Maskew Cowper, born Kew, Melbourne, 5 October 1940.

Test career 1964–8: 27 Tests, 2,061 runs, 5 centuries, average 46.84.

The MCC side that went to Australia in 1965–6 under the captaincy of Mike Smith was determined to be positive and by the Fifth Test they had largely succeeded. The First and Second were drawn, England won the Third by an innings and 93 runs, Australia won the Fourth by an innings and 9 runs. A question loomed: with the Ashes riding on the Fifth Test (Australia held them, and a draw would have been enough) would the positive cricket be played or would Melbourne be cast in the same concrete as Old Trafford two years before? Simpson was still the Australian captain.

England batted first and Barrington, the ultimate symbol of English cricket abroad, made 115 and wicketkeeper Parks made 89. Although Barrington had been aggressive, the England innings lasted until some half an hour before tea on the second day.

Lawry and Simpson opened for Australia but, at 15, David Brown, the strong Warwickshire fast bowler (*The Age* described him as 'rangy, awkwardly running'), pitched one on the leg stump, which moved sharply across and hit Simpson's stumps. Grahame Thomas came in but, after tea, swung at Glamorgan's Jeff Jones (*The Age* described him as the 'crinkly-haired Welshman') and Titmus caught it. At 36 for two Australia were in maximum danger.

Bob Cowper, a powerful left-handed batsman, had a command of all strokes but particularly favoured leg glances of the subtle kind, hooking and square cutting. Like Lawry a Victorian, he'd been playing Test cricket for two years now and in this series scored 22, 99 and 5, 60 and 0, but had then been dropped for the Fourth Test. Lawry welcomed him back by driving Brown into the covers and they ran four.

Positive cricket or the blight of the little urn again? *The Age* described how 'the two Victorians concentrated on playing only deliveries that were pitched at or near the stumps. Never did either batsman make any serious attempt to look for runs'. *The Age* went further, pointing out that 'confirmation' of the Australian mind-set – runs of secondary importance to time – came just after five o'clock with Australia still in maximum danger at 66 for 2. Lawry and Cowper appealed against the light, but neither would have 'entertained' an appeal of that sort if the side had been in a run-chase rather than in trouble.

Cowper looked settled and, the appeal against the light refused, he and Lawry batted safely to the close with Australia 101 for 2 (Lawry 43, Cowper 32). Simpson accepted that 'the match is still pretty even' but 'we still have plenty of batting left'.

Heavy rain fell overnight and that changed everything as Lawry and Cowper came out to begin the third day. The play would be 'sadly lacking in distinction, grace, and humour. The outfield on the scoreboard side of the ground had the consistency of a water-meadow, and play had not gone on for long before the ball became a soggy slimy object fit to break the hearts of bowlers obliged to use it'.[1]

E.W. Swanton smelt 'a sniff of stalemate in the air'[2] and, perhaps reflecting so much of England v Australia in the 1960s, suggested that when you have weak bowling and exceptionally easy pitches 'only two captains of real flair and daring – some heroes perhaps out of the golden age[3] – could rise superior to circumstances.' Swanton did not expect the rest of the match to disturb that view.

Play began on time, although the outfield was wet enough for the fielders to slither, or rather sink ankle-deep, into it. Reportedly players on both sides said subsequently that these were the worst conditions they had ever played Test cricket in. The wicket itself had been protected, had somehow gone to sleep and wouldn't be waking up.

Smith used pace for the opening hour and, in the first over, Jones made one cut away from Lawry. It excited Jones and the fielders but did not excite Lawry at all. Not much on a cricket field seems to have ever done that. He would not make another mistake until the tea interval was in sight. Attrition, concentration, accumulation, patience – this was the air Lawry breathed. He was so angular he might have been drawn by L.S. Lowry, and so obdurate he might have been giving lessons on how geometry – his geometry – is rarely wrong.

Brown did get Cowper into trouble twice in his first over but Lawry's fabled obduracy appears to have got to Brown who, in his third over, gathered a ball Lawry had prodded on to the leg side, and 'suddenly took it into his head to hurl it with a kind of savage, despairing fury, to miss Lawry by inches and knock out the leg stump, though the batsman appeared to be in his ground. At the end of the over Smith had a word with his bowler and I doubt it was to congratulate him on the excellence of his eye'.[4]

Lawry and Cowper risked nothing but they were scoring runs. *The Age* murmured to its readers that Smith might have considered giving Bob Barber (an occasional but effective leg-spinner) or Barrington (ditto) some overs if only to introduce uncertainty, and to see what, if anything, happened next. Smith had given Barber a single over, which went for 10, on the second day. He didn't put him on again now.

There were only nine overs in the first hour and from them the batsmen took 40 runs. It was respectable enough then and would be respectable enough these days too with an outfield like that.

Lawry had gone to his 50 in 7 minutes under 3 hours (five 4s).

Both batsmen were strong off their legs against the England bowling, which lacked accuracy. Apart from medium-pacer Barry Knight of Essex, a genuine front-line bowler, the field was set with only three men on the leg side. The line of attack was clearly off-stump but, lacking the accuracy, runs were coming on the leg side.

After an hour, at 144, Titmus came on but in these wet conditions he abandoned any thoughts of spinning the ball, marked out his longer run and bowled medium-pace. Such was the sensitivity about defensive cricket that the MCC tour manager, Billy Griffith, came up to the Press Box to explain that Titmus couldn't dry the ball enough to grip it for his off-spinners. The decision for him to bowl medium-pacers was not defensive in intent but enforced by the conditions.

Titmus and Knight slowed the scoring. In the second hour Lawry and Cowper managed 35 off 12 overs and by lunch the total had gone to 172 for 2 (Lawry 81). That meant 99 had been added during the morning, again respectable then and now.

After lunch *The Age* reported that the pair 'went through a slow, almost motionless first hour but even so Lawry did not lose his appearance of invulnerability.' Titmus was now trying to spin the ball and a couple of deliveries troubled Cowper. Lawry reached 94 and Cowper pushed a ball from Knight to Jones at square leg. The batsmen set off for a dubious single and Lawry had only reached mid-pitch as Jones seized the ball. Jones would have made it a deadly single if he'd picked the ball up cleanly and thrown it to Parks, but he didn't. Lawry, unmoved, continued to his century in 5 hours and 20 minutes.

At 211, and in the 66th over, Jones forced Cowper into an edge over first and second slips when the new ball had been taken, and that was the first boundary (as opposed to all-run 4s) of the day. That statement seems barely credible but, of course, the soggy outfield explains it. Cowper now broke (mildly) loose and hooked Brown to the boundary. That shot sailed towards Knight at long-leg but Knight seemed to lose it against the background and, as he advanced to where he thought it was, it went over his head. At 90 Cowper tried to cut Jones but sent the ball over the slips. Lawry, suspecting that the nervous 90s were making Cowper very nervous indeed, applauded Cowper's shot, as if perhaps to say well played but concentrate.

Cowper moved to his 100 in the same over by pulling Jones for three. It had taken him 5 hours and 10 minutes but, as tea approached, the partnership was broken. Lawry tried to play a cover-drive off Jones and sent a two-handed catch waist-high to Edrich in the gully. Lawry had been at the crease for more than 6 hours.

Doug Walters, nimble and adept on Australian wickets, might have banished the negative but, instead, settled into the rhythm of the innings. Cowper, meanwhile, was playing more strongly, although he had difficulty getting the ball through the inner ring of fieldsmen and, whenever he did, the wet outfield dragged the ball to a halt. The drying only began during the afternoon.

At 291 Barber finally came on to partner Titmus but Cowper and Walters moved to their 50 partnership in 1 hour and 20 minutes.

E.W. Swanton noted that Barber plied seven tidy overs towards the close of play but before that had only had the one over on the second day for the 10 runs. Any leg-break bowler (before Shane Warne and some of the Indian masters) traditionally operated at two levels: expensive because leg-breaks were difficult to discipline, deadly because there was always the chance of the unplayable ball. How many overs a leg-break bowler was given often represented a window into the mentality of the captain. Swanton wrote, acerbicly, that the fact Barber hadn't been given the ball until 7 and a half hours into the Australian innings 'explains as graphically as anything else the whole nature of the exercise'.[5]

At 315 Cowper spooned up what appeared to be a bat and pad catch off Barber, which Parks sprinted forward to catch, but the umpire ruled it hadn't hit bat and at the close Australia were 333 for 3 (Cowper 159, Walters 35). Since tea Cowper had scored 47 and Walters only 35.

Bill O'Reilly, one of the earliest of an interesting breed – a leading player who become a perceptive day-by-day commentator – set Cowper's innings into context by stressing that if Lawry had set the tone, Cowper followed him, and he 'attempted no shot which contained the slightest element of danger. His square cut, for instance, was shelved. His hook shot, a favourite with him, appeared no more than twice in the early session'. However, O'Reilly endorsed this approach, describing the innings as mature and lifting his stature within the side. O'Reilly was thoroughly impressed by how Cowper 'used the full face of his bat to drive confidently on either side of the wicket'.[6]

Overnight rain fell and continued to fall the next day – one source speaks of an inch

The Age

Page 22

TELEPHONE: 63 0341; CLASSIFIED ADVERTISING: 63 0301.

MELBOURNE, TUESDAY, FEBRUARY 15, 1966

'ASHES' ARE SAFE FOR AUSTRALIA

Lawry-Cowper partnership stops England

By Percy Beames

BOB COWPER and Bill Lawry resolutely batted Australia well beyond danger of defeat in the fifth Test at the MCG yesterday and the Ashes are certain to stay in Australia's keeping for another series.

The two Victorian left-handers were mainstays of a batting effort that saw 232 runs scored for the loss of only one wicket for the day.

Lawry stopped serving Australia's needs only after making 108, but Cowper, not out 159, lives to fight yet another day.

Purtell is keen to be officia

By Tony Kennedy

Jack Purtell, one of the best joc Australia has produced is planning retirement.

ABOVE: Century-maker Bob Cowper snicks a ball between the hands of slips fieldsman Ken Barrington (left) and Colin Cowdrey during play in the fifth Test yesterday. BELOW: The two heroes of the day, Cowper and Bill Lawry partners in a stand of 212, are happy men at the end of the day.

Lawry now one of the 'greats'

By Lindsay Hassett

BILL LAWRY'S worth to Australia was well recognised before the start of this summer — but he must now be accounted one of Australia's great opening batsmen.

and a half – and by the afternoon play was abandoned for the day. It rendered the final day meaningless in terms of a match, which seemed a fitting epitaph for something so grim in concept and execution by both sides. Someone used the word charade for this long, final gasp. It did, however, give Cowper his conjunction of circumstances and it might be the only conjunction he ever did get. He can't have known that it would be, although he had a business career to pursue and his Test career wouldn't last too much longer.

Brown bowled a hostile maiden to Cowper and then Walters. Knight was the other opening bowler. Early on Cowper was uncertain against Brown outside the off-stump when he was pushing at the ball, but he was clearly laying a foundation. After an hour Jones replaced Brown and at that point only 32 runs had been scored.

Walters, still defensive, reached 50 in 200 minutes and Cowper reached his double century after almost 9 hours (10 4s). Cowper now, according to *The Age*, began to show his 'challenging side'. He 'held command over every England bowler. But even more important, Cowper proved he could unfold an attractive range of attacking strokes without resorting to methods that involved more than normal risks'.

At 412 Barber came on and, in his second over, took a return catch from Walters who had taken 1 hour 45 minutes to add 25, and was almost morbidly out of touch. That was 420 for 4 and Ian Chappell bustled in.

Cowper was now confident enough to lift Titmus and at lunch had reached 226. The first of the records had gone because he was past Simpson's 225, made in the Fourth Test of this series, and was now highest scorer. Hereabouts he gave a semi-chance when he cracked the ball past gully and Titmus couldn't get a hand to it.

By now the Australians in the Press Box were understandably getting excited. The conjunction continued to offer him a chance, a whole afternoon and evening where he had every record, even the 365 of Sobers, within his reach and with the match neutered there were no other pressures bearing down on him. After Chappell, a batsman described as one of Australia's young eagles and who might be expected to stay and prosper, there was Keith Stackpole, who, as it happened, was another of the young eagles. Cowper was not faced with a short tail and could continue to bat properly, which he was doing with mounting freedom. Chappell seemed inhibited and watched as the records fell.

At 271, Cowper had passed Bradman's 270 at Melbourne in 1936–7 and so now he had made the highest score by an Australian against England in Australia. R.E. Foster's 287, the highest by a player from either country in Australia, was at hand. By the time he'd reached it Chappell had gone, caught behind the wicket off Jones with Australia 481 for 5. They overtook the England first innings total shortly after, although they had taken 11 overs to get there.

In the last over before tea Cowper moved to 303, beating Bradman's 299 (not out) against South Africa at Adelaide in 1931–2 and becoming only the third Australian to score a Test triple hundred. If he maintained his concentration and simply kept on, steadily, he could easily pass Sobers before the match ended. The whole final session invited Cowper to help himself.

John Clarke, reporting for the *London Standard,* noted 'an atmosphere approaching ecstacy' among the Australians in the Press Box as they contemplated how close 365 might prove to be. Everything else aside, no Australian had held the world record since that August day in 1938 at The Oval when Hutton had cut Fleetwood-Smith for four to take it from Bradman.

Time is a curious dimension. How many of the crowd of 10,000 at Melbourne had been born then? We can't know that, although you'd have to be more than 28, but we can know that Bill O'Reilly, watching so intently in the Press Box (but not perhaps in ecstacy, he wasn't that kind), had been bowling at the other end to Fleetwood-Smith...

Cowper was tired, visibly tired. Someone used another word, weary, which is not quite the same thing. He resumed but had cramp in his right thigh and couldn't seem to shed it. His timing had gone and Stackpole, who had batted an hour for 9, couldn't help because Knight bowled him and in came Veivers, who couldn't help Cowper much either. Veivers attempted to sweep Titmus and was bowled, making Australia 543 for 7 although that had no real relevance.

At this point Cowper had sunk into a sort of paralysis. In the 33 minutes since tea he had scored 4 and now he played an exhausted push at Knight and dragged the ball on to the leg stump.

He had been at the crease for 12 hours and 6 minutes, faced 589 deliveries and hit 20 4s. Significantly, he had needed 7 and a half hours to accumulate the 159 on the first two days, but the 148 he added on this final day had taken only 4 and a half. More than that, only 57 runs had come at the other end while he was adding the 148. This was a very, very fine innings.

Because of its context it could not compare with Hutton's 364, either of the Bradman triple hundreds or the Sobers 365 – as each of those had been constructed to create victories, and even Simpson's 311 at Old Trafford had had a distant edge to it. He too might have been creating a platform for a win at the same time as making Australia safe. The state of the match on the final day, after it had been drowned by the rain of the day before, gave Cowper so much but took away a certain degree of credibility. Cowper, of course, could do nothing about that.

Simpson declared as soon as Cowper was dismissed, and England lost 3 wickets in the 75 minutes remaining. It made John Clarke (among, no doubt, many others) wonder what might have happened if Simpson had declared at lunch, albeit 59 behind.

It wasn't that kind of era.

Former England fast bowler Frank Tyson, writing in *The Century Makers*, caught the era. 'Cowper was one of those imperceptible scorers who seldom gave the impression of tearing an attack limb from limb, yet, when you took stock, was always 40 runs more than when you last looked at the scoreboard. [...] Above all Cowper placed the ball superbly, tugging the fieldsmen this way and that with artistic touches supplemented by fleet running between the wickets. In four years at the top he played in only 27 Tests, cutting short his sporting ambitions to follow his chosen business career at the age of 27. The wastage of Cowper in 1968 was an eloquent commentary on the financial martyrdom to which players of his era had to submit themselves. Had Cowper been born nine years later, in more affluent times, [the Packer revolution, replete with dollar bills] he would have survived in international cricket much longer'.[7]

Notes

[1]   *With England In Australia,* Clarke.

[2]   *The Daily Telegraph.*

[3]   The Golden Age is widely regarded as from 1899 to 1914, when World War One began. In this time many of the game's most romantic figures – Charles Fry and K.S. Ranjitsinhji, Victor Trumper and Archie MacLaren prominent – played, but the phrase tries to capture more than that by implying the game itself was being played in a golden way. And they were not all romantics: in Yorkshire, for instance, George Hirst and Wilfred Rhodes were business cricketers who scored thousands of prudent runs and took thousands of wickets.

[4]   Clarke op. cit.

[5]   *Daily Telegraph.*

[6]   *Sydney Morning Herald.*

[7]   *The Century Makers,* Tyson.

Australia v England
Played at Melbourne, 11, 12, 14, 15, 16 February 1966

ENGLAND

G. Boycott	c Stackpole b McKenzie	17	lbw b McKenzie		1
R.W. Barber	run out	17	b McKenzie		20
J.H. Edrich	c McKenzie b Walters	85	b McKenzie		3
K.F. Barrington	c Grout b Walters	115	not out		32
M.C. Cowdrey	c Grout b Walters	79	not out		11
M.J.K. Smith	c Grout b Walters	0			
J.M. Parks	run out	89			
F.J. Titmus	not out	42			
B.R. Knight	c Grout b Hawke	13			
D.J. Brown	c and b Chappell	12			
I.J. Jones	not out	4			
	b 9, l-b 2, n-b 1	12	l-b 2		2
	(9 dec)	485	(3 wkts)		69

	O	M	R	W		O	M	R	W
McKenzie	26	5	100	1		6	2	17	3
Hawke	35	5	109	1		4	1	22	0
Walters	19	3	53	4		2	0	16	0
Simpson	5	1	20	0					
Stackpole	10	2	43	0		3	0	0	10
Veivers	15	3	78	0					
Chappell	17	3	70	1		2	0	2	0

AUSTRALIA

W.M. Lawry	c Edrich b Jones	108
R.B. Simpson	b Brown	4
G. Thomas	c Titmus bJones	19
R.M. Cowper	b Knight	307
K.D. Walters	c and b Barber	60
I.M. Chappell	c Parks b Jones	19
K.R. Stackpole	b Knight	9
T.R. Veivers	b Titmus	4
N.J.N. Hawke	not out	0
	b 6, l-b 5, n-b 2	13
	(8 dec)	543

Did not bat: A.T.W. Grout, G.D. McKenzie.

	O	M	R	W
Brown	31	3	134	1
Jones	29	1	145	3
Knight	36.2	4	105	2
Titmus	42	12	86	1
Barber	16	0	60	1

MATCH DRAWN
Failed by 59 runs to beat the record

West Indies v England, Bridgetown, March 1974

*Lawrence George Rowe, born Kingston, Jamaica,
8 January 1949.*

*Test career 1971–80: 30 Tests, 2,047 runs, seven centuries,
average 43.55.*

The Test career of Lawrence Rowe, nicknamed 'Yagga,' remains enigmatic. He showed immediate maturity because on his debut as a 23-year-old against New Zealand at Sabina Park in 1972 he made 214 and 100 not out. It was one of the best innings ever played by a Jamaican.

By 1973–4 he was an established opener in the West Indies side as they faced a resolute England team led by Mike Denness. Their openers, Geoff Boycott and Dennis Amiss, were in prime form, Keith Fletcher was a prolific scorer at all levels of the game, Alan Knott one of the best wicketkeeper batsmen and Bob Willis an explosive windmill of a fast bowler.

West Indies won the First Test by 7 wickets, built around an innings of 158 by little Alvin Kallicharran, a left-hander of beautiful balance and savage power. The Second Test was drawn, England building that around an unbeaten 262 from Amiss, although in the West Indian innings of 583 Rowe made 120.

The Third Test began on a damp, heavy morning at Bridgetown. West Indies captain Rohan Kanhai won the toss and put England in. It seems a wise risk because at one stage England were 130 for 5 but combative all-rounder Tony Greig made 148. Even so, England's first innings total of 395 left them vulnerable.

Roy Fredericks opened with Rowe and took strike. There was a sub plot here because Rowe had gained the reputation of only scoring big runs on his home ground, Sabina Park. He was about to make that into nonsense. He took the fight to the England bowlers and Fredericks, sensing the mood of the moment, was content to support him. The launch of the innings, however, was in marked contrast to England who had needed until tea on this second day to get to their 395, and, more than that, the 395 would quickly be seen to be vulnerable.

The crowd had been contemplative and subdued. Now Rowe sent the power, grace and energy of his stroke play out to them, altering and lifting their mood. The 50 partnership came up in eight overs, slightly over a run per ball. It had taken 40 minutes.

The Barbados *Advocate-News* wrote that 'with about 12,000 supporters giving the two openers wholehearted support, Rowe hit a sizzling 48 and Fredericks contributed 24 to lay a solid foundation from which West Indies could build a good lead'.

The elegant Rowe laid into the bowling, pulling, hooking, driving and cutting 'majestically'. 'He had the crowd cheering lustily whenever he made a scoring stroke'.[1] Rowe had them cheering very lustily indeed when Willis bowled him a bouncer. So fleet of foot and initial movement, Rowe moved into it and hooked it high over square leg into the grandstand. It travelled with 'staggering speed, a thrilling, magnificent shot'.[2]

In 16 overs – 10 minutes were lost to a shower, and an appeal against the light cut the final 6 minutes – Rowe and Fredericks put on 83. This appeal evidently irritated Denness because by now medium-pacer Chris Old and Greig had begun to contain the onslaught and might even have taken a wicket. At the close Rowe had struck six 4s as well as the hammer-blow into the grandstand.

The Friday was a rest day and when play resumed on Saturday most of Barbados seemed to be trying to get into the ground. It was full to brimming two hours before play was due to start, and more people were inside than had ever been before. Security broke down under their numbers. People came over the walls and simply sat in whatever seats they wanted whether they were for ticketholders or not. Others climbed on to the roofs of the stands.[3] The entrances were so crowded that journalists – local and those with the tour – were themselves reduced to climbing over the wall.

The wicket remained docile and played true, dictating that the initial England tactic must be containment. Willis and Old opened the bowling and concentrated on the line of the off-stump, pitching just short of a length to a field with a third man and long-leg. Rowe got his own innings moving with a business stroke, a gentle push into the covers for a couple. Old, however, was repeatedly called for no balls and was soon out of the attack. Willis fired a couple of yorkers at Rowe. The off-stump line hampered Fredericks, who felt something akin to claustrophobia, but Rowe sailed on largely untroubled.

Fredericks fumbled a couple of times outside the off-stump, and when Old came back on he beat him twice in an over. Fredericks needed 17 minutes to score his first run and was visibly unsettled to the point where he didn't regain his composure.

Amazingly at 51 Rowe equalled his highest Test score outside Jamaica. Whatever state Fredericks was in the pair moved well together: at one point Rowe elegantly drove Old to long-off and they ran four. He had the huge and bustling crowd on their feet as, elegantly again, he drove the next ball to the boundary to bring up the 100 partnership in 1 hour and 42 minutes. Rowe 'kept sections of the mammoth crowd whistling and blowing whistles, had some dancing and clapping and left some just dumbfounded as he tore into England's bowling'.[4]

Old came off and Geoff Arnold, Surrey seamer, replaced him. Rowe punched a delivery from Arnold to the boundary, the ball thundering between two fielders in the covers. He moved on to the back foot and steered Willis past where third slip would have been for another boundary. And when Greig came on he glanced him so fine that fine leg couldn't stop it. *Wisden* (1975 Almanac, page 924) wrote that 'on this sort of pitch there was a languid ferocity about him that owed everything to his timing and his perfect balance. His cutting, driving and hooking were fearsome, yet there was always more poetry than brutality about his play.'

After an hour (and 13 overs in it), West Indies had added 43 and this with England trying containment. Fredericks had made 8 of them. Greig was bowling like a giant, moving the ball off the seam and refusing to be intimidated by Rowe.

Fredericks went shortly after the first drinks break, nicking a ball from Greig. It turned from the off, took an inside edge and struck the leg stump. He had made 32 and West Indies were 126. Kallicharran came in, this Kallicharran who scored at a tremendous rate, this Kallicharran who wouldn't be contained, this Kallicharran who would match Rowe stroke for stroke and run for run. A great examination of control and psychological strength was coming to Mike Denness and his bowlers.

Rowe got to his century – his first, of course, outside Jamaica – in 3 hours and 28 minutes shortly after the lunch interval. He did it with a straight-driven boundary and then a glance for a couple. The 100 contained 12 4s and the 6 from the day before. The crowd invaded the pitch to congratulate him, although this was by definition entirely good natured and, the congratulations done, they went obediently back to whatever vantage point they had been able to secure. That said, Greig and Arnold, concentrating on Rowe's off stump, had caused him some discomfort from time to time.

Rowe, Kallicharran Rip England Attack

By LOUIS BRATHWAITE
(Sports Editor)

THE West Indies' two young batting stars, Lawrence Rowe (25) and Alvin Kallicharran (24) figured in a sensational record smashing second-wicket stand as they tore the England bowling apart yesterday — the third day of the third Test match at Kensington Oval.

Rowe, with the elegance and grace reminiscent of Barbados and the West Indies' former great batting hero, Seymour Nurse and the late captain, Frank Worrell; and exhibiting the terrific power and ruthlessness of the legend Everton Weekes, hammered an undefeated 202. His innings was the main driving force as the West Indies ended the day on 394 for three wickets — one run behind England's first innings total of 395. Rowe had continued from 43.

The left-handed Kallicharran, who stroked the ball with consummate venom and amazing skill belted the bowling in a masterful innings of 119, matching Rowe all the way in their attractive and memorable 249-run stand smashed the record for a second-wicket partnership for the West Indies against England of 228 scored by R. K. Nunes and George Headley at Sabina Park in 1930. The stand also bettered the previous ground record for the West Indies against England of 222 by J. K. Holt and Frank Worrell in 1954.

A record crowd of about 20,000 spectators from all parts of the island, and 1,000 more from England who are in Barbados specially to watch the Test, packed the Oval from about 2 hours before the start of play. It was inevitable that a capacity crowd would have filled every vantage point yesterday after Rowe and Roy Fredericks had set a blistering pace at the start of the Barbados innings on Thursday, slamming 83 in 77 minutes.

Journalists, and these included visiting members of the Press, had to climb over a wall to enter the Oval. Some fans not only did likewise from as early as two hours before the start of play, but some also watched the day's proceedings from the tops of the Kensington and Eric Inniss Stands.

Perhaps most people came to the Oval to see the Jamaican Rowe break the jinx of scoring his first first class century outside of his home-ground, Sabina Park, for he had scored all 10 of his previous first class centuries there. Not only did Rowe break the Sabina Park spell, but he also satisfied with his sparkling double-century — the second double of his Test career. He started his career with 214 against New Zealand in 1972. This was Rowe's fourth Test century, his second in succession against England and he has so far struck 25 fours and one six. His previous highest score outside of Jamaica in a first class innings was 84 versus Notts on the English tour last year.

Rowe has now been displaying his exquisitely delightful shots for 437 minutes — the duration of the West Indies innings, and more thousands are expected to pack the Oval today with two objectives — to see if Rowe can pass 300, and if he can proceed to break Gary Sobers' highest Test world record of 365 not out.

Rowe's first hundred included 12 fours and a six, and was compiled in 208 minutes, while he has so far struck 25 fours and one six in his double century.

Kallicharran's 119 took him past the 1,000-run mark to 1,116. It was his second century against the touring team, he having also pounded out 158 in the first Test and also his fourth Test century. The 100 took him 174 minutes and included 15 fours, while he struck another three fours before his innings and the partnership ended after 252 minutes. He was bowled by England's vice-captain Tony Greig.

Rowe and Kallicharran's first 50-run stand took 57 minutes and they added 100 runs in 102 minutes. They posted 200 runs in almost a run a minute. All the bowlers felt the effect of the slashing blades of the two batsmen as they exhibited every shot in the book. The ovation which the batsmen got was as superb as their fine knocks. Some spectators displayed their tremendous enthusiasm by racing on the field and congratulating the two heroes.

It was noticeable from the start of play that the Kensington strip had remained docile and was therefore playing true to expectations. And it was however not surprising that England decided to contain Rowe and Fredericks as much as possible.

The Englishmen succeeded somewhat with their plan by concentrating on bowling outside the offstump or on a good length, with a partly defensive field with fielders posted on the third man and long leg boundaries.

But while Fredericks, who had continued on 24, seemed to be worried by the opponents' tactics and did not look comfortable, Rowe's concentration never wavered and he played just as confidently as he had done on Thursday afternoon when he enlivened the proceedings.

Rowe did not seem particularly savage then, but his effortless strokeplay and precision timing still had the English fielders scrambling to cut off balls which could have raced to the boundary.

Fredericks had two edges along the ground and was beaten twice outside his offstump in the first over from Old, and took 17 minutes to increase his score. He seemed unsettled by this shaky start and never regained calmness. It was not surprising therefore that he did not last much longer.

The usually dashing Fredericks stayed at the crease long enough to add eight runs in just over an hour. But he must have been extremely happy to see Rowe approaching his eagerly awaited century with the grace and classical skill for which the Jamaican has become known.

Rowe's first scoring stroke for the morning was a gentle push into the covers which brought him two runs. When he had scored 51 he had equalled his highest ever Test score outside of Sabina Park. It was at Kensington in 1972 that he knocked 51 of the New Zealanders.

Rowe and Fredericks displayed their excellent running between the wickets by racing for four when Rowe elegantly drove a delivery from Old towards the longoff boundary. Arnold sprinted from extra cover and managed to stop the ball from hitting the boundary, but the two openers had already completed four — all run. Rowe brought the crowd to their feet when he majestically cover drove the next ball for four to send the partnership to 100 in 102 minutes.

Rowe kept sections of the mammoth crowd whistling and blowing whistles, had some dancing and clapping, and left some just dumbfounded as he tore into England's bowling.

He got on the backfoot and steered a well controlled shot off Willis through a vacant third slip for four; he was nearly yorked next ball; punched an Arnold delivery between the two cover fielders for another four; meticulously glanced Greig's first ball of the day to fine leg which was too fine for the long leg fielder to stop.

He was mainly responsible for the West Indies adding 43 in 13 overs in the first hour despite England's gallant effort to limit the scoring rate to a slower pace.

Fredericks fell in the first ball after the first water break when he played across lazily at an inswinger from Tony Greig bowling slow to medium, and dragged the ball unto his leg stump. The West Indies were then 126 for one.

Fredericks' dismissal brought in Kallicharran. And the way Rowe and he knocked around the English bowlers, will be long remembered by all those who saw the fantastic exhibition of batting.

After Kallicharran's departure, Rowe played cautiously, content to get his second double century and wait to strike more terrific blows against the English attack today. But England picked up another wicket when big six-footer Clive Lloyd, after coming in to bat at 4.50 p.m., fell with eight minutes remaining for play.

Lloyd, who began his innings with a powerful sweep for four off a Pocock delivery, was also determined to play defensively for the remainder of the day's play, but lost the battle by not relying on his usual type of aggressive play. He had scored eight when he prodded forward to a Greig offbreak which popped of a good length, and provided Keith Fletcher with a simple catch at third slip. This was Greig's third victim and he finished the day with 3 for 87.

Speedster Vanburn Holder was sent in to bat as nightwatchman and survived until the end. The West Indies had enjoyed another glorious day of Test cricket. And the thousands of spectators enjoyed it too.

● Diminutive Guyanese batsman, Alvin Kallicharran, appears to be caressing this delivery from England vice-captain, Tony Greig, but the ball raced through the off side field for one of the left hander's 18 boundaries. Kallicharran scored 119, his fourth Test century in a record-breaking second wicket partnership with Jamaican Lawrence Rowe yesterday at Kensington Oval.

Others in picture are wicket-keeper Alan Knott, while Keith Fletcher is at slip.

he West Indies' new g sensation, Lawrence Rowe, is pictured executing one of numerous graceful cover drives during his dazzling knock of 202 not out, as the West Indies replied with 394 to England's first innings total of 395 at Kensington Oval yesterday. This was Rowe's highest first class century outside of his native land, Jamaica.

Scoreboard

ENGLAND 1st Innings	395
WEST INDIES 1st Innings (continued from 82 without loss)	
R. Fredericks b Greig	32
L. Rowe not out	202
A. Kallicharran b Greig	119
C. Lloyd c Fletcher b Greig	8
V. Holder not out	4
EXTRAS (1 lb, 26 nb)	29
TOTAL (for three wkts)	394

Wickets fell at: 126, 375, 393.
BOWLING: G. Arnold 21—5—[illegible]—0; R. Willis 15—1—61—0; A. Greig 26—2—87—3; C. Old 20—3—[illegible]—0; P. Pocock 17—3—30—0.

22 Schools Enter Girls' Athletic Contest

Twenty-two schools are expected to participate in the Barbados Girls' Interschools Athletic championships which start on Tuesday at the National Stadium.

The championships will be divided into six section meets, each comprising three or four schools, with competition starting at 9 a.m. each day. The individual winners of each event from each section meet, regardless of which school they are from, will compete in the finals on March 22.

Points will be awarded for the first three places in each event at the section meets and the first four places at the finals thus determining the overall champion school, the champion school in the four divisions and the individual champion for each event.

Tuesday's competition will bring together the Alleyne, Federal, St. Lucy's Secondary and Springer Memorial; while on Wednesday, the Co-operative, St. George's Secondary, Parkinson and the Metropolitan will meet.

St. Michael's Girls, the defending champions, Ellerslie and St. Ursula's will meet on Thursday, while Friday's competition will see athletes from Alexandra, St. Leonard's, the Unique and the Modern in action. On Monday, March 18, Princess Margaret, Industry High and West St. Joseph will meet, while the final section meet will see Foundation, last year's runners up, St. Patrick's, Queen's College and Codrington High in action.

Competitors for the finals will be all girls from the section meets who placed first in any of the sprints, relays and field events, plus the two best from all the second places. From the long distance events, the first three girls from each section will run in the finals.

Barbados Polo Club Edge Out Visitors

The Barbados Polo Club rounded off the season in fine fashion, defeating the San Flamingo team from England five goals to 4½ in the final match of the four-match tour of the island by the visitors, at the local club's grounds Holder's, St. James, yesterday.

Barbados defeated their guests 4½ goals to four in the opening match last Saturday, while the visitors defeated a local team 6—1 in their second match at the new polo arena, Mangrove, St. Philip, on Tuesday.

The home team then came back to win the third match 4½ goals to four on Thursday.

San Flamingo went into yesterday's match with a half goal advantage, but despite two goals from John Kidd and Roger Gooding, who was filling in for the tourists, they were unable to capitalise on their advantage.

Barbados were piloted to victory by captain Othneil "Cow" Williams, who score two goals, while the other goals came through Arthur Williams, Andy Dowding and Owen Deane.

The Barbados team not only maintained an unbeaten record against the touring team this series, but are yet to lose a series at home to San Flamingo.

Barbados defeated San Flamingo 2—1 last year during their first tour of the island.

Meanwhile, despite the official close of the local season, arrangements are being made for the playing of matches at the new arena at Mangrove. Matches will be played on Thursday and Saturdays at 4.30 and 4 p.m., respectively.

Arrangements are also being made to stage a gymkhana and jumping show at the Holder's grounds later this year.

Gibbs Tops at Campus

Laura Gibbs was voted the most outstanding women player in the Cave Hill Campus of the University of the West Indies Lawn Tennis tournament on Friday, when the tournament concluded at the Cave Hill courts.

Gibbs who had already won the singles title and shared the women's doubles title with Sandra Osbourne, teamed up with David Clarke on Friday to register a 6—4, 6—4 victory over Al Cummings and Holly Bromfield to win the mixed doubles title and become the first triple winner in the tournament.

Clarke, who was also the men's singles champion, was the most outstanding male player, while the men's doubles title went to Monty Eustace and Terry North.

Patterson, Griffiths On To Semi-Finals

PETER Patterson and Ron Griffiths, the number three pair in the men's doubles of the Barbados Lawn Tennis Association's grass courts tournament, advanced to the semifinals on Friday, when the tournament continued at the Garrison.

Patterson and Griffiths were made to work hard for their 6—2, 4—6, 6—1 victory over Richard Marshall and Brian Hart in their quarter final encounter.

Meanwhile, Michael Tucker and Andrew Gittens had an easy passage to the semi-finals, winning by default from the number two pair, Basil Denham and Gordon Sumpter.

Monty Eustace qualified for the final of the Plate competition when he defeated Mickey Tasker 7—5, 4—6, 6—0, and will come up against Brian Hart when the competition continues tomorrow at the Garrison.

In the men's doubles semifinals also carded for tomorrow, Gregory Adams and Peter Symmonds, the number one pair, will come up against David Clarke and Gerald Cozier, while the number three pair, Peter Patterson and Ron Griffiths will play Mickey Tasker and Andrew Gittens.

Today's Sport

(LOCAL)

CRICKET:
Fourth day's play in the third Test match between England and the West Indies at Kensington Oval — 10.30 a.m.

HOCKEY:
Barbados Women's Hockey Association's trial sessions in preparation for the Caribbean championship continue at Wildey — 6 30 a.m.

● CONSERVE YOUR POWER EVERY HOUR

Todds in Fine Bridge Victory

MR. and Mrs. William Todd won the east-west competition on Thursday night in the Hastings Bridge Club's weekly game at the Ocean View Hotel.

The Todds had the best score of 141 match points in the 10-table Skip Mitchell movement. Second were Noel Mapp and Hayden Forde with 133½ match points, while Peter Lashley and Leroy Lynch were third with 128½ match points. In fourth spot were Eithne Goddard and Tony Watkins with 121½ match points.

Bert Brathwaite and Herman Alleyne won the north-south competition with 137 match points, while Gladstone Holder and Orlando Marville were second tied with St. Elmo Thompson and Gilpin Jones on 121 points, while Blyden Callender and Keith Roach

HARRISON LINE

FORTNIGHTLY SERVICE FROM LONDON
(IN CONJUNCTION WITH SAGUENAY LTD.)

VESSEL	FROM	LEAVES	DUE BARBADOS
"EXPLORER"	London	Mar. 15	Mar. 26
"NATURALIST"	London	Mar. 29	Apr. 8

FORTNIGHTLY SERVICE FROM GLASGOW AND LIVERPOOL

"WESTBURY"	Liverpool	Mar. 13	Mar. 24
"ADMINISTRATOR"	Liverpool	Mar. 27	Apr. 6

HOMEWARD OPPORTUNITIES

VESSEL	TO	LEAVES BARBADOS
"DALESMAN"	London	Mar. 27

For further information apply to:—

DA COSTA & MUSSON LTD., Agents

However, Christopher Martin-Jenkins wrote: 'the ferocity of his attacking strokeplay contrasted with his calm, undemonstrative manner at the crease. So early did he pick up the line and length of the ball that it seemed impossible for him to become unbalanced or ungainly. On this pitch at least it mattered nought that he seemed almost exclusively a back-foot player'.[5]

In just under an hour Rowe and Kallicharran had made 50, in 1 hour and 42 minutes they had made 100 and they maintained this pace so urgently that the 200 partnership came up in virtually even time. They were playing the full range of strokes and it didn't matter who was bowling at them: Arnold, Willis, Greig, Old or off-spinner Pat Pocock.

Kallicharran went to his century in 6 minutes under 3 hours (15 4s) and hit three more boundaries before Greig bowled him for 119 at 375, just 20 behind England. Greig had now changed from his medium-pace to bowling off-breaks and bowling them well. Kallicharran was out at 4.50pm. He and Rowe had put on 249, a new West Indian Test record for the second wicket.

At last Rowe slowed, his double century within sight, and meanwhile Clive Lloyd tried to defend so he, too, would be there at the close of play. For a naturally aggressive batsman, defence made Lloyd vulnerable. He prodded forward at Greig, and Fletcher caught it at third slip. Before the close Rowe did get to the double century (25 4s, the 6). The closer he'd got to it the harder he'd had to work for it: Greig and Pocock were bowling tight. He finally reached it with a swift single to mid-wicket. John Jameson fielded the ball and threw down the wicket but Rowe had made it safely. The crowd invaded the pitch again to congratulate and celebrate him, although this time the police prevented them from reaching the actual wicket and one senior officer took advantage of his position. As the crowd melted back towards their seats he went up to Rowe, face wreathed in a vast smile, and shook his hand.

At the close West Indies were 394 for 3, night-watchman Vanburn Holder 4 not out. With Rohan Kanhai, Sobers, Derrick Murray and bustling Bernard Julian to come, England faced a further onslaught when play began again.

It didn't happen. Denness might have taken the new ball the night before but chose not to and chose not to again now, although the old one had been in use for 97 overs. Superficially this seemed a surprising gambit. Denness opened with the spin of Pocock and Greig. The assumption was that Denness did not want to squander any of the new ball's shine on Holder, although there was another dimension to this because a tail-ender might nick and glance a few from the pace attack but spin would torment him. It worked, Greig caught and bowled him. Before that, however, Rowe had had a moment of genuine alarm. From the non-striker's end he set off for a single and was half way down the pitch before Holder sent him back. Denness, fielding the ball at deep mid-off, couldn't capitalise on the moment.

When the new ball was taken, at 456 for 4 and 112 overs, Arnold bowled Kanhai for 18, ripping out his middle stump. Sobers came in and, of course, every time he came to the wicket in a Test match he did so as the highest scorer of all. Willis found the edge of Sobers's bat and Greig, diving, scooped the ball up. Sobers was gone before he'd scored. E.W. Swanton noted that Rowe's 'new stature' had grown to the point where the dismissal of Sobers, and for a duck, was received by this excitable crowd with something approaching equanimity.[6] All eyes were on Rowe, all anticipation of how far he might go, beyond Sobers and the 365? Soon enough they saw Rowe go past George Headley's 270 at Kingston in 1934–5, the highest innings against England by a West Indian.

Obdurate Derrick Murray was in and would put an end to any suggestion of the West Indian innings collapsing.

Meanwhile, Rowe hit two successive Willis deliveries to the boundary and even when Old made a ball rear sharply enough to strike him on the shoulder he regained his composure straight away. At lunch, when Denness led his tired troops off to put their feet up, Rowe was 274 and 116 runs had been scored in the morning session. Here, of course, was the eternal dilemma. The match was into its fourth day and West Indies, heading towards a lead of 100, were looking for the win when England batted a second time. The dilemma was how much time to bat for and how much time to leave to bowl England out a second time. Would Rowe be given time to beat Sobers? In the morning session he had scored 72. He was still 91 short of Sobers so that, maintaining his striking rate, he'd be into the final session before he got there. That lunch time the crowd waited and wondered.

After lunch Rowe moved to his triple century with a gloriously pure drive to the cover boundary. It had taken him 10 hours and it had taken its toll. Almost immediately, at two o'clock, 'fatigue overpowered him'.[7] He lofted Greig to deep mid-wicket where Arnold took the catch. Greig punched the air, while Rowe turned slowly away. He had been at the crease for 10 hours and 10 minutes, although only 140 overs, and hit 36 4s as well as the 6.

Curiously, however weary he may have felt, Martin-Jenkins noted that he 'looked as cool and smart and fresh' making his back back to the pavilion as he had looked 'making his way from the pavilion to begin his innings three days before'.[8]

West Indies declared at tea on 596 for 8. Imagine if Rowe had still been there, but it was still well short of Sobers. Luckily Kanhai did not have to face the dilemma.

England stumbled into trouble replying and at one stage were 40 for 4. Fletcher played an heroic 129 not out, Knott made 67 and at 277 for 7 they'd escaped with a draw.

The enigma remains. During this innings, as all who witnessed it seem to agree, Rowe was announcing himself as a potentially great batsman on the world stage. He had already made runs, good runs, at his home ground of Sabina Park but now, with the 302, he had outgrown that. He simply couldn't sustain it and one source suggests that Rowe discovered he suffered from hayfever.[9] Evidently this hadn't mattered on the 'burnt pitches of his native Jamaica' but it did elsewhere and he had to 'fight against a streaming nose and other niggling injuries.' In the late 1970s he found runs harder to get, played in Packer's World Series and captained a rebel West Indies tour to South Africa. It was a long way from the 302.

West Indies v England
Played at Bridgetown, 6, 7, 9, 10, 11 March 1974

ENGLAND

M.H. Denness	c Murray b Sobers	24	lbw b Holder	0
D.L. Amiss	b Julien	12	c Julien b Roberts	4
J.A. Jameson	c Fredericks b Julien	3	lbw b Roberts	9
G. Boycott	c Murray b Julien	10	c Kanhai b Sobers	13
K.W.R. Fletcher	c Murray b Julien	37	not out	129
A.W. Greig	c Sobers b Julien	148	c Roberts b Gibbs	25
A.P.E. Knott	b Gibbs	87	lbw b Lloyd	67
C.M. Old	c Murray b Roberts	1	b Lloyd	0
G.G. Arnold	b Holder	12	not out	2
P.I. Pocock	c Lloyd b Gibbs	18		
R.G.D. Willis	not out	10		
	l-b 5, n-b 28	33	b 7, l-b 5, n-b 16	28
		395	(7 wkts)	277

	O	M	R	W		O	M	R	W
Holder	27	6	68	1		15	6	37	1
Roberts	33	8	75	1		17	4	49	2
Julien	26	9	57	5		11	4	21	0
Sobers	18	4	57	1		35	21	55	1
Gibbs	33.4	10	91	2		28.3	15	40	1
Lloyd	4	2	9	0		12	4	13	2
Fredericks	3	0	5	0		6	24	0	0
Rowe						1	0	5	0
Kallicharran						1	0	5	0

WEST INDIES

R.C. Fredericks	b Greig	32
L.G. Rowe	c Arnold b Greig	302
A.I. Kallicharran	b Greig	119
C.H. Lloyd	c Fletcher b Greig	8
V.A. Holder	c & b Greig	8
R.B. Kanhai	b Arnold	18
G.S. Sobers	c Greig b Willis	0
D.L. Murray	not out	53
B.D. Julien	c Willis b Greig	1
A.M.E. Roberts	not out	9
	b 3, l-b 8, n-b 35	46
	(8 dec)	596

Did not bat: L.R. Gibbs.

	O	M	R	W
Arnold	26	5	91	1
Willis	26	4	100	1
Greig	46	2	164	6
Old	28	4	102	0
Pocock	28	4	93	0

MATCH DRAWN
Failed by 64 runs to beat the record.

Notes

1. *Advocate-News.*
2. *Testing Time,* Martin-Jenkins.
3. *Wisden,* 1975 Almanac, page 923.
4. *Advocate-News.*
5. Martin-Jenkins op. cit.
6. *The Daily Telegraph.*
7. *Advocate-News.*
8. Martin-Jenkins op. cit.
9. www.sporting-heroes.net/cricket-heroes/displayhero.asp?HerolD=602

England v India, Lord's, July 1990

Graham Alan Gooch, born Leyton, 23 July 1953.

Test career 1975–95: 118 Tests, 8,900 runs, 20 centuries, average 42.58.

Graham Gooch bristled at the wicket as if sometimes he was restless within his own strength. His driving, particularly straight, was as ferocious and glorious as anything Ted Dexter of the generation before could do; that straight drive came off the bat like a gunshot as if the restlessness of the strength was all distilled within it.

In a radio discussion about fast bowling, he said that he had only once been genuinely afraid and that was against the West Indies pace attack. He realised that the ball was outpacing his reactions and he could be physically hurt because he couldn't do anything about it.

That apart, he was a formidable opponent, although he'd describe himself as shy, who, in 1990, was at the height of his reputation and his powers.[1] This alone makes the events of 26 July at Lord's very hard to understand.

It had been a dry summer and the Indian batsmen had loved that. Sanjay Manjrekar made 158 not out against Yorkshire, Ravi Shastri and the skipper, Mohammad Azharuddin, both made 105 against the minor counties, Sachin Tendulkar made 105 not out against Derbyshire but, more importantly, all the front line batsmen were in the runs.

Azharuddin won the toss at Lord's, the First Test of three (the New Zealanders had toured for the first part of the summer). Nobody – except, presumably, Azharuddin himself – could quite believe what happened next. He put England in to bat and that was the bit that was hard to understand. The England captain, Gooch, surmised that Azharuddin made the decision entirely by himself because he had heard that when Azharuddin got back to the Indian dressing room the coach, Bishen Bedi, was 'furious.' From nowhere Gooch was strapping his pads on.

Sunil Gavaskar, writing in *The Daily Telegraph,* said that it was 'difficult to understand Azharuddin's decision. There was a cloud cover when the toss was made but the weather forecast was good'. Gavaskar added that, precisely because the front line batsmen were in the runs, they didn't require 'protection'. Perhaps, Gavaskar ruminated, Azharuddin was influenced by the fact that two of his bowlers, Kapil Dev and Manoj Prabhakar, would be able to exploit the cloud cover and that Lord's had a reputation for helping bowlers in the first hour of the day.

Gooch had, of course, seen the cloud cover and seen that the morning was humid and early movement could be expected. He had an ear infection and had, two days earlier, been involved in a hectic run-chase at Colchester against Lancashire. Gooch made 177 from 152 balls and Essex won by 6 wickets.

At Lord's, when he strode out with Mike Atherton to open the innings against India, he was in prime form, however much discomfort he was feeling from the ear. He set his innings in motion by flicking a half-volley from Manoj Prabhakar to the boundary.

When the score was 14 in the sixth over Atherton got a nasty ball from Kapil Dev and misjudged its line. It beat the bat, struck the front pad and was deflected into his off stump.

David Gower came in and Gooch greeted him by striking three boundaries in four balls: two were half-volleys from Prabhakar, one went thundering to long-off and the other to square leg. Kapil appealed for lbw but the ball was missing the leg stump, and now Gooch struck Kapil to long-off. Gower had little of the bowling and, while this was going on, managed a single in 23 minutes.

John Thickness in the *Evening Standard* wrote that when Gower was facing his ninth ball he 'hit Kapil crisply down to the Tavern and his 12th when, against Prabhakar, he followed with one of those curtseying cover-drives of his that make the women swoon'.

If Gooch didn't intend to make the Indian bowlers swoon he certainly would have them wilting. When he'd reached 35 he completed 30,000 runs, but in 10 balls he'd been beaten four times by Prabhakar. At 36 and England on 61 – it had taken an hour and a half – Gooch ought to have been caught by wicketkeeper Kiran More off Sharma. As Gooch himself realised, if that had happened – England two wickets down – Azharuddin's decision might have looked quite different.

After lunch Gooch cover drove to the boundary, pulled Shastri into the Mound stand, cover-drove again and he had 50. Gower untypically took 2 hours and 35 minutes to make 40 (off 109 balls, four 4s) and was then caught at silly point. His partnership with Gooch was worth 124. By now the Indian attack was wilting.

Perky, cheeky Allan Lamb was in and as the afternoon unfolded Gooch was blasting leg-spinner Narenda Hirwani to the boundary to a field that had no square leg, and Lamb was pulling Sharma's short deliveries with such power to the short Mound Stand boundary that umpire Dickie Bird, a lively mover at the best of times, was 'waving a handkerchief as a white flag' because he was in fear of 'life and limb'.[2]

At this point some 33 runs were taken off four overs and between lunch and tea, 127. When Gooch reached his century it was his 10th in Test matches and – arcane but worth recording all the same – he had become the first batsman to make four hundreds in Lord's Tests. (If you're wondering, Bradman's sequence was 254 and 1; 36 and 13; 18 and 102 not out; 38 and 89: 'only' two). You could sense by the controlled, minimalistic way he raised his bat to acknowledge the applause that he saw this as a beginning not an end. He used his right boot to re-make his mark. It meant 'work in progress'.

He and Lamb put on 150 between tea and the close from 28 overs and Gooch finished the day on 194 not out (285 balls, two 6s, 27 4s). Lamb was 104 and the partnership worth 218.

Gooch was tired now but due to have dinner with Doug Insole, a former Essex player and something of a mentor. Insole had booked a table at Primrose Hill but Gooch could 'hardly keep my eyes open from the first course onwards'.[3]

Next day, at the ground, he prepared in his usual ritualistic way. He had an early net. It was a hot morning, close and sticky. He moved into the ritual, which was important to him, whenever he was going out to bat. He set it out in his autobiography. Between 10.30am and 11am he'd have a cup of tea, strip off, he'd had a net, towel himself then put his whites on quickly. At a Lord's Test the ritual went further because he always changed in 'exactly the same position'.

All this done, Gooch would go and sit along on the balcony outside the dressing room composing himself. He'd examine the state of the match and ask a sequence of questions based around that. He'd think about the needs of the team, think about the bowlers and 'particularly' the fielders. He'd try to replay what he had done against them before and concentrate on the successful parts.

The start was slow because, in truth, there was no reason for undue haste. Gooch thought the tactic was to get the England total up to 600 and declare to have a thrust at the Indians before the close but that was some 5 and a half hours away and two attacking batsmen on a good pitch can score an awful lot of runs in 5 and a half hours. Kapil Dev bowled two maidens to Lamb, Prabhakar bowled a maiden to Gooch and even got one past him. No run was scored from the 27 deliveries in the first quarter of an hour, and, although India had taken the new ball, Gooch was content to play a couple of maidens against that. He recited to himself the mantra: *no undue haste, let the ball come to you.* Lamb was judging the situation the same way because he took 25 minutes to get his score moving again.

Then Gooch sent Prabhakar to the square boundary to move past his highest Test score: he'd had 196 against Australia at The Oval in 1985 (and as a point of comparison that had taken him 7 hours and 3 minutes, 27 4s; here at Lord's he'd been at the crease for exactly 6 hours). He could afford a little haste now because, two balls after beating his own record, he on-drove three. This second hundred had taken him 131 balls, an amazing 59 fewer than he'd needed to get to his first hundred but, equally amazing, containing fewer boundaries. Certainly this early in the day's play Kapil Dev and Prabhakar were making the ball move enough to cause discomfort, if nothing more serious than that.

The double century revitalised whatever tiredness Gooch had been feeling. Antibiotics were beating the ear infection and as he moved on from the double hundred a curious thing happened: he was sustained by the public address system announcing the various records as he reached them.[4]

At 206 Gooch became the highest scorer against India at Lord's. He unleashed his straight-drive twice against Prabhakar in one over and Lamb, taking England to 400, was timing the ball so sweetly that he leant into the delivery from Kapil Dev and caressed it to the boundary at the Nursery end. Yes, the public address was busy. When the total reached 449 Lamb had a go at Sharma and was caught low and two-handed by Manjrekar in the gully. It was his highest Test score and had lasted 4 hours and 36 minutes, the partnership worth 308. This represented the highest England stand for any wicket against India but was still well short of the 370 made by Compton and Edrich against South Africa in the golden summer of 1947.

No respite for the Indian attack, however. Robin Smith of Hampshire, another who'd been born believing that cricket balls had been manufactured to be hit, came in. At 240 Gooch went past his own highest score in 'England' matches, the 239 against Jamaica set earlier in the year. A run later he was past Hammond's 240 against Australia in 1938, which had stood as the highest England score at Lord's.

England were 466 at lunch so 97 had come in the session and that included a brief break for a shower.

Gooch now moved into his lunchtime ritual. He washed, towelled-down again, put his sweaty shirt into the drying room, then got out and arranged his kit so it would be ready when he wanted to put it on. He put his feet up, ate some chicken and a roll, then dressed. These are the moves of a careful, methodical, experienced man who knows his trade and yet – and this is the great secret – has found a method of retaining that unsullied almost boyish delight of seeing the ball early, locking the body into the classical position and screaming the ball along the ground past the bowler so that it cannons against the pavilion railing, while the old men behind that railing are boys again themselves. Graham Gooch was everybody's idea of a professional and everybody's idea of what an amateur had been in the days when, from this same pavilion, Gentlemen came from one door and Players from quite another.

At 247, soon after lunch, Gooch was past Boycott's 246 and that was the highest score any England batsman had made against India. Smith, however, was bearing the brunt of the Indian attack and at one point despatched Prabhakar for three successive boundaries. Imperceptibly, the tiredness seemed to come back to Gooch, at least later in the afternoon.

At 255 he went past the highest Test innings at Lord's, the 254 of Bradman in 1930. He'd remember that as the public address announced this he suddenly understood 'how momentous the day was becoming.' Ordinarily Gooch did not permit himself to look too far forward in an innings; he'd set a target of the next 20 runs and when he'd achieved that he'd set off for the next 20. An innings became a sequence of small increments which cumulatively might make something very big. Now, however, he allowed himself to muse on a specific number, 275, his highest first-class score. He'd made it at Chelmsford against Kent two years before and he hadn't forgotten that after getting out so close to a triple century he'd vowed to himself that if he ever got that close again it wouldn't escape him a second time.

In the midst of this his touch seemed to have deserted him because although he was trying to sweep the spinners he couldn't connect. He drew up to the 275 with a boundary, exceeded it with a single and, at 278, drinks came out. He drank avidly from a bottle of water. He'd earned it.

At 286 Gooch went past the highest score an England captain had ever made, the 285 of Peter May at Edgbaston against the West Indies in 1957. He'd remember an on-drive for a couple to take him to 291 and suddenly he felt a 'flutter of nerves.' The professional in him dealt with that because he also felt an 'overpowering determination' to reach the 300. He'd remember how patient he was, how he'd played the equivalent of three overs working his way through the 290s until, in the final over before the tea interval, he had 299 – and the strike. He noticed Smith at the other end eager to run a single if Gooch put the ball anywhere where that was possible, so Gooch wouldn't have the tea interval preying on him. Gooch reacted by signalling to Smith to *calm down*.

And that's a professional.

The run didn't come and he went to tea at 299. As the players headed off, Gooch left his helmet in the middle, 'work in progress'. The afternoon harvest had been 133 runs for England from 33 overs.

Back in the dressing room Gooch faced an anxious wait. He drank a cup of tea but ate nothing. He left his pads on but changed his shirt. He intended to follow his original tactic and declare the innings closed in order to have a thrust at the Indian batting before the close. He was thinking as a captain, evaluating what was best for the side rather than helping himself to history at the expense of that.

In the first over after tea he steered a ball from Shastri to fine leg for a single and he became the fifth Englishman to score a triple hundred joining Sandham, Hammond, Hutton and John Edrich. It was the 12th time it had been done in all Tests. Unfortunately

BBC television had switched to horse racing and so missed the 300th run, which meant that Gooch's wife missed it as well as everybody else and many of those people were not pleased. They said the BBC had lingered too long at the racing after the race was over. The BBC countered that they were contracted to show the races, which they'd billed to show, and anyway a recording of the run had been played soon after.

These things happen.

The triple century seemed to release him, seemed to reinvigorate him, although he had been batting for 10 hours. He set about the Indian attack with the same vigour as he had in the earlier part of his innings. At least six significant milestones lay ahead, some of them outright records, and the public address might well be much, much busier.

Gooch, of course, knew all about Sobers's 365 and the ultimate. As he said, who didn't? At 306 Shastri might have caught-and-bowled him but it was a sharp chance. The weather was clouding over and with the score now beyond 600 he pondered the declaration. A single later took him to face Shastri and he drove him against the sightscreen at the Nursery End.

311.

He was past Edrich's 310, the highest score by an English batsman in a Test since the war. Now, off the next ball, he played a tremendous stroke, striking Shastri into the far distance for 6.

317.

He was past Simpson's 311, the highest score by a Test captain (Woodfull had captained the Australians in 1930 when Bradman made 334) and, as the breathless public address announced, he was also past the 316 of Jack Hobbs for Surrey against Middlesex, 1926, the highest first-class score ever made at Lord's.

The weather closed in further and light rain was falling.

324.

They came off and stayed off for around 20 minutes. The crowd, eager to see if Gooch could establish a new record, didn't like that and began slow handclapping. Gooch didn't see it like that. England's opening bowler Devon Malcolm was genuinely fast and, in this light, the umpires would have brought the players off. He might as well bat on and if he was going to do that he might as well have a go at the record. In the end it was a simple matter shorn of complications or permutations.

A few moments after the resumption he was past Sandham's 325. He pressed on until, at five o'clock, he'd reached 333. He tried to drive Prabhakar – a 'lazy, airy sort of drive,' as he'd say himself – and the ball came back between bat and pad, striking the off-stump. He turned away, weary, while the whole ground rose to him. The volume of applause and the depth of emotion that it contained, moved him deeply.

Ahead, by respectively 4, 32 and 33 runs (to beat them), lay the last three basecamps – pitched by Hammond, Hutton and Sobers – before the summit of Everest. For Graham Gooch, from a moment after five o'clock on 27 July 1990, they would be forever too high.

Typically, when he was asked about how he felt about the innings, Gooch said 'it was just one of those things,' which was exactly the kind of thing he did say in public. 'Once I got past 300 and then 330 I was going to go on. I wasn't batting to get the record but

I knew it was possible. Then I missed the ball and got bowled. Initially when I was out I felt a little bit disappointed but not really now. I am happy with what I got.'

England manager Mickey Stewart was more eloquent. 'I would like to have seen him get the record because of the way he has dedicated himself to both the technical and physical side of the game. You need guts and determination to play an innings like that, and, having shown both those qualities, it would have been nice for him to have chalked up something for himself.'

Gooch had batted for 10 hours 28 minutes, received 485 balls, hit three 6s and 43 4s. He and Smith had put on 192, and when Smith was out – century completed in 3 hours and 14 minutes – Gooch declared. The record breaking did not end there, however. India survived the 65 minutes to the close and eventually made 454. Kapil Dev hit four consecutive 6s and they took the Indians to the one run they needed to avoid the follow-on.

This produced a great irony because ordinarily if you make 333 and other batsmen in the side make hundreds too you bat yourself out of a chance for a serious second innings. Gooch's 333 was, as we've seen, the 12th in Test history. Sandham had had a

34 THE DAILY TELEGRAPH, SATURDAY, JULY 28, 1990 •

SPORT

CRICKET — FIRST CORNHILL TEST

Triple-centurion Gooch beaten only by fatigue

By Peter Deeley
at Lord's

Second day of five: India, with all their first-innings' wickets standing, are 605 runs behind

WHEN this extraordinary day had long ended, people were still queuing for a replica scorecard, no doubt to be produced as evidence in years to come that they were at Lord's when Graham Gooch scored his memorable 333, the third largest individual total by an England batsman.

There can rarely have been more tension in a rather one-sided day's Test play in recent history than that manifested by the near-capacity 20,000 crowd from the moment when the England captain, struggling against physical fatigue in mid-afternoon, finally reached his 300.

It happened with the first ball after tea. From that moment on, Gooch seemed to shrug off the effects of 10 hours at the crease and once more picked up the momentum with which he had earlier destroyed a very average Indian attack.

Then it dawned on me, spectators and participants alike, were sharing in a very rare moment. Gooch was no longer like a marathon runner whose legs have gone; he had his second wind and was looking at the ultimate prize — Sobers's first-record 365.

True, on 306, he gave a sharp caught-and-bowled chance to Ravi Shastri, but this surely was a day, we felt, when the gods were with him. In another over from Shastri, he was despatched one ball to the Nursery End sight-screen and then, off the next, hit a huge six that must have carried more than 100 yards.

That took Gooch to 317, the highest individual total posted on a Lord's scoreboard, passing Sir Jack Hobbs's 316 for Surrey in 1926.

On 324, drizzle intervened. When the umpires were an unconscionable time getting play going again, even members joined in the slow handclap, so anxious were they to see Gooch atop of the Test Everest.

But the final steps are always the most challenging. Nine runs later, Gooch essayed a drive at Prabhakar and the ball

nipped back between bat and pad, taking off-stump.

So this son of Leytonstone trudged wearily back up the pavilion steps to the Long Room, dwarfed by walls of applauding admirers, those legs suddenly feeling a good deal more than 37 years old.

It was precisely 5pm and Gooch had been at the centre of affairs for 10½ hours, since 11 o'clock the previous morning, collecting a mind-boggling 43 boundaries and three sixes along the way.

He had been fortunate in the latter part of his innings to have as his companion Robin Smith, who took the brunt of the strike in the afternoon when his captain was flagging.

The first portion of play had

So near to Sobers record

MICKY STEWART, the England manager, was more disappointed than Graham Gooch after the captain had failed by 33 runs to better Sir Garfield Sobers's record Test innings of 365.

While Gooch, 37, shrugged off his dismissal as "just one of those things", Mr Stewart summed up the thoughts of almost everyone else inside the ground.

"I would like to have seen him get the record because of the way he has dedicated himself to both the technical and physical side of the game," said Mr Stewart. "You need guts and determination to play an innings like that, and, having shown both of those qualities, it would have been nice for him to have chalked up something for himself."

Gooch was content to say: "I'm happy with what I've done."

seen Gooch and Allan Lamb scattering records to all parts of the ground. Their 308-run partnership, scored in 276 minutes, was the highest England stand for any wicket against India, and, on this ground, is second only to Edrich and Compton's 370 against South Africa in 1947.

So dominant were the batsmen that it came as a surprise when Lamb, having reached 139 — his highest Test score — slashed at Sharma, and Manjrekar took a very good, low, two-handed catch in the gully.

Despite another short break for slight rain, the first session had produced 97 runs. The afternoon was even more predictive, 133 runs coming from 33 overs with Smith setting the

tempo as he hit Prabhakar for three successive fours. Then he changed his bat twice, the handle of one eventually coming away from its body.

This was the time when Gooch was continually sweeping at the spinners and missing. On 278, he consumed almost a whole bottle of tonic water, and there was a glimpse of what appeared to be a stifled yawn from Test debutant John Morris, who had been sitting padded up for what must have felt like an eternity.

At tea, Gooch, one run short of the third hundred, left his helmet in the middle as if to say, in the words of a famous American general, "I shall return."

When Gooch was finally out, he and Smith had made 192 for the fourth wicket, a statistic which rates only a footnote on this day. But Smith deservedly went to his century in 3½ hours and Morris had the chance at least to feel what it was like in the middle before England declared at their fifth-highest total.

All credit to the Indian openers for surviving the final 65 minutes. The light was poor and they must have felt exhausted. Whether they can last three days remains to be seen.

Cricket — P32-33

LORD'S SCOREBOARD

India won the toss
ENGLAND—First Innings

*G A Gooch b Prabhakar (43 4's, 3 6's, 828mins, 485 balls)	333
(wild shot to good length inswinger)	
M A Atherton b Kapil Dev (1-0-22-20)	8
(between through the gap, ball brushed top of pad)	
D I Gower c Manjrekar b Hirwani(4-0-150-109)	40
(caught attempting to bind the ball off with his pads)	
A J Lamb c Manjrekar b Sharma(22-0-276-187)	139
(square cutting ball through the gully)	
R A Smith not out(14-0-194-155)	100
J E Morris not out(1-0-23-21)	4
Extras(b 2, lb 21, w 2, nb 4)	29
Total (4 wkts dec, 653 min, 162 overs)	653

Fall of wickets: 1-14 (Atherton), 2-141 (Gower), 3-449 (Lamb), 4-641 (Gooch)
Did not bat: I R C Russell, C C Lewis, E E Hemmings, A R C Fraser, D E Malcolm.
Bowling: Kapil Dev 34-5-120-1 (1w), Prabhakar 43-6-187-1 (3nb), Sharma 33-5-122-1 (2nb, 1w), Shastri 22-0-99-0, Hirwani 30-1-102-1.

INDIA – First Innings

R J Shastri not out(13-0-63-62)	27
N S Sidhu not out(0-43-45)	20
Extras(nb 1)	1
Total (0 wkts, 63 mins, 16 overs)	48

To bat: S V Manjrekar, S R Tendulkar, *M Azharuddin, D B Vengsarkar, †KS More, Kapil Dev, M Prabhakar, S R Sharma, N D Hirwani.
Umpires: H D Bird & N T Plews

Robin Smith on his way to an undefeated century

Graham Gooch shows the strain after his record-breaking triple century at Lord's

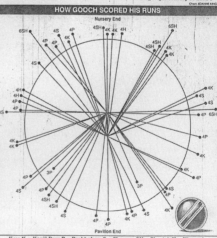

HOW GOOCH SCORED HIS RUNS

Key: K = Kapil Dev; P = Prabhakar; S = Sharma; SH = Shastri; H = Hirwani

Picture: PHILIP BROWN

Day that record wa missed by 33 ru

SUNI
GAVASI

TWENTY years from ... when Graham Gooch e... Wisden to look at the hi... individual scores in Tes... tory, he will sigh and thin... his name could have bee... top of that roll-call.

Tiredness and the des... score runs quickly to d... and let his bowlers loose... which left him so near an... so far from the summit.

Gooch is not a records... but it makes more sense... after a record when around, and if it is not go... hamper the team's chance...

Everything was in favou... him breaking Gooch's fir... Although looking a weary towards the end, h... fortunate to have had a ... of unscheduled interru... due to a light drizzle.

There was no questi... these stoppages affectin... wicket or his concentrati... fact, the breaks helped h... recharge his batteries ... speak, but mentally h... aware that with the inte... tions he had lost valuable...

The hallmark of Gooch... ting in this Test has bee... straight-driving. Wh... played this shot it was a ... example to those wa... youngsters how the bat s... come down on the ball a... low through after contac...

Gooch still does not li... to his drives as much ... coaches would like, but h... ing makes up for this ... tional weakness. Again... pace of the Indian bowle... deficiency in the fron... movement was not dange...

Maybe against bowlers... calibre of Alderman an... lee he might be in some... ble, and Kapil in his f... would also have give... some anxious moment... Kapil is now four years ... and the wicket did not h... bounce that he would ... liked.

Yes, July 27, 1990, is ... Gooch will remember. ... Not for the 333 runs he... but for the 33 he did not...

second innings (and made 50), nobody else until Hanif (who made his 337 in the second innings), then nobody else except Simpson who had had time to make only 4 in his second innings before the 1964 game at Old Trafford mercifully came to an end.

Now, because of the attacking tempo adopted by both sides, two sessions and a full day remained. Gooch set off at a gallop again, setting the tone with a boundary off Kapil Dev. England scored at 5 an over and when Gooch was out he'd scored 123 in 2 hours 28 minutes, with four 6s and 13 4s. In the match, therefore, he had scored 456 runs and that took him past the previous record held by Greg Chappell in 1973–4 for Australia against New Zealand in Wellington (Chappell 247 not out and 133). Gooch's second innings opening partnership with Atherton, 204, was a new record for England against India but by now, perhaps, everyone was satiated with records.

England moved in for the kill on the final day and although Sharma, India's number 10, made 38 and the match ended with a touch of theatre. The ball went to mid-on and Sharma set off. Mid-on seized the ball and threw down the middle stump at the bowler's end running Sharma out and completing the England victory by 247 runs.

Guess who the fielder at mid-on was?

Yes, it really had been Graham Alan Gooch's match.

Notes

[1] Gooch had a nice sense of humour but somehow he kept it hidden in public all those years, often sounding dour. When he retired he gave expert summaries on the BBC's *Test Match Special* and one time when rain stopped play (and the *TMS* were chatting) he recounted how, playing for Essex against Somerset, the great and feared Viv Richards was striding to the wicket and a young Essex spinner, making his debut, tried to *stare Richards out* as he made his journey to the wicket. Gooch went over to the spinner and said DON'T DO THAT TO HIM!!! Viv Richards was a murder of bowling in affable mood. When he was upset, vacate the stands, women and children first. A cricket ball is hard.

[2] *The Daily Telegraph.*

[3] *My Autobiography*, Gooch.

[4] Ibid.

England v India
Played at Lords, 26, 27, 28, 30, 31 July 1990

ENGLAND

G.A. Gooch	b Prabhakar	333	c Azharuddin b Sharma	123
M.A. Atherton	b Kapil Dev	8	c Vengsarkar b Sharma	72
D.I. Gower	c Manjrekar b Hirwani	40	not out	32
A.J. Lamb	c Manjrekar b Sharma	139	c Tendulkar b Hirwani	19
R.A. Smith	not out	100	b Prabhakar	15
J.E. Morris	not out	4		
	b 2, l-b 21, w 2, n-b 4	29	l-b 11	11
		(4 dec) 653		(4 dec) 272

Did not bat: R.C. Russell, C.C. Lewis, E.E. Hemmings, A.R.C. Fraser, D.E. Malcolm.

	O	M	R	W		O	M	R	W
Kapil Dev	34	5	120	1		10	0	53	0
Prabhakar	43	6	187	1		11.2	2	45	1
Sharma	33	5	122	1		15	0	75	2
Shastri	22	0	99	0		7	0	38	0
Hirwani	30	1	102	1		11	0	50	1

INDIA

R.J. Shastri	c Gooch b Hemmings	100	c Russell b Malcolm	12
N.S. Sidhu	c Morris b Fraser	30	c Morris b Fraser	1
S.V. Manjrekar	c Russell b Gooch	18	c Russell b Malcolm	33
D.B. Vengsarkar	c Russell b Fraser	52	c Russell b Hemmings	35
M. Azharuddin	b Hemmings	121	c Atherton b Lewis	37
S.R. Tendulkar	b Lewis	10	c Gooch b Fraser	27
M. Prabhakar	c Lewis b Malcolm	25	lbw b Lewis	8
Kapil Dev	not out	77	c Lewis b Hemmings	7
K.S. More	c Morris b Fraser	8	lbw b Fraser	16
S.K. Sharma	c Russell b Fraser	0	run out	38
N.D. Hirwani	lbw b Fraser	0	not out	0
	l-b 1, w 4, n-b 8	13	b 3, l-b 1, n-b 6	10
		454		224

	O	M	R	W		O	M	R	W
Malcolm	25	1	106	1		10	0	65	2
Fraser	39.1	9	104	5		22	7	39	3
Lewis	24	3	108	1		8	1	26	2
Gooch	6	3	26	1					
Hemmings	20	3	109	2		21	2	79	2
Atherton						1	0	11	0

ENGLAND WON BY 247
Failed by 33 runs to beat the record.

West Indies v England, St John's, April 1994

*Brian Charles Lara, born Cantaro, Santa Cruz,
Trinidad and Tobago, 2 May 1969.*

*Test career (as at 3 May 2005), 1990–: 115 Tests,
10,487 runs, 28 centuries, average 53.50.*

To quantify the impact that Brian Lara made in 1994, or more precisely between April and June, you have to go directly back to Bradman, *c.*1928–30. Nothing that happened in between Bradman then and Lara will stand the comparison. Nor is the similarity drawn into just one dimension, that of success far beyond the reach of others. Both men were in their twenties (Lara 25, Bradman 22), both were small, had neat, compact builds and an appetite about them that led you to understand that 100 was an introduction to an innings, a first base camp low in the foothills, both had the eyesight and reactions of a bird of prey, a full repertoire of strokes, and both could apply formidable concentration. Their careers in 1928 and 1994 had no recognisable limits at all.

We've already discussed how difficult it is comparing eras and now here is another conundrum. Of all the batsmen from 1930 to 1994 – and taking the whole of first-class cricket globally that must be thousands – you can understand how some achieved competence, some achieved what can loosely be called greatness but only these two redrew the possibilities of the game. Others worked within the possibilities, exploiting and occasionally expanding them. Bradman and Lara represented the possibility of entirely new beginnings.

Why them and not many of the others too? I hope I've pointed (in the first paragraph here) to at least something of what both men had, but that doesn't explain it because many of the others must have had those qualities, or commensurate qualities, and they never did anything like this. Nor does the C.L.R. James point – Bradman lacked the inhibitions of those going before him – help much. Presumably Lara did not have those inhibitions either, but you don't score runs on that scale simply because you lack inhibitions, however much that helps.

Watching films of both men (as a way of equalising the experience, unfair to be able to watch Lara in person but not Bradman, for the sake of this argument) there is a communality about them. You can *feel* a dynamo inside them but they are controlling it absolutely so that it can be made into a dynamic force or a method of denial as they play ball after ball for days on end. They can alter the balance between the dynamic and the denial without significantly increasing the risk factor. In short, Bradman could play several different strokes to the same ball, almost as if he was exploring the outer regions of his own ability, and so could Lara.

For example, in Lara's innings and even against a bowler as lively as Andrew Caddick he had time to look at a ball outside the off-stump, glide into position as he looked, then drive it through the covers to the boundary. That, incidentally, was at 21 for 2, it was his first shot in anger (as the saying goes) and he had the composure of a man who'd been batting for a week. Clearly, against such as the left-arm spin of Phil Tufnell, he'd have more time and I want to isolate one delivery to illustrate that. Tufnell is bowling round the wicket and Lara shifts his weight on to his back foot as Tufnell's arm comes over. The ball begins its flight to him and Lara is coming on to the front foot but this is an instinctive, primary movement: he is already re-assessing the pitch of the ball and transferring his weight on to the back foot again. His right leg is swivelling wide creating as much space as he'll need for the pull shot. At the instant of contact he is able to whipcrack the ball away from off-stump into the wide green acres of the leg side.

It was all done in time – this moment between the bowler releasing the ball and it reaching the batsman – that is so brief that it makes the game a cramped, constricted, stab-at-it experience for the competent, more spacious for the great but, as it seems, happening at a completely different pace if Bradman or Lara is on strike. We have already had one illustration. In 1930, albeit against a spin bowler, Bradman went up the track, turned, fell headlong on to his side facing the wicket and still cut the ball for runs. In 1994 if the same thing had happened to Lara he'd have done that or something similar too: nothing to do with the dynamo, everything to do with slow-motion.

Lara was born in the village of Cantaro not far from Port of Spain. He had a natural ball sense and his father gave him a small bat when he was three. At 20 he was Trinidad and Tobago's youngest captain and although he made his Test debut in 1990 he was not given a regular place until 1992. When the West Indies toured Australia he made 58 and 0; 52 and 4; 277; 52 and 7; 16. This was in the nature of a prelude as the England touring party were to discover the following winter.

The West Indies was still a forbidding place to go and Curtly Ambrose underlined that when, in the Third Test at Port of Spain, he broke England to 5 for 3 and bowled them out for 46. It was in the nature of a continuation: after two decades of this sort of thing the West Indians had established a psychological advantage over England built around prolific batsmen, big totals and forbidding fast bowlers.

West Indies had won the First Test at Kingston by 8 wickets (Lara 83 and 28), won the Second by an innings and 44 (Lara 167) and won the Third by 147 runs (Lara 43 and 12), followed by the Ambrose destruction. The talk was of them winning all five Tests – the fabled whitewash – and there seemed no particular reason why they shouldn't. This England side, captained by Atherton, was resilient, however. They struck back at Bridgetown in the Fourth Test with Alec Stewart making 118 and 143, Angus Fraser taking 8 for 75, and, when the West Indies were chasing 446 – no side had ever made that many to win a Test – Andy Caddick took 5 for 63, including Lara who mis-hooked him.

Lara would write that he felt the West Indian's mental approach hadn't been right and, going in to that Fourth Test, they were simply too confident. The psychological advantage of the decades had made that a danger, perhaps an ever-present danger.

The Wisden Trophy was inaugurated in 1963 as something to be played for like the Ashes, and up to 13 April, 1994 – when Chris Lewis bowled Ambrose to seal the Fourth test victory – there had been 68 matches, of which England had now won 10 and the West Indies 36. No England side had won a series against them since 1969. Atherton had been born in 1968...

More to the point, the West Indies had won the previous 12 Tests at Bridgetown and England tour manager Keith Fletcher felt that even a draw would be an achievement[1]. Yet in the match England outplayed the West Indies, establishing a useful first innings lead of just over 50 and, thanks to Stewart, 59 from Graham Hick and 84 from Graham Thorpe, set up the win, which Caddick bowled them to.

The West Indies did not intend to allow this to happen again and it gave the Fifth Test in Antigua a different atmosphere. This might be a real contest and it might be even more than that. If England won it that might lead to a profound psychological shift: the

West Indian fast bowlers were nearer the end of their careers than the beginning and the batting, Lara and Haynes aside, was no longer blitzing Test attacks all round the world.

Antigua might be a pivot.

The West Indies captain Richie Richardson was injured and Courtney Walsh took over. He won the toss and batted with a makeshift opening pair because Desmond Haynes was injured. The openers, Phil Simmons and Stuart Williams, did not last long even though the pitch was, in Lara's own words, 'a marble top.'[2] Williams went with the total at 11, caught by Caddick off Fraser, and Lara came in.

Antigua was alive and not just because of Lara, although he was being given a 'carnival-like reception' as he made his way to the wicket. Lara would describe the crowd at the Antigua Recreation Ground as one of the most 'animated,' containing as it did 'some of the Caribbean's best-known characters, including Chickie, whose instruments blast out non-stop, and the acrobatic Gravy and Mayfield who entertained all day with their antics and comments'. As if this wasn't lively enough, the All Saints Iron Band was positioned on the far side of the ground and letting everybody know they were there.

Before Lara had scored a run Simmons was lbw to Caddick making the total 12 for 2. Jimmy Adams came in.

Before the series Lara had set himself the target of two centuries. He'd scored the 167 at Georgetown and was now determined to make another. That dictated how he approached the innings. He was certainly not gazing beyond a century at this stage. Others, gazing back, would say they could see records already, but hindsight is 20/20 vision every time. What anybody could not mistake was the conjunction of circumstances that might at least make something extraordinary possible.

Lara was quite content to proceed circumspectly even though the bowling was not particularly penetrating and the wicket truly marble but he had time, plenty of that. The only disadvantage was the slow outfield, which Lara would describe as 'long, coarse grass'. It had the effect of making boundaries into 2's, in retrospect a staggering thought because a fast outfield would eventually have taken him who knows where?

Soon enough he exchanged the helmet for the chocolate West Indian cap – no bowler was going to hit Lara on this wicket – and, still proceeding circumspectly, took 51 balls to get himself into double figures and 121 to get himself to his 50 (seven 4s). He reached it with a lovely pull shot, all anticipation, balance, timing, power. He accelerated after that, taking three boundaries in an over from Lewis including a spoon-cut and a lashing of the ball – cross-batted, chest high – through the covers off the back foot. He galloped along to his century in 8 minutes under 4 hours. Phil Tufnell, round the wicket, bowled a short one outside the off-stump that turned. Lara made room and smote it to the boundary in front of square leg. He punched the air and raised his arms. He pointed out himself that his second 50 had occupied him no more than 59 balls, which was twice as fast as the first 50.

Adams had bustled to 59 (with a couple of 6s) out of 191 when he was caught by Nasser Hussain, on as substitute, off Fraser. Keith Arthurton helped push the score along to 274 by the close, Lara 164. The extent of his mastery is contained in a statistic: during the day he struck 24 boundaries, and only 6 had come from his partners (including the two Adams 6s). He'd been at the crease for 6 hours and 2 minutes, and faced 256 balls. He had played all his shots and made no semblance of a mistake. Some people judged that, whatever happened, Lara simply could not bat any better.

He went to bed early. He was rooming with Junior Murray at the Royal Ramada Hotel and he was glad about that because Murray 'is just the sort of quiet person who fits in with anything you want to do'. Lara might have had much on his mind because the team's poor over-rate in the previous Test had led to heavy fines. In strictly financial terms Lara could ameliorate that with a double hundred. There was a £50,000 award for any batsman who did that and it would be pooled.

Lara woke 'around 5.30' that second morning and went to a nearby golf course because he found that hitting the balls helped him to relax. When he reached the Recreation Ground to resume his innings he felt that other people thought 'something special was going to happen.' *The Gleaner* caught that mood when it quoted an (unnamed) Jamaican at breakfast as saying 'this is it. Lara is going to break Sobers's record today. The man is batting so well there is no way the English can get him out'.

When play did resume Lara played a maiden from Fraser then another from Caddick. There was no hurry now any more than there had been yesterday. After that, as *The Gleaner* reported with some gusto, Lara 'set the drummers to work when he posted his first runs of the morning with his trade-mark stroke as he went up on the left leg and whipped a short delivery from Caddick to the mid-wicket boundary'. His eye was in, the wicket was still marble and he 'went around the compass with a diadem of strokes – hooking and pulling, driving and cutting with an arrogance that reminded of [Viv] Richards'. Meanwhile, Arthurton had injured his hand and that inhibited what shots he could play so much that he managed only a single in the first hour. Lara would have to make the main weight of the runs and he'd be doing that all right.

He reached his double century, to a drum roll, in mid-morning off 311 balls after 7 hours and 6 minutes, steering Lewis to leg from outside the off-stump. For this fourth 50 had needed only 71 balls and, when it was completed, he raised his cap and bat simultaneously. He was beaming broadly and sweat covered his forehead but his body language of delight seemed to be understated. The double hundred was no more than second base camp and the mountain remained.

He was 225 at lunch, moving into full stride, and the afternoon stretched away to eternity for the English bowlers.

Sobers was at the ground watching ardently and during the lunch interval he received a plaque from the government and people of Antigua and Barbuda for all he had done for West Indian cricket. Sobers, by nature gracious, said 'I do not want to be long because I know you want to see a young man – a young man of quality and promise – get past 365. In fact, I would like to see it also, and I wish him good luck in his quest. He is a great little player but then you have to be to score like that'. Sobers, like Bradman, accepted that such records were by their nature temporary and in the fullness of time they'd go.[3]

Arthurton was still there but lasted only 17 minutes when play resumed. Caddick had him caught behind by Jack Russell. He and Lara had shared a partnership of 183 in 4 hours and 7 minutes.

Shivnarine Chanderpaul, only 19, became the fourth left-hander in succession to come to the wicket, and Chanderpaul would be no sleeping partner. As *The Gleaner* reported, he 'pulled Caddick to the mid-wicket boundary to get off the mark, played a couple of drives through the off-side, impishly pulled Caddick to the long-on boundary and then, when Lewis replaced Caddick next over, moved down the pitch and clipped the pacer past the square leg umpire as the crowd greeted each stroke with approval'. Chanderpaul was matching Lara stroke for stroke, run for run, and Lara sensed the England bowlers were 'rapidly losing their enthusiasm for the task'.[4]

Eternity was ever further away and now frustration had crept in. Fraser, *The Gleaner* reported, 'was involved in a heated exchange with vice-captain Alec Stewart and the bowler kicked the ground in disgust when shortly after he was on-driven by Lara for another boundary'.

Lara went to 250 off 377 balls but there was rain in the air and they came off briefly. (There were to be four stoppages, a loss of 23 overs: Lara would feel that if he had had those 23 overs, he might well have been spared a nervy night of pressure and the unnamed Jamaican's confident breakfast forecast would have been vindicated). He moved past his own highest Test score – the 277 – and Fraser will 'probably take to the grave' how Lara had drawn level with the 277: 'an audacious stroke which saw the little man rocking back and pulling the big pacer, the ball flashing past his left heel on the way to the long-on boundary'.[5]

At 286 Lara played what he describes as his first false stroke. Caddick was bouncing and got one to lift more than Lara had anticipated. Lara was trying to steer it down to third man but instead got an edge and the ball almost went to wicketkeeper Jack Russell's left hand. Lara differentiated this from an actual chance – Russell didn't lay his glove on the ball – but understood why Caddick roared in frustration.

In *The Gleaner's* considered opinion this false stroke was Lara's sole 'blemish' of the whole day. Oh, and the ball sped to the boundary, of course.

It is impossible to know if any of the other triple-centurions got so far before playing their first false stroke – no accounts of the innings are that complete, and mostly real chances are recorded – but it seems unlikely, even by Bradman himself. Lara had exercised mastery of a complete, all-embracing and, in terms of duration, perhaps unique kind. No ball of the day would beat him and no ball the day before had beaten him either.

Chanderpaul repeatedly told Lara to maintain his concentration and not give the whole thing away. Lara was openly grateful, and amazed that a 19-year-old could do it. Lara wasn't tense and was beginning to realise that, if he did keep his concentration, the summit would come into view.

He moved on towards his triple century, straight-driving Caddick to the boundary and that was 298. In the same over he got a short ball outside the off-stump, opened the face of the bat and ran it down towards Fraser, who set off towards it from third man. Lara immediately saw the possibility of two runs and covered the first run so fast that he was almost on Chanderpaul as he turned to embark on the second. Fraser's throw went high forcing Russell to back away from the stumps and leap to catch it, and by then Lara was 300.

The ground erupted. Some say the ovation lasted a full five minutes. He'd batted 10 hours and 10 minutes, faced 432 balls and struck 38 boundaries. The England attack had been pulled, driven (and literally as well as figuratively) cut to pieces.

Soon enough he was past the 302 of Rowe and in a purely West Indian context only Sobers lay ahead. Lara finished the day on 320 out of 502, Chanderpaul – who'd slowed in the on-offing for the showers – 41. The instant play finished, in fact as the umpires lifted the bails, Lara turned his concentration to Sobers and the 365. He would soon know that the whole cricket world had turned their attention to him. He lingered for an hour in the dressing room, getting everything into perspective and straightening his mind for what lay ahead.

At the hotel, the fax machines incessantly chattered out the messages and Lara would remember some of them 'already congratulating me'. He 'tried to read as many as I could, using them as a means of motivation'.[6] In his room Junior Murray acted as valet and protector. He deflected the rush of inbound phone calls by saying 'sorry, he's asleep'.

Lara didn't sleep well, woke up at 4am and simply couldn't find sleep again. His mind was working now, deciding against golf at dawn, thinking of the people who'd always said he'd break the record one day, facing the bowling as if play had begun again and charting the basecamps ahead – Sandham, then Gooch, then Bradman, then Hammond, then Hutton, then 'the big one'. And it was the big one not just because it was the highest, not just because it was by a fellow left-hander, not just because it was by a fellow West Indian but because of its historical weight. Ignoring Hammond's 336, the *real* record had been held by Bradman at 334 until Hutton in 1938 and Hutton had held it until Sobers in 1958 and that was it. To score a triple-century may or may not have been devalued by the overall increase in their number across the years from 1930, but Bradman-Hutton-Sobers represented an imperial dynasty: Bradman the best batsman who had ever lived, Hutton either the best or second best England opener who had ever lived (Hobbs the other),[7] and Sobers the best all-rounder who had ever lived.

Lara, on the morning of 18 April 1994, was only 46 runs away from extending the dynasty to himself.

Now, in the hotel, he felt nervous to a degree he had not experienced before and – the way of the world – he had so much time that he almost missed the team bus to the ground. The ground seethed with people. The gates had been open at 8am and as Lara arrived it was fit to burst. People wanted to slap him on the back, give him a word. He reached the dressing room and sat – it must have been a private moment in all the bustle – thinking of his late father, and he wanted to cry. His father had always said, as a sort of creed: *if you want to achieve anything, you need dedication, discipline and determination.* It could scarcely have been bettered as a precis of Brian Lara or the 320 he had scored so far. He would continue the creed when play began. He had, he would say, taken a decision to apply as much caution as he possibly could.[8]

He felt the tension reaching into him and he wanted play to begin because that would end this waiting and worrying and wondering. When he reached the crease he understood that the tension had affected his strokeplay. After a couple of overs the new ball was taken and Lara sent it over cover's head from Caddick – and Caddick didn't

Lara: the world at his feet
...smashes Sobers' 36-y-o record with majestic 375

BRIAN LARA: Broke Sobers' 36-y-o Test batting record of 365 runs with a scintillating knock of 375.

From
TONY BECCA

BWIA
We are the Caribbean.

ST. JOHN'S — The King is dead! Long live the King!

That was the chant around Antigua yesterday as Brian Lara was crowned king of batsmen after a world record 375 runs at the Antigua Recreation Ground.

Starting the day as the Prince of Trinidad and Tobago, the 24-year-old lefthander ended the third day of the fifth and final Test against England as the king of the world after erasing Sir Garfield Sobers' 36-year-old record of 365 not out against Pakistan at Sabina Park in 1958 and powering the West Indies to a commanding first innings of 593 for five declared.

At stumps on a day which ended in anti-climax after Lara's brilliant performance — the silence a stark contrast to the continuous cheering which accompanied him during his march to glory, England, weary and demoralised after over two days of leather-hunting in the hot Caribbean sun, were going well on 185 for two with Mike Atherton on 63 and Robin Smith on 68.

For England however, the harsh reality was that with two days to go they were not only 408 runs off the West Indies total, not only 209 runs away from saving the follow-on, but all of 190 runs adrift of Lara's personal tally.

Resuming at 320 after becoming only the 12th batsman in the history of Test cricket to reach 300 runs in a single innings, and sitting eighth on the all-time list, Lara moved to the top 19 minutes before lunch when, after pulling level with Sobers with a fluent drive through extra-cover off Andrew Caddick, he hooked Chris Lewis to midwicket as thousands of jubilant fans invaded the field for the coronation of the new king.

In a touching scene, Sobers — the old king — strolled onto the field, fought his way through the throng of spectators, and offered his hand in congratulations; and after that — after dragging himself away from the ecstatic fans, Lara knelt and kissed the pitch which he had, up to that time, occupied for 748 minutes and faced 530 deliveries while stroking 44 boundaries.

Batting like a man who had decided that, come hell or high water, he was going to fulfil his boyhood ambition, Lara, understandably, was not as fluent as he was during the preceding two days. Every stroke however, every run, every boundary was greeted with cheers and the pulsating beat of drums as another full house urged him on.

"I had made up my mind to do it as cautiously as possible," said Lara minutes after he was dismissed — caught by wicket-

keeper Jack Russell off Caddick in the last over to lunch, "and so I decided to take it one run at a time, one milestone at a time."

And that he did — for most of the time.

After stepping past Lawrence Rowe's 302, Don Bradman's 304, Bob Cowper's 307, John Edrich's 310 not out, and Bob Simpson's 311 on the second day, Lara eased past the others one by one, or rather two by two — the relegation of each marked by superb boundary strokes.

Andy Sandham's 325 at Sabina Park in 1930 — the previous highest in West Indies/England encounters — was the first to go when Lara drove Caddick to the cover boundary, and then it was Graham Gooch's 333 and Bradman's 334 when he smashed Angus Fraser off the backfoot to the backward point boundary to reach 335, and then it was Wally Hammond's 336 not out and Hanif Mohammed's 337 when he drove Fraser off the backfoot to the extra-cover boundary to reach 359.

With the crowd humming in the excitement of it all, Lara took his time to 351, and as the tension mounted, he sprinted for three twos in one over from Lewis to reach 357; and then, as if remembering his early morning promise to himself, he moved into the 360s — to 361 — with four singles.

Such is the genius of Lara however, such is his arrogance, that with the crowd chanting and whistling, he drove the last ball of an over from Caddick through extra-cover to reach 365, and then, after Shivnarine Chanderpaul had sensibly tucked away the first ball of the following over from Lewis for a single, after captain Atherton and Lewis had pulled in the field after a long deliberation, he promptly hooked the second to the vacant mid-wicket boundary.

The scene was something to behold — on the pitch were thousands of spectators, in the stands, thousands and thousands cheered and danced to the beat of drums and pan, and in the players' enclosures — both of them, all the players stood and applauded.

The most touching moments however, apart from Sobers' gesture, came when, after the police had cleared the field, one by one, went up and shook his hand or patted him on the back, and, at the end of it all, after he was finally dismissed after 766 minutes, 538 deliveries and 45 boundaries, when the England reserves stormed down the steps and took pictures of the record-breaking batsman as he lifted his bat on the way in.

Throughout Lara's final assault yesterday, Chanderpaul was at the other end, and on another day, he would have been the toast of the gathering, not because of his undefeated 70 while sharing a fifth-wicket partnership of 219 with Lara, but because of his delicate stroke-play — the kind which, along with his wonderful temperament, suggested once again that

another West Indies star in the way.

Joining the action on the second day at 374 for four, Lara on 239, Chanderpaul batted for 266 minutes and deliveries while keeping Lara company, and three of his boundaries — two straight es and an extra-cover drive Caddick yesterday — strokes of class.

Left with nothing to play but a draw after captain C ney Walsh had called the d ration at Lara's dismissal, gland started confidently reached 40 without loss be Alec Stewart hooked Ken Benjamin to Curtley Ambro backward square-leg, and Ramprakash, after two ele drives through extra-c shouldered arms to Ken Benjamin and was leg b wicket at 70 for two.

With Atherton and S playing some lovely strokes ever, especially Smith who the pacers with relish, En recovered well through an broken third-wicket partne of 115 in 157 minutes.

England however, may have been in trouble at clo both batsmen were fortuna survive the leftarm spin of Adams — Atherton, whe was dropped on 45 at 14 Phil Simmons at silly point Smith, minutes before the when he was dropped on 166 by Winston Benjamin covers.

West Indies 1st inning (resumed at 502 for 4 wick)
Phil Simmons lbw b Caddick
Stuart Williams c Caddick b
ser ....
Brian Lara c Russell b Cadd
Jimmy Adams c substitute
sain) b Fraser ....
Keith Arthurton c Russ
Caddick ....
Shivnarine Chanderpaul no
Extras(lb3, nb 23)........
TOTAL (for 5 wickets decl
Fall of wickets: 1-11, 2-1
191, 4-374, 5-593.
Bowling: Fraser 43-4-1
(nb12) Caddick 47.2-8-
(nb2) Tufnell 39-8-110-0
Lewis 33-1-140-0 (nb8) Hi
3-61-0

England 1st innings
Mike Atherton not out 63
Alec Stewart c Ambrose b
ny Benjamin ....
Mark Ramprakash lbw b H
Benjamin 19 ....
Robin Smith not out 68 ....
Extras (byes 2, legbyes 3, n
6)................................
TOTAL (for 2) ....
Fall of wickets: 1-40, 2-70.
Bowling: Ambrose 12-5-
Walsh 12-2-54-0 (nb4), Wa
Benjamin (nb1), Kenny E
min 13-4-34-2 (nb1), Cha
paul 5-1-22-0, Adams 5-0-17

King Lara promises to keep on hunting

from TONY BECCA
Senior Sports Editor

ST. JOHN'S — Minutes after breaking the world record for Test cricket's highest individual score at the Antigua Recreation Ground yesterday, Brian Lara promised to keep on hunting.

Flushed with excitement after erasing Sir Garfield Sobers' 36-year-old record of 365 not out with a glorious 375, the Trinidadian hero said that records were made to be broken, he was happy that he had broken one, and would not stop.

"It is a great feeling," said Lara, "and I suppose I just have to keep going, and who to tell, break my own record."

While many of his fans believed that it was destined to happen at any time, Lara said that he 'never expected to reach this far so early in my career, but now that I have done it, I am just gonna keep on living.

"I know things will change, but I won't get swell-headed or anything like that. I will always be the same."

Was it a lot of pressure out there, especially with everyone expecting it?

"It was, and when I got the ball over midwicket, I was so happy. I had done it."

For the excited Lara, the disappointment was that his deceased father was not around to see it, and that his mother was not in Antigua for the moment, "but I want to thank them for everything. They gave me life, and they encouraged me."

According to Lara, he played a few rounds of golf with Sobers on the eve of the Test, and the Great One not only encouraged him but was quickly on the field to congratulate him.

"It is nice to know that he respects me, and that he thought I could do it. It was also nice of him to come out and congratulate me. That is one of the greatest moments of my life, of my career, and I will never forget it. He is a great man."

Speaking about the innings itself, Lara, who was 320 not out on the previous day, said that he started playing his way to the

world record from 4 a.m. while he was in bed.

"I did not want to miss this opportunity," said the batsman who scored 277 in the third Test against Australia at Sydney last January.

How do you feel now?

"Great, I believe. It was when I got into the shower afterwards that I realised what a great innings I had played. I will never forget this day."

For Sobers, there was no regrets at having lost the record.

"Records are made to be broken," said the game's greatest all-round cricketer.

"It had to go some day, and who better to do so than this guy. From the first time I saw him bat, I believed that he would be the one, and I am happy that he did it. No one can bat like him. He does not play with his pad; he plays with his bat. He is a lovely stroke player."

File photo
BRIAN LARA

Hart Cup 100 for Broomfield

MONTEGO BAY — A brilliant knock of 103 by openner Teddroy Broomfield, his third century of the season, guided Riahs CC to first innings honours over St. James Youth as action continued in the 1994 St. James Hart Cup Cricket Competition last weekend.

In the game played at Barnett Oval, Riahs took first knock and took the 'Youths' attack to task,

declared. Broomfield, who struck twelve fours in his innings, was the main-stay of the batting while Carlton Tomlinson and Steve Alcott, with good scores of 42 and 39 respectively, gave valuable support.

Bowling for 'Youths', Oniel Ellis, with figures of three wickets for 41 runs off 10 overs, and Kenroy Virgo, with two for 31, were the only bowlers to figure

unslaught of the Riahs batsmen.

In their reply, 'Youths' failed to come to grips with the Riahs attack and could only manage 167 all out, losing first innings points by 72 runs. Conroy Thompson, who top-scored with 38, and Conrod Thompson and Kirk Nembhard, with scores of 29 and 16 respectively, were the only batsmen to get among the

care for that. Chanderpaul resumed his role as adviser and protector: *take care, concentrate*. The boundary off Caddick took Lara past Sandham's 325.

Lara would remember edging another ball to third man, and he attributed that to the nerves.

Fraser was bowling and, off the back foot, Lara belted the ball to the boundary through backward point.

335.

Lara faced Fraser and moved on to the back foot, drove him cleanly to the extra-cover boundary and was past Hammond and Hanif with the one shot. It made him 339.

Hereabouts, he played and missed at Fraser who said 'I don't suppose I can call you a lucky bugger when you are 340'.

He took his time reaching 351. From 335, four dot balls, a single, a dot ball, a single, five dot balls, a single, a 2, a 3, 10 dot balls, a single, a dot ball, two singles, two dot balls, a single and that was the 351. The crowd's rising excitement, and noise, had not seemed to affect him, not even Gravy, wearing Santa Claus uniform, in the West Indies Oil Stand. Up to the 350 he had batted 721 minutes, faced 511 deliveries and struck 42 boundaries. He got there by working Lewis – round the wicket, and on the line of the off-stump – towards deep square leg for a couple. It was an easy, polished stroke, all economy of movement and risk. He didn't take his cap off but just waved the bat. He smiled but it might almost have been a sigh.

The crowd of 10,000 were hand-clapping rythmically as though that might carry him to the record.

When he was ready he set about Lewis and did it with absolute confidence. He'd stroke the ball to a fielder in the deep and they'd scamper two. So he stroked the ball to Mark Ramprakash at square leg, scampered. Ramprakash threw to Russell who broke the stumps, but Lara knew he was safely in.

353.

He stroked the ball towards Ramprakash again. 'Come two!' Chanderpaul could scamper, all right, and so could Lara.

355.

He stroked the ball to Fraser at third man, scampered again.

357.

In the next over he drove at Lewis and, as it seems, this was his first genuine mistake as against a false shot. He missed the ball and it almost struck the off stump. Chanderpaul advanced towards him, resuming his role as adviser and protector. Lara now ignored the tumult and eked out four singles.

361.

The crowd were whistling and chanting. Caddick had already bowled five balls and now Lara drove him to the extra-cover boundary.

365.

Lara saw 'the crowd on their feet, hundreds of them seemed to be massing on the boundary line'. Chanderpaul was to face Lewis and tucked him away for a single from the first ball – Chanderpaul minimising the suspense and anxiety for Lara. Now Lara was to face Lewis, but Lewis and Atherton were in lengthy conversation about the setting of the field. All Lara needed was a single. Up came the fielders to cut that off.

Lewis was bowling over the wicket. Lara *read* into the way Lewis ran up to bowl that a short ball was coming and instinctively he found himself 'moving into the hook shot before the ball was bowled'.[9] The ball was very short and rose – almost steepled – shoulder high outside the off-stump. Instantly Lara was into a thundering pull rather than a classical hook, and the ball fled to the mid-wicket boundary.

Three policeman sprinted past it towards the middle. They knew what was going to happen, and already some spectators had out-sprinted them.

369, where no man had ever been before.

The time was 11.47am.

The Gleaner reported that 'the scene was something to behold – on the pitch were thouands of spectators, in the stands thousands and thousands cheered and danced to the beat of drums and pan, and in the players' enclosures – both of them – all the players stood and applauded.'

Lara hoisted his bat aloft and took that chocolate cap off, and spectators were moving towards him like a great tide. Chanderpaul changed roles because Lara no longer needed advice or protection. Chanderpaul hugged him. The police were trying to get the crowd under some sort of control and they managed to clear a path for Sobers.

The Guardian reported that in all the excitement a figure who resembled Nelson Mandela came from the pavilion in all his dignity and, flanked by policeman, made his stately path towards Lara.

Sobers, the gentleman, clasped Lara and congratulated him. Sobers told Lara that he'd felt he was the one to break the record. Sobers said later: 'It had to go someday, and who better to do it than this guy? From the first time I saw him bat, I believed that he would be the one, and I am happy that he did it. No one can bat like him. He does not play with his pad, he plays with his bat. He is a lovely stroke-player.'[11]

When Sobers had gone Lara went down and kissed the pitch.

When the pitch had been cleared by the police, the England players made their way to Lara and each of them congratulated him, shaking his hand and patting him on the back.

Lara thought briefly of trying to go on to 400 but his concentration had been broken and he couldn't get it back. He scored a couple more singles, another boundary and then – wear and tear, perhaps – inside-edged an outswinger from Caddick's last ball before lunch to Russell. As Lara moved towards the pavilion Caddick shook his hand. That was 18 minutes and 8 balls on from the 365. He'd taken 12 hours 46 minutes, faced 538 deliveries[10] and struck 45 4s.

Lara was gracious about Sobers too. 'It is nice to know that he respects me, and that he thought I could do it. It was also nice of him to come out and congratulate me. That is one of the greatest moments of my life, of my career, and I will never forget it. He is a great man.'

An aspect to ponder is that Lara had struck 45 boundaries but no 6.

He felt tired.

Walsh declared immediately but on such a wicket even this West Indian attack was unlikely to bowl England out twice, and didn't. By a statistical freak, England were dismissed in their only innings for 593, exactly the same score as Walsh had declared at. There was now only time for West Indies to make 43 without loss in their second innings.

Warwickshire signed Lara and the boy was bursting with runs. On his debut at Edgbaston in late April he made 147 against Glamorgan and four days later against Leicestershire, 106 and 120*. He didn't play against Oxford University, which must have meant he was entitled to a rest or Warwickshire were demonstrating the quality of mercy to the students, and made 136 against Somerset at Taunton and 26 and 140 against Middlesex at Lord's. This astonishing sequence – the 26 was the only innings since the 375 when he had not made a century – was no more than a prelude.

Durham came to Edgbaston, batted and declared at 556 for 8. Warwickshire lost an early wicket and Lara came in, his form suddenly and inexplicably gone from him. He was bowled by a no-ball and, at 18, dropped. He was so dissatisfied with himself that in the tea interval he went into the nets to work on his technique. Rain ruined the third day and here was a conjunction of circumstances: Lara could bat the match out. Before lunch on the fourth (and of course final) day he scored more boundaries (25 4s, seven 6s) than Trevor Penney scored runs (27) at the other end.

He murdered Durham, taking his third hundred off 58 balls, his fourth hundred after 72 more and, in a great climactic moment in cricket's long history, 77 balls to move to 501.

West Indies v England
Played at St John's, 16, 17, 18, 20, 21 April 1994

WEST INDIES

P.V. Simmons	lbw b Caddick	8	not out		22
S.C. Williams	c Caddick b Fraser	3	not out		21
B.C. Lara	c Russell b Caddick	375			
J.C. Adams	c sub (N Hussain) b Fraser	59			
K.L.T. Arthurton	c Russell b Caddick	47			
S. Chanderpaul	not out	75			
	l-b 3, n-b 23	26			
	(5 dec) 593		(no wkt) 43		

Did not bat: J.R. Murray, W.K.M. Benjamin, C.E.L. Ambrose, K.C.G. Benjamin, C.A. Walsh.

	O	M	R	W		O	M	R	W
Fraser	43	4	121	2		2	1	2	0
Caddick	47.2	8	158	3		2	1	11	0
Tufnell	39	8	110	0		6	4	5	0
Lewis	33	1	140	0					
Hick	18	3	61	0		8	2	11	0
Ramprakash						3	1	5	0
Thorpe						2	1	1	0
Stewart						1	0	8	0

ENGLAND

M.A. Atherton	c Murray b Ambrose	135
A.J. Stewart	c Ambrose b K.C.G. Benjamin	24
M.R. Ramprakash	lbw b K.C.G. Benjamin	19
R.A. Smith	lbw b K.C.G. Benjamin	175
G.A. Hick	b K.C.G. Benjamin	20
G.P. Thorpe	c Adams b Chanderpaul	9
R.C. Russell	c Murray b W.K.M. Benjamin	62
C.C. Lewis	not out	75
A.R. Caddick	c W.K.M. Benjamin b Adams	22
A.R.C. Fraser	b Adams	0
P.C.R. Tufnell	lbw b W.K.M. Benjamin	0
	b 9, l-b 20, n-b 23	52
		593

	O	M	R	W
Ambrose	40	18	66	1
Walsh	40	9	123	0
W.K.M. Benjamin	41.1	15	93	2
K.C.G. Benjamin	37	7	110	4
Chanderpaul	24	1	94	1
Adams	22	4	74	2
Arthurton	2	1	4	0

MATCH DRAWN

New world record by 10 runs. The old record stood for 36 years 2 months.

Notes

1   *Wisden,* Almanac 1995, page 1008.

2   *Beating The Field,* Lara.

3   One sporting record that seemed safe from the ravages of time was Bob Beaman's long jump of 29ft 2.1in (8.9 metres) in the Mexico City Olympic Games (British long jumper Lyn Davies actually thought Beaman had jumped clean out of the pit). In an activity where centimetres are important, Beaman had destroyed the 8.35m of Ralph Boston and Igor Ter-Ovanesyan. Beaman's jump was a freak, and a freak set at altitude. It was not beaten until 1991 when Mike Powell did 8.95m in the Tokyo World Championships. So Beaman's record hadn't been safe. That is a way of introducing how a record might be, though: Jim Laker's 19 wickets against Australia in the Old Trafford Test of 1956. Forever is a long time *but* it was done by an extreme conjunction of circumstances: a pitch which suited Laker's off-breaks perfectly, an Australian side which seemed mesmerised and, most crucial, an inexplicable inability by Tony Lock at the other end to take more than one wicket. (Inexplicable? The received widsom is that Lock tried too hard, and the more wickets Laker took the harder he tried; whereas, on such a wicket, wickets came to you). Laker went past the 17 of Sydney Barnes (for England against South Africa, Johannesburg, 1913–14) – so that had stood for almost half a century. As I write these words, Narenda Hirwani is third on the list with 16 for India against the West Indies at Madras in 1987–8.

4   Lara, op. cit.

5   *The Gleaner.*

6   Lara, op. cit.

7   At the risk of a verbal flogging by cricket historians, I have not included W.G. Grace because I don't think of him as an opener, more the pillar around which recognisable modern cricket was constructed.

8   Quoted in *The Gleaner.*

9   Lara, op. cit.

10 The *cricinfo* website explains that in fact Lara received 537 balls. One was added by the official scorer to 'cover up for umpire Darrell Hair's mistake in allowing a five ball over'.

Sri Lanka v India, Colombo, August, 1997

*Sanath Teran Jayasuriya, born Matara, Sri Lanka,
30 June 1969.*

*Test career (as at 3 May 2005), 1991–: 96 Tests, 6,465 runs,
14 centuries, average 43.10.*

It was a long time coming: no country had been given Test match status since Pakistan in 1954, although Sri Lanka (as Ceylon) had long been a staging post for England touring sides on the way to Australia. For instance, on the way to the Bodyline series England played All Ceylon at the Sinhalese Sports Club and Jack Hobbs wrote: 'Natives climbed tall trees overlooking the pitch, matting sun-shelters were dotted round the enclosure, and the stands were packed with local people, among whom women were predominant'.[1] The folklore was that after such a match – at four yearly intervals, of course – the stands were burnt down in celebration.

Rather quaint, in fact so quaint that when Sri Lanka played in the 1979 Prudential World Cup in England many spectators were surprised by the skill of their spin bowlers and the natural, unfettered aggression of their batsmen. They toured again in 1981, playing against the counties, and were granted Test status. There were questions about how they'd cope with cricket at that level and they lost their inaugural match, against England at Colombo in February 1982, by 7 wickets, but at Lord's in 1984 they charmed and impressed everyone by drawing with a full England side after making 491 for 7 declared in their first innings (Sidath Wettimuny made 190, the longest Test innings at Lord's).

By 1997, when India made a two-Test tour, the surprise of a generation before had become complete acceptance and the Sri Lankan victory in the World Cup of the year before – beating Australia in the final in Lahore – cemented that.[2]

The batsmen did like to hit the ball. In that World Cup left-handed opener Sanath Jayasuriya flogged India for 79 off 76 balls at Delhi – Sri Lanka were 42 after the first three overs – and he flogged England all over Faisalabad in the quarter finals, 82 off 44 deliveries, and because he hit 13 4s and three 6s, only 12 of the 82 had actually been run.

There was no history of cricket in the Jayasuriya family, but there doesn't have to be. He was good early, established by the age of 19 and a Test player since 1990. He was a devastating one-day player and if any doubts lingered over his suitability for the five-day game he was about to banish them as India came to Colombo in August 1997 for the first of the two Tests.

India won the toss on a placid, welcoming wicket and batted. Three batsmen – Navjot Sidhu, Sachin Tendulkar and Mohammad Azharuddin – made centuries and India declared at 537 for 8, leaving Sri Lanka to bat out 10 overs of the second day. Jayasuriya opened with Marvan Atapattu, and Atapattu liked to hit the ball, too. He hit five 4s off 26 deliveries in just 42 minutes then tried to drive left-arm spinner Nilesh Kulkarni and was caught behind. It was Kulkarni's first ball in Test cricket and if he thought Test cricket was going to be easy, by the time he had bowled another 419 of them he knew the truth.

Atapattu's wicket ended play for the day, Sri Lanka on 39 (Jayasuriya 12).

In time, Jayasuriya would sense that bowlers were trying to 'cramp' him – bowling straight, giving him no width – and he'd have to adjust the way he played. This would involve keeping his score ticking along and when a delivery came into one of his 'strong areas' he'd punish it, rather than blast everything he could reach. Perhaps this innings was the beginning of that.

The experienced Roshan Mahanama came out with Jayasuriya who was now preparing to demonstrate, given his record and reputation, almost superhuman self-denial. He moved to his 50 off 71 deliveries and still the pitch was welcoming, although Mahanama was in trouble early. Opening bowler Venkatesh Prasad had a confident appeal against him turned down and there wouldn't be another moment like that until near close of play. At lunch Sri Lanka had reached 136 (Jayasuriya 72, Mahanama 36) and already the innings had a definite shape. Jayasuriya would go on and on until the follow on had been avoided, guaranteeing Sri Lanka against defeat and Mahanama would cast himself in a supporting role. Jayasuriya put it this way: 'I batted to save the match for my team – my priority was to put the match beyond the Indians' reach.'

After lunch, Jayasuriya moved to his century off 138 deliveries and briefly abandoned the self-denial to get there. Kulkarni was bowling his 14th over (of the 70 he'd have bowled by the end of the Sri Lankan innings). Jayasuriya was on 85 and successively struck the spinner for 2, three boundaries, another 2. He had been at the wicket for 3 hours and 21 minutes and hit 14 4s.

He moved serenely on to 150 off 235 deliveries (19 4s) – it took 5 hours and 20 minutes and was now far beyond his previous best score in a Test, 113 against Pakistan, and a moment later was past the 151 of Mahanama, which represented the highest score by a Sri Lankan against India, at Colombo in 1993–4.

At the other end this same Mahanama moved circumspectly; he would only reach his century (off 244 deliveries, 10 4s) with seven overs of the day left and he pulled Prasad to the mid-wicket boundary to get there. He was, however, vulnerable. At 109 and heading towards the end of the day, he moved out to try and drive Rajesh Chauhan but edged the ball. Wicketkeeper Nayan Mongia didn't catch it and, on the same total, missed a stumping chance.

Jayasuriya finished the day with 175 off 299 deliveries (20 4s) in 2 minutes short of 7 hours. Mahanama was 115 off 277 deliveries (14 4s) and together they had put on 283 in 6 hours and 16 minutes – comfortably the best partnership in Sri Lanka's 75 Test history. The newspapers were already speaking of Lara's record even if that meant Jayasuriya batting through the fourth day and full into the fifth. That was his conjunction of circumstances. That evening of the third day, Sri Lanka needed no more than 16 to avoid the follow-on and the moment that was reached the match died. Jayasuriya could bat right to the end of the fifth day if he wanted and if he could…

He had spent this third day, as the Sri Lankan *Daily News* reported, batting 'very comfortably against the Indian pace cum spin combination'. There was no suggestion that the morrow might be any different, and if Mahanama stayed with him a whole raft of cricketing records stretching back to the 1930s and the Bradman era became vulnerable.

There's a lovely description of the Jayasuriya innings: 'To put this innings in perspective, one needs to consider the degree to which a batsman has to stretch himself both physically and mentally. The heat in Colombo isn't easy on a player and the humidity makes it worse. Home conditions sure, but when an innings stretches over such a long period of time, then this advantage is whittled away. There are moments when everything is a blur, when the heat and the dust make one wish that it would all end. And at that point, it is only sheer will that makes a man carry on.'[3]

However, as if to contradict this, Elmo Rodrigopulle in the *Daily News* wrote that Jayasuriya, 'with a frame that every bodybuilder will envy,' never showed signs of being tired throughout the day.

From his overnight 175 Jayasuriya went to his double century in another 28 deliveries (25 4s) and two runs later had made the highest Test score in Sri Lanka, beating the 201* of Don Kuruppu against New Zealand at Colombo in 1986–7. Six runs further on and he'd broken his own first-class score, 207* in 1988–9 when he was playing for Sri Lanka B against Pakistan B.

It was going to be that kind of day.

'I honestly did not think of any records while I was batting,' he'd say. 'The wicket was good and I thought if I could stay out there the runs would come.' They would and they did. He needed 98 deliveries to get to his 250 while, at the other end, Mahanama proceeded with the same caution as the day before.

Jayasuriya had one moment of alarm, at 265, when he was struck on the pad – on the back foot – by a delivery from Chauhan. In the next over he beat the 267 of Aravinda de Silva, scored at Wellington against New Zealand in 1990–1, and was now the highest Sri Lankan Test scorer.

When he moved past the 285 of Frank Worrell he'd become the highest scorer in any first-class match ever played in Ceylon/Sri Lanka. All else aside, that demonstrated how far Sri Lankan cricket had come. Worrell had been a member of a Commonwealth side – these did a kind of missionary work in spreading and encouraging the game, and were by no means a repository for the elderly, the halt and the lame. The main part of that 1950–1 Commonwealth tour was to India, with four matches in Ceylon at the end. The side included the West Indian spinner Sonny Ramadin, who had just mesmerised England, Jim Laker, arguably the greatest off-spinner of all time, and so on. Worrell, a batsman of great grace and presence, made the 285 in 4 hours 30 minutes (five 6s, 31 4s). By passing Worrell, Jayasuriya was helping give Sri Lankan cricket a legitimacy of its own.

He drove Kulkarni to the long-on boundary to reach his triple century off 518 deliveries in 12 hours and 3 minutes (one 6, 32 4s), giving more legitimacy. Now a Sri Lankan had a triple century and of the old-established Test playing countries, New Zealand didn't have one and neither did South Africa. Jayasuriya pressed on towards 326 by the close, scored off 568 deliveries in 13 hours and 2 minutes. (two 6s, 33 4s). As he and Mahanama came back to the pavilion 'fire crackers exploded outside the ground'.[4] It was time for celebration, reflection and anticipation.

The celebration was that Jayasuriya was already past all but Gooch, Bradman, Hammond, Hutton, Sobers and Lara.

The reflection was that, with Mahanama on 211, the pair had scored 548 together, which was a huge distance beyond the existing Test record, 467 by Martin Crowe and Andrew Jones for New Zealand against, as it happened, Sri Lanka at Wellington in 1990–1; even further on, of course, than the 451 by Bradman and Ponsford at The Oval in 1934, and Jayasuriya and Mahanama hadn't finished.

Sri Lankans wryly pointed out that never before had two batsmen batted through two days of Test cricket and still been together.

Well Sobers and Worrell had done that at Bridgetown against England in 1959–60, hadn't they? No. They'd come together at 4.50pm on the Friday and stayed together until 11.40am on the Tuesday (no play on the Sunday, a rest day). That too had been a placid, welcoming wicket. In reply to England's 482, West Indies lost three wickets for 102 when Worrell joined Sobers. They were respectively 21 and 8 not out at the close. Next day Sobers went to 100 and Worrell to 91 but rain washed out the final hour's play. Resuming on the Monday, Sobers went right through to the close on 216 and so did Worrell, 177. They'd have done the full two days except for that hour lost to the rain.

Jayasuriya and Mahanama truly did have a new record.

The anticipation was that the Lara 375 had now become a real possibility. Just another 50 would do it. The government decreed that next day the spectators be let in free, and 30,000 would come to be witness, many from Matara, a fishing town in the extreme south of the country, formerly famous for curd and treacle[5] and now perhaps about to become world famous for something else altogether.

The *Daily News* entertained no doubts because it carried this headline:

SANATH 326 N.O., SET FOR LARA'S MARK

Rodrigopulle, predicting that the whole of Sri Lanka would come to a halt as Jayasuriya resumed his innings, entertained no doubts either. He wrote that 'knowing Jayasuriya as I do, he is not one who will let this opportunity slip'.[6]

The eternal verity, present since the first ball in cricket's whole history had been bowled who knows when, had never changed. All prophecy is dangerous about a batsman's prospects in an innings because one ball is always enough and that can *always* be *any* ball.

Sri Lanka did come to a halt. The *Daily News* reported that soldiers in the northern war zone fighting against the Tamil Tigers[7] stopped and watched the cricket on television.[7] Office workers in Colombo did the same.

Anil Kumble, the Indian spinner who had toiled for so long for no reward, opened the bowling and Jayasuriya stroked him through to the boundary.

330.

Mahanama caught the theme and, to general astonishment, battered Kulkarni for three 4s in an over.

Jayasuriya faced Kumble and drove him to the cover boundary.

334.

He was past Gooch, a significant moment because Gooch's 333 stood as the highest Test score ever made against India. Kumble bowled and Jayasuriya cut it to the boundary.

338.

He was past Bradman and Hammond, and into the 30-run gap between them, Hutton and Sobers. He took a single, took another and then Mahanama went. He played back to Kumble, missed the ball and was lbw. He'd made 225 from 561 deliveries (27 4s) and they'd put on 576. Ah, but the eternal verity and the one ball.

'Golden memories and silver tears' as Sanath is dismissed

COMMENT

by Elmo Rodrigopulle

Thirty six runs eluded the technical perfection and authority of Sanath Jayasuriya yesterday when he was unlucky to pop a catch to silly point Ganguly off Chauhan to end an innings of monumental endurance of 340 played mostly in torrid heat and energy sapping conditions.

It was not only a personal tragedy for the brilliant allrounder from downtown Matara whose eyes were moist with tears at coming so close to Brian Lara's magical 375 assured in the record books for another lease of life.

EVERY RIGHT

Strangely, Sanath Jayasuriya has earned every right to be identified in Lara's class for what he has already achieved. He is known more than Lara for his habit of destroying a bowler like Vivian Richards was wont to do. The bowler who has faced his assault has often been taken away from the cricket scene.

In many ways Jayasuriya can be reckoned a more complete cricketer than Lara for he is an allrounder. His leg spin often baffles the best of batsmen. Well might Jayasuriya have said with the great poet when leaving his crease *"Weep not for for me – few are my sorrows"*.

Although the individual record is not against his name, there is still another world record in his name — — the fastest 50 in one–day cricket and that against a Pakistan side that included the mighty Waqar Younis, Mushtaq Ahmed and Saqlain Mushtaq.

Records apart, his departure was a singular moment of sorrow to the spectators who journeyed all the way in big numbers to see their hero.

While his innings grew in stature from the time it started on Sunday, it always dispensed charm and excitement to the spectator.

The match was memorable not merely for the high scores on both sides, but for the fact that it was a niche for so many other records.

TRIPLE CENTURY

Sanath Jayasuriya made a triple century. Mahanama made his best ever test score of 226. The world record second wicket stand and for that matter any wicket in Test cricket, the highest total in Tests and many many more records too numerous to mention.

While his innings grew in stature what joy and excitement he dispensed. In fact, he astonished and stunned everyone when he became the first Sri Lankan cricket to go over the dream 300–run mark. Then he brought life to a standstill when he passed the immortal Sir Donald Bradman's mark of 334, made against England at Leeds in 1930.

Sir Donald is no mere mortal. He was and is still the greatest batsman that the world of cricket has seen and will ever see. Going past the great Sir Don was an achievement itself, that will be writ in letters of gold in the game's history.

● ILLUSTRIOUS

Jayasuriya is now only behind Brian Lara, Sir Garfield Sobers and Sir Leonard Hutton the only illustrious willow wielders ahead of him.

Anyway performances like these are what 'golden memories and silver tears' are made of as sung by that great balladier Jim Reeves.

When play resumed in which one was expecting the miracle, Jayasuriya started off beautifully middling the ball well and sending the ball to the fence with magnificent timing.

Undoubtedly, Jayasuriya was in no trouble with expectations that he would not only equalise the elusive Lara record but also go past it. But that off spinner from Chauhan which turned, held back and popped off his bat, saw Ganguly gleefully accepting the catch and throwing it up to the heavens.

● BLACK SUPERMAN

It was moving to see all the Indian fielders rallying round Jayasuriya and patting him on his back, sad, but yet happy that they had got rid of this 'black superman' who not only bashed and blasted them in the limited over game, but also made them toil and sick of the game of Test cricket.

While giving credit to all his masters, principals, coaches and his mates who helped him achieve this batting record, it will not be fair if the name of that once great Sri Lankan off spinner who did much to bring Sri Lanka cricket to what it is today – Abu Fuard is not mentioned.

It was Fuard who fought against all odds to break the stranglehold that was held by the elite schools and clubs and gave cricketers from lesser known schools and provinces the break into the big league. And today, Fuard's foresight and thinking has paid rich and unforettable dividends,

● GREAT INNINGS

Roshan Mahanama too played a great innings. With his double century, he has cemented his place as the one drop batsman for a longtime to come. He too was very correct in his strokeplay and the world record partnership for any wicket in Test cricket with Jayasuriya will not be broken for a long, long time to come.

Well played Jayasuriya. Well played Mahanama!

Jayasuriya misses Lara's record

Sri Lankan opening batsman Sanath Jayasuriya reacting after being caught at silly point by Saurav Ganguly off the bowling of Rajesh Chauhan in the first Test against India. Jayasuriya was dismissed 35 runs short of Lara's record of 375. (Photo by Anuruddha Lokuhapuarachchi – Reuters)

Sri Lanka make highest Test total – 952 for six

By SA'ADI THAWFEEQ

After all the excitement generated in the past 24 hours of Sri Lanka's champion opener Sanath Jayasuriya attempting to break West Indian Brian Lara's world record score of 375, it all boiled down to nothing.

What the 30,000 odd spectators admitted in free were left to relish were two world records: for any wicket in Test cricket, and the highest–ever total ever made in a Test.

After five days of record–breaking performances at the R. Premadasa Stadium where the first Test between Sri Lanka and India ended in a draw, the eventual winner was not the game of cricket, but the pitch.

Had it not been fot the interest produced by Jayasuriya going for Lara's world record and for the world record partnership between Jayasuriya and Mahanama, which produced 576 runs for the second wicket, this Test could easily have been played to almost empty stadium.

Pitches of this nature are not going to encourage Sri Lanka to produce match winning bowlers if they are to become a force in the longer game by the year 2000.

Unless the R. Premadasa Stadium pitch is relaid and made more competitive to both bowlers and batsmen, Test matches should not be played there.

Coming to the game, the disappointment of Jayasuriya not breaking Lara's record – he fell short by 40 runs was somewhat compensated by Sri Lanka hitting up the highest–ever total in Test history when they amassed 952 for six wickets on the fifth and final day yesterday.

After the first two days were occupied by India in compiling a total of 537 for 8 declared, Sri Lanka's batsmen dominated the final three days on a pitch which proved to be a heart–break for bowlers.

Jayasuriya made a monumental knock of 340 in 799 minutes off 578 balls with two sixes and 36 fours in an immaculate display of concentration and endurance with Mahanama, whose innings of 225 occupied 753 minutes (28 fours). They put on a world record stand for any wicket of 576 which would take some beating.

Even after their dismissals two balls of each other, the hapless Indian bowlers had no respite as vice–captain Aravinda de Silva (126), skipper Arjuna Ranatunga (86) and Test debutant Mahela Jayawardena (66) flayed them around for Sri Lanka to go past England's 59–year–old world record total of 903 for seven declared against Australia at the Oval.

De Silva completed his 12th Test century batting 293 minutes and facing 211 balls. He had 16 fours. With Ranatunga, whose 87 came off 110 balls with 14 fours. De Silva added 175 runs for the fourth wicket in 150 minutes. During the course of his innings, Ranatunga became the first Sri Lankan batsman to top the 4,000 run mark in Test cricket playing in his 70th match.

De Silva forged another century (131) stand with Jayawardena for the fifth wicket which took Sri Lanka past the world record total. Jayawardena was out for 66 scored in 133 minutes with 10 fours.

Jayasuriya began the day on 325 and confidently moved to 340 with three fours and two singles before popping up a simple catch to silly point fielder Saurav Ganguly. The ball from off–spinner Rajesh Chauhan bounced a little more than he anticipated and therein ended Jaysuriya's chance of breaking the world record.

The anguish in Jayasuriya's face was quite evident as he hit the bat on the ground to convey his disappointment. All the Indian fielders ran to congratulate him as he departed with his head held down. They applauded him all the way to the pavilion from where he got a standing ovation.

Jayasuriya's marathon and chanceless innings of 340 was the fourth highest in test cricket, after Lara's 375, Garry Sobers' 365 (not out), and Len Hutton's 364.

Mahanama's departure in the previous over probably seemed to have an effect on Jayasuriya. Mahanama playing back to leg–spinner Anil Kumble was ruled out lbw.

ARAVINDA DE SILVA who also made a century back cutting a ball in his innings of 126. (Picture Nishantha Sumanadasa)

From SA'ADI THAWFEEQ at R. Premadasa Stadium

1997

INDIA – 1ST INNINGS 537 (for 8 decl.)

SRI LANKA – 1ST INNINGS (587 for one contd.)

S. T. JAYASURIYA c Ganguly b Chauhan	340
M. S. ATAPATTU c Mongia b Kulkarni	26
R. S. MAHANAMA lbw b Kumble	225
P. A. DE SILVA c Prasad b Ganguly	126
A. RANATUNGA run out	86
D. P. M. JAYAWARDENA c Kulkarni b Ganguly	66
R. S. KALUWITHARANA not out	14
U. C. J. VAAS not out	11
EXTRAS (B–27, LB–10, W–7, NB–14)	58
TOTAL (for 6 wkts at stumps, 271 overs, 1126 mins)	952

DID NOT BAT: K. R. Pushpakumara, M. Muralitharan, K. J. Silva.

FALL OF WICKETS: 1–39, 2–615, 3–615, 4–790, 5–921, 6–924.

BOWLING: Prasad 24–1–88–0 (W–4), Kuruvilla 14–2–74–0 (NB–4), Chauhan 78–8–276–1 (W–3, NB–5), Kumble 72–7–223–1 (NB–5), Kulkarni 70– 10–195–1, Ganguly 9–0–53–2, Tendulkar 2–1–2–0. Dravid 2–0–4–0.

RESULTS: Drawn.

MAN OF THE MATCH: S. T. Jayasuriya (Sri Lanka).

1938

Given below is the scoreboard of the England innings against Australia which stood for 59 years as the highest–ever total achieved in Test cricket, until Sri Lanka surpassed it.

England batting first scored 903 for seven declared and bowled out Australia for totals of 201 and 123 to win by an innings and 579 runs. The match was played at the Kennington, Oval, London.

ENGLAND – 1ST INNINGS

L. HUTTON c Hassett b O'Reilly	364
W. J. EDRICH lbw b O'Reilly	12
M. LEYLAND run out	187
W. R. HAMMOND lbw b Fleetwood Smith	59
E. PAYNTER lbw b O'Reilly	0
D. C. S. COMPTON b Waite	1
J. HARDSTAFF Jnr not out	169
A. WOOD c and b Barnes	53
H. VERITY not out	8
EXTRAS (B–22, LB–19, W–1, NB–8)	50
TOTAL (for 7 wkts decl. 333.2 overs)	903

DID NOT BAT: K. Farnes, W. E. Bowes.

FALL OF WICKETS: 1–29, 2–411, 3–546, 4–547, 5–555, 6–770, 7–876.

BOWLING: Waite 72–16–150–1, McCabe 38–8–85–0, O'Reilly 85–26–178–3, Fleetwood Smith 87–11–298–1, Barnes 38–3–84–1, Hassett 13–2–52–0, Bradman 2.2–1–6–0.

Congrats from 'SB'

Minister S. B. Dissanayake, has sent the following congratulatory message to Duleep Mendis, Manager, Sri Lanka cricket team.

"Let me congratulate the Sri Lankan cricket team on their fantastic achievements in the first Test against India. Records after records were broken by the Sri Lankan cricket team leaving cricket researchers to start rewriting cricket records. It indeed is a fantastic achievement.

Sanath Jayasuriya and Roshan Mahanama, with their elegant stroke playing stamina and courage showed the whole world that we are no longer one-day champions only. We are a force in Test cricket too. We have reached Himalayan heights in the international cricket arena.

We are all proud of this young band of cricketers led by Arjuna Ranatunga. The Sri Lankan team showed the cricket world that records can be broken with team spirit, concentration and courage along with love for the country."

Miracle to win

ATHENS, Wednesday (Reuter) – Double Olympic champion Marie Jose Perec admitted on Wednesday she would need a miracle to win a medal in the women's 200 metres at the world championships after working hard to win her first–round heat.

Perec, who won the 200 and 400 metres titles at last year's Atlanta Olympics, has been in indifferent form all season and had originally decided not to come to the Athens event because she said she had no chance.

Printed and Published by the Associated Newspapers of Ceylon Ltd., at No. 35, D.R. Wijewardene Mawatha, Colombo, on Thursday August 07, 1997.

They had come as close as it was possible to get to the highest first-class partnership of all, 577 by V.S. Hazare and Gul Mahomed for Baroda against Holkar at Baroda in 1946–7. That was in the final of the Ranji Trophy Tournament and they took 8 hours and 53 minutes to do it. Jayasuriya and Mahanama had taken 12 hours and 33 minutes, although comparing a Ranji Trophy match just after the war with a modern-day Test is unfair and unwise.

Next over and two balls later it was all over. Chauhan bowled a delivery, which bounced a little, spun and popped up off the bat to Sourav Ganguly at silly point. Ganguly clasped the ball in both hands – tightly.

Jayasuriya's 340 had come off 578 deliveries (the two 6s, 36 4s) and taken 13 hours and 19 minutes. In annoyance he hit the ground with his bat. There was anguish on his face and, as he moved away, his head was down. That did not stop the Indian fielders coming up to congratulate him – it was the fourth highest Test score after all and he was applauded all the way back. The crowd stood to him.

The *Times of India* reported that many of the Colombo office workers who'd stopped work to watch on television were crying.

Sri Lanka batted out the day to draw the match and, at 952, had gone clean past England's 903 at The Oval in 1938. The *Daily News* bemoaned the Colombo wicket and said it should be relaid to make cricket more competitive. Across the five days, 1,489 runs had been scored and only 14 wickets had fallen, an average of 106 for every wicket.

Bosser Martin, a rotund gentleman in suit, waistcoat, collar and tie and homburg hat, had stood, hands in pockets, on the morning of 20 August 1938 watching as Hammond spun the coin and Bradman called wrong. Martin had his back to the pitch he'd created, the 1,000 run pitch.

Maybe there were mixed feelings about the pitch at the R. Premadasa Stadium, Colombo, on 2 August 1997 when Tendulkar and Sri Lankan captain Arijuna Ranatunga came out to toss but, if Bosser Martin had been transported through time to it, he surely would have approved, and been disappointed Sri Lanka fell 48 short.

No matter. The *Times of India* quoted one of those who'd watched Jayasuriya's fifth day attempt on 375 on his office television. He was an accountant called Manoj De Soyza and he said: 'Even when we won the World Cup we weren't taken seriously by the rest of the cricket world. But now everyone can see that Sri Lankan Test cricket is for real'.

It was.

Sri Lanka v India
Played at Colombo, 2, 3, 4, 5, 6 August 1997

INDIA

N.R. Mongia	c Jayawardene b Pushpakumara	7
N.S. Sidhu	c Kaluwitharana b Vaas	111
R.S. Dravid	c & b Jayasurtya	69
S.R. Tendulkar	c Jayawardene b Muralitharan	143
M. Azharuddin	c & b Muralitharan	126
S.C. Ganguly	c Mahanama b Jayasuriya	0
A. Kumble	not out	27
R.K. Chauhan	c Vaas b Jayasuriya	23
A. Kuruvilla	c Atapattu b Pushpakumara	9
	b 10, n-b 12	22
	(8 dec)	537

Did not bat: N.M. Kulkarni, B.K.V. Prasad.

	O	M	R	W
Vaas	23	5	80	1
Pushpakumara	19.3	2	97	2
Jayawardene	2	0	6	0
Muralitharan	65	9	174	2
K.J. Silva	39	3	122	0
Jayasiriya	18	3	45	3
Atapattu	1	0	3	0

SRI LANKA

S.T. Jayasuriya	c Ganguly b Chauhan	340
M.S. Atapattu	c Mongia b Kulkarni	26
R.S. Mahanama	lbw b Ganguly	225
P.A. de Silva	c Prasad b Ganguly	126
A. Ranatunga	run out	86
D.P.M.D. Jayawardene	c Kulkarmo b Ganguly	66
R.S. Kaluwitharna	not out	14
W.P.U.J.C. Vaas	not out	11
	b 28, l-b 9, n-b 14, w 7	58
	(6 wkts)	952

Did not bat: K.R. Pushpakumara, M.Muralitharan, K.J. Silva.

	O	M	R	W
Prasad	24	1	88	0
Kuruvilla	14	2	74	0
Chauhan	78	8	276	1
Kumble	72	7	223	1
Kulkarni	70	12	195	1
Ganguly	9	0	53	2
Tendulkar	2	1	2	0
Dravid	2	0	4	0

MATCH DRAWN
Failed by 36 to beat the record

Notes

1   *The Fight For The Ashes 1932–3*, Hobbs.
2   For an overview of Sri Lankan cricket history, see the feature Years of Preparation, *Wisden*, 1997 Almanac, page 30.
3   www.gnubies.com/lanka/lanka4.htm
4   *Times of India*.
5   *Wisden* Five Cricketers of the Year, 1997 Almanac, page 45.
6   *Daily News*.
7   The Tamil Tigers (Liberation Tigers of Tamil Eelam) have been fighting the Sri Lankan army and attacking political targets for many years. Their core is 'deprived Tamil agricultural workers whose families lost their livelihood due to economic reforms in the late 1970s, as well as unemployed urban Tamil youth who faced economic and social discrimination.' (BBC)

Australia in Pakistan, Peshawar, October 1998

Mark Anthony Taylor, born Leeton, New South Wales, 27 October 1964.

Test career 1988–99: 104 Tests, 7,525 runs, 19 centuries, average 43.49.

334 no

17 OCTOBER 1998

SNAPSHOT

HANDS OFF
JIMMY

n Symes is not up for grabs,
Australia tells Ireland

AGE 2

MATCHPLAY
WOES

art Appleby falls to "buzzsaw"
s Westwood

PAGE 16

FRESH
CYCLE

Tyler-Sharman is changing
image, and pushing for
ges to Australian cycling

PAGE 19

ORTS INDEX

KET	21	RACING 17,18,20
TBALL	19	GOLF 16
NG	14	MOTOR SPORT 14
KETBALL	19	RESULTS 14

ONLINE

ow the Test as it happens
have your say via e-mail on
fascinating live cricket site at
w.theage.com.au

Bradman's mark met by Taylor

By MARK RAY
PESHAWAR, FRIDAY

With his teammates urging him on from the players' balcony as dusk fell here this evening, Australian captain Mark Taylor equalled Sir Donald Bradman's highest score of 334 by an Australian in Test cricket.

A weary but smiling Taylor left the field through a hastily organised guard of honor formed by his teammates and said later that he would discuss with the team later tonight whether Australia should declare at its overnight score of 4/599 or bat on for a while to make some quick runs before trying to bowl Pakistan out twice and win the match and the series. "If we bat on tomorrow, we'll be going for it from the word go," Taylor said.

Asked whether he wanted to bat on to pass Brian Lara's world record highest score of 375, Taylor dismissed that scenario out of hand.

"The record doesn't mean anything," he said. "Obviously a world record is a world record but it doesn't mean a lot. I'd prefer to win this game. That's what I'm here for, to win this game."

If his teammates think that a declaration first thing in the morning is the best tactical move, Taylor would remain in the record books alongside Bradman, a prospect which seemed to delight him.

"I'm more than happy to sit with The Don," he laughed. "I don't think I'm going to get his average though."

Typically the modest Taylor admitted, with no prompting, that he was dropped on 325, late in the day, by keeper Moin Khan off the left-arm spin of Aamir Sohail. Other than that Hemish and one wild swing in the middle session, Taylor

made no errors and played at a steady pace throughout, adding a healthy 222 to his personal tally for the day, most of them off the middle of the bat. As the light faded in the final over, Taylor, who has now batted through the first two days of this Test match, failed to score the single he needed off the last few balls of the day to pass Bradman's 68-year-old record. But Taylor had already climbed the mountain peaks of Test batting records here today.

At stumps on the second day of this second Test, Taylor is encamped safely on 334 and Australia in an impregnable position at 4/599, with Ricky Ponting not out on 76.

In a wonderful feat of physical and mental stamina, Taylor passed a number of records on the way. Those records included:
■ The highest score by an Australian against Pakistan, beating Graham Yallop's 268 made in Perth in 1983-4.
■ The only triple century made in Pakistan
■ The 15th triple-century in Test history, with Taylor the 14th batsman to make one
■ The equal highest score by an Australian, equalling Don Bradman's 334, made at Leeds in 1930
■ The highest score by an Australian captain, passing Bob Simpson's 311 made at Manchester in 1964.

Taylor passed Bradman's career aggregate of 6996 and when he passed 321 he also went past Greg Chappell's 7110 to be in third place behind Allan Border on 11,174 and David Boon's 7422.

Apart from one wobbly period in the middle of the day when he swung wildly at a few deliveries with his head flopping back, Taylor played at

Continued page 21

On Guard: Mark Taylor's teammates honor their captain, whose undefeated 334 equalled Sir Donald Bradman's record.

SCOREBOARD

AUSTRALIA first innings

	R	M	B	4s
MARK TAYLOR not out	334	720	564	32
MICHAEL SLATER c Mahmood b Shoaib	2	50	27	–
JUSTIN LANGER c Moin b Azhar	116	362	212	10
MARK WAUGH c Moin b Sohail	42	123	107	3
STEVE WAUGH c Moin b Shoaib	1	15	3	–
RICKY PONTING not out	76	166	147	6
Sundries (9lb 3w 16nb)	28			
Four wickets for	599			

Fall: 16 (Slater) 295, (Langer), 418 (M Waugh) 431 (S Waugh)
Bowling: Shoaib Akhtar 31-6-107-2 (1nb) Mohammad Zahid 16-0-740 (1w 9nb) Mushtaq Ahmed 46-3-153-0 Azhar Mahmood 23-2-82-1 (2w 2nb) Aamir Sohail 42-8-111-1 (2nb) Salim Malik 16-0-63-0 (2nb), (2nb).

Ton lifts weight off captain

Ton lifts weightOnly those who toss a coin to decide innings can appreciate the draining effect of captaining a professional cricket team. It is a unique experience in sport.

Soccer and football captains also shoulder responsibility but once the whistle blows, they're swallowed up in the action. Moreover their games last 90 minutes or so and afterwards the spotlight is upon their coach.

A cricket captain is an isolated figure working within a team at the closest quarters and yet also duty bound to provide direction and morale. From sunrise to nightfall the captain carries this weight.

It is exhausting. A captain cannot relax. During the hours of play he has a thousand tiny decisions to make.

Throughout he must set the tone. Once his head drops, the day has been lost. He must not stop pressing or else the game will drift and his team will disintegrate. At stumps, he must give interviews, as colleagues let their hair down.

Meanwhile, the captain must score runs or take wickets. He is two people, a cricketer and a leader. He

cannot allow his own poor form to affect his approach, cannot grow defensive merely because his own game is in disarray.

Australia has been fortunate during the past 13 years to possess two men of extraordinary stamina. Allan Border hardly missed a match and he did not rest upon the field, continually scrapping in his cussed way.

Now it is Mark Taylor's turn to remind all and sundry of his remarkable powers. It's part of his attraction that he manages to be both intelligent and straightforward. Moreover, he is thoughtful without being intense, so that failures bring a shrug and some constructive thought rather than internal panic. He has a

strong will and great faith in h
Qualities he has needed.

Others might have been u
by the unproductive season
werg so well documented,
have convinced themselves
deterioration was permanent,
was never beaten in his own
and that was critical. Nor c
make excuses. Rather, he su
thought things over and emb
upon the long haul back. Cle
has returned to basics. It's not
idea in hard times. He has re
the pull stroke, a trademark
early years. Repeatedly he s
ball to the boundary at Pesh
the bowlers dropped a fractio

Continued p

Last-minute horseplay

By TONY BOURKE

In a sensational last-ditch bid to get Our Unicorn into today's Caulfield Cup, its trainer, Colin Alderson, last night was believed to be trying to negotiate with the New Zealand owners of veteran Count Chivas to buy the horse and scratch him.

Alderson was at Melbourne airport yesterday evening to meet Richard Wood, the managing owner of Count Chivas, when he arrived from NZ to see his horse run in the Caulfield Cup.

The only way Our Unicorn, who is first emergency, can get into the cup is if there is a scratching at 8 am today, and until Alderson's desperate move last night, there was no suggestion of any other horse coming out. Count Chivas, a seven-year-old gelding, has run in the past three Caulfield Cups, finishing second to Doriemus in 1995, and he also finished second to Saintly in the 1996 Melbourne Cup. Although Count Chivas last days seem to be behind him, his connections decided to press for his fourth Caulfield Cup after he finished fourth to It's All In Fun in the Coongy Handicap at Sandown last Sunday.

Earlier yesterday, Alderson said he felt "extremely frustrated" about not having Our Unicorn in the cup after the debacle during

the week surrounding Taufan's Melody.

The VATC committee had acted to exempt Taufan's Melody from any ballot on the cup, although he had not met all the qualifying clauses, but chose not to use its discretionary powers to include Our Unicorn, who has been one of the best-backed horses in the race.

Our Unicorn missed out on making the field, which is limited to 18 starters plus two emergencies, because he was 19th on the list of qualifiers, and Taufan's Melody was included above him.

The chief steward, Des Gleeson, last night said there was no problem as far as the stewards were concerned with any pending sale of Count Chivas, and the horse could be scratched up until 8 am today.

Count Chivas was a 50/1 chance for the Caulfield Cup in the latest markets, and if Our Unicorn gets a start he will be third favorite, at 7/1, according to the doubles bookmaker Micahel Eskander.

There was heavy support yesterday for Our Unicorn, with Tabcorp's national Sportsbet, and he firmed from $16 to $12 for a $1 investment.

Alderson said Our Unicorn had never been in better shape, and if he ran in the cup "whatever beats him will win."

"We had his blood done this week, and it

came back 10 out of 10," Alderson said.

As the winner of $1,908,587 from hi
starts, it is hard to know what sort of valu
owners now place on Count Chivas, par
larly with the $1.5 million prizemoney on
today. Apart from the $828,000, inclu
trophies, for first prize, there is $240,00
second, $120,000 for third, $65,000 for fo
and $50,000 for fifth; and a $40,000 stan
rebate for horses finishing down to tenth

Count Chivas, now trained at Ballara
Simon Morrish, has not won a race since
1996 Sydney Cup, and his most recent pla
was a second to Marble Halls in the
Craiglee Stakes at Flemington.

Alderson is in a double bind with
Unicorn because the four-year-old need
finish in the first five in the Caulfield Cu
qualify for the Melbourne Cup at Flemin
on 3 November.

He considers his other qualifying opt
the Geelong Cup next Wednesday, or Th
day night's Grosby Gold Cup at Moc
Valley, not really viable.

"If Our Unicorn can't run (today) I m
pull the pin and hope he can get an invita
to run in Hong Kong in December,
said.

Of all the triple centurions Mark Taylor is perhaps the hardest to fit into a neat summary. His Test career had several dimensions that interacted, sometimes against each other. He was able to accommodate this, flourish and then retire at exactly the right time having won universal respect as a good man and true. Those are the dimensions, but the core of the man himself is contained within the asterisk after 334 on page 141.

To an Australian, Bradman's 334 represented a totemic feat both in where it was scored – the mother country, then a quite different concept to now, if it remains a concept at all – and how it was scored. Since then (or more accurately since Bradman's 304 at Leeds in 1934) only two other Australians had reached the triple century, Simpson and Cowper, as we have seen. That Australia had played so much cricket between 1930 and 1998 and, of all their batsmen, only these two had climbed to within sight of the 334, lent it an almost mystical, timeless quality.

If Mark Taylor had cared to become the first Australian to beat it that was absolutely within his power on 17 October 1998, the third day of the Second Test at Peshawar. He was captain of the side and had the 334 not out overnight. Every cricketer would have understood if he'd given himself an hour more to move past Bradman and set off toward's Lara's 375 – only, of course, 41 runs away. Instead he weighed up the state of the match and decided that the total, 599, was enough. He was much more interested in bowling Pakistan out twice and winning the match than even a quick-run single to have the record from Bradman.

It was an attitude that explains how he was able to achieve what he did achieve as captain.

Scyld Berry, writing in the *Daily Telegraph*, paid him a lovely tribute in 1999 when Taylor had announced his retirement. Berry began by suggesting that Taylor's successor, Steve Waugh, was fortunate to be his country's most 'effective' batsman because if he wasn't he'd find Taylor 'an impossible act to follow'. During the five years he was captain, Berry said – in a very striking phrase – Taylor demonstrated to the whole world of cricket 'how Test matches should be played.'

He was a Mike Brearley who was also able to score centuries (of this, more in a moment) and he 'heightened the level of cricket debate by educating press conferences and the wider public beyond'. That's another very striking phrase. Berry concluded by pointing out that Australia had been at a low ebb only 12 years ago, rugged Allan Border broke the losing habit and then Taylor taught Australia how to win Test matches again, and did it with a basic lesson: the best way to do it is by attack.

There had been a problem, potentially very awkward indeed, the year before the Pakistan tour. Taylor had become the most successful Australian captain by winning seven consecutive Test series but by then his form had deserted him. Scyld Berry's comparison with Brearley is not a careless one. Brearley was an England captain of rarest perception who could, and did, get the side to win matches by his intellect but as an opening bat he was not a high-level Test player (39 matches, 1,442 runs, average 22.89). The problem was the same as for an off-form Taylor: was he worth his place even without the runs? In 1997–8 Taylor lost his place in the Australian one-day side but remained captain of the Test side.

He made 3 in the First Test at Rawalpindi, a match that Australia won by an innings and 99. Here, in a sense, was the dilemma restated. Pakistan made 269 and in reply Australia amassed 513 (Slater 108, Steve Waugh 157, Lehmann 98, Healey 82) so that Taylor's runs were not needed. Ten days later they were in Peshawar.

The *Melbourne Age* reported that 'during the lead-up to this critical second Test, Taylor, for the first time on this hectic tour, had begun to show a little strain. He had been annoyed that the match-fixing[1] hearings at the Lahore High Court had dimmed the afterglow of his team's fine win at Rawalpindi.'

Now, at Peshawar, he won the toss and batted. Although Pakistan had lost the great Wasim Akram through a throat infection and influenza, Taylor and Slater would face a hostile and sustained pace attack from the two young bowlers Shoaib Akhtar and Mohammad Zahid. Taylor, always candid, expressed relief that Wasim wasn't playing because Pakistan were not the same team when he wasn't.

Akhtar's first few overs were very, very lively, while Taylor almost played on to Shoaib in the third over of play – the ball went to the boundary. Slater lasted doggedly for 49 minutes and was then caught in the gully off Shoaib Akhtar for 2 when the score was 16. Subsequently Taylor estimated that the bowling was faster than anything he'd ever faced before and, at the beginning, the tactic was simply survival.

Langer came out and might have gone straight away but survived a confident appeal for lbw from Shoaib from his first ball. He responded by taking the bowling on while Taylor searched for his form. Twice, before he'd reached 30, Taylor was dropped and both times by Saeed Anwar off leg-spinner Mushtaq Ahmed. At 18, Taylor sent a catch to extra-cover and at 27, cutting, he spooned a easy catch to point.

Langer cut and hooked so effectively that he went to his 50 off only 68 balls and now, into the second hour, the Pakistani pace attack had slowed. Any early moisture that the wicket might have had was gone now, the ball was softer and the Pakistani bowlers lacked length. That gave Taylor a rare chance to play his hook, and he did five times against Akhtar. Taylor wasn't searching for his form any more, he was visibly finding it. Then a curious thing happened.

As Peter Roebuck wrote in *The Age*: 'Langer was also fluent against the leg-spinner, sweeping at every opportunity, an approach calculated to keep the score moving and to disturb Mustaq's equanimity. Not every sweep found the middle of the bat but the bowler became frustrated and fell on to the defensive. Pretty soon, Taylor, Langer's redoubtable partner, was following suit as Pakistan's inexperienced and threadbare attack was gradually tamed.'

Taylor moved to his 50 by pulling Zahid hard to the boundary and now, with the pace bowlers pitching short of a length, he began to outscore Langer. When he'd reached 93 he unleashed a mighty hook for 6 off the first ball of a new spell by Akhtar and from 97 took three singles for his century. The light was deteriorating and play ended at 4.19pm, 21 overs early, with Taylor on 112, Langer 97 and Australia 234: three deliveries from Mohammad Zahid forced Taylor to take extreme evasive action. Afterwards Taylor said that he had not been offered the light and even if he had he'd have stayed on, at least until Langer got to his century.

Both batsmen had repeatedly refused offers of the light before this. The wicket was still playing beautifully, the Pakistani bowling wasn't going to frighten anybody and there were clearly a lot more runs to come. That evening there were two imponderables, how many runs and how fast?

Taylor resumed in a confident mood, playing his shots on both sides of the wicket. He was 'more confident' and 'ruthlessly' hooked, pulled, cut and drove 'the erratic and purposeless Pakistani bowling'.[2]

Roebuck wrote: 'Clearly he has returned to basics. It is not a bad idea in hard times. He has restored the pull stroke, a trademark in his early years. Repeatedly he sent the ball to the boundary at Peshawar as the bowlers dropped a fraction short. These were not glamorous strokes, but they were efficient and conclusive. Tellingly he's also recaptured his ability to leave the ball alone. Of course the circumstances were not demanding. The Pakistanis were resigned to their fate. Some tripe was sent down. Still, Taylor did not make a discernable mistake as he moved quickly towards his second hundred. Throughout he was imperturbable.'[3]

That second hundred came when he straight drove Mushtaq Ahmed to the boundary. It had come off 360 balls (22 4s, one 6).

Langer was out when he'd made 116 (in 6 hours and 2 minutes, 10 4s) and Australia were then 295. That made the partnership worth 279, the highest for any Australian wicket against Pakistan, beating the 259 by Wayne Phillips and Graham Yallop at Perth in 1983–4.

There followed a mini-collapse with the Waugh brothers both out by 431 but that only let Ricky Ponting in. Only in the middle of the day did Taylor's confidence seem to waver: head back, he lashed at several deliveries. Between lunch and tea, the Pakistanis draw their fielders back but Taylor and Ponting maintained their scoring rate by playing hit and run. Anything short, anything that could be hit on the rise, and Taylor sent them away with his pull. He went past 268 made by Yallop in that stand with Phillips, which was the highest score by an Australian against Pakistan. Taylor was now master of all he surveyed, playing freely and imperiously. The only real chances he'd given were run outs, with Salim Malik the worst offender. He missed the stumps with Taylor far from safety.

When Taylor reached 300 he had the first triple century in Pakistan and had overtaken Bradman's career aggregate (6,996). The next basecamp was Simpson's 311, the highest score by an Australian captain, then Greg Chappell's career aggregate of 7,110 to make Taylor the third heaviest Australian Test scorer (Allan Border 11,174, David Boon 7,422). Taylor got there when he moved past 321. But at 325 he was dropped at the wicket off left-arm spinner Aamir Sohail.

Towards the very end of the day he was within touching distance of Bradman's 334 and the Australian players came out onto the balcony to acclaim him if he beat it. The light was getting worse and worse as he faced the final over. He might even have made it off the final ball, when he played Aamir Sohail towards square leg, but Ijaz stopped it – and stopped the single.

After this last ball, as Taylor made his way off, the Australian players formed up outside the pavilion making a guard of honour for Taylor to pass through. Taylor was smiling as he went. Taylor went into the pavilion and at the top of the stairs the Pakistani coach, Javed Miandad, was waiting to congratulate him and offer him a soft drink. Taylor had batted for exactly 12 hours, faced 564 balls, hit a 6 and 32 4s.

Inevitably the imponderables had to be pondered again. Surely he'd give himself enough time to move on past Bradman and even have a go at the Lara 375?

Wisden (Almanac 2000, page 1145) reported that 'there were a number of team meetings that evening, and several players urged Taylor to bat on and beat Lara. But it was typical of his approach to the game that he should be aware of the record without being obsessed with it.'

Taylor said he would talk the situation over with the other players about attempting the record and balance that against giving his bowlers the maximum time to bowl Pakistan out twice. 'The record doesn't mean anything,' he'd say. 'Obviously a world record is a world record but it doesn't mean a lot. I'd prefer to win this game. That's what I'm here for, to win this game. I want to win this series in the sub continent.' He'd add that Australia hadn't done that 'for years'.

He smiled. 'I'm more than happy to sit with The Don. I don't think I'll get his average, though.'

He declared and one immediate reaction was that he did not want to usurp Bradman's record but it was much more pragmatic: he wanted to give his bowlers as long as possible to bowl Pakistan out twice, itself a major task on this wicket.

His decision to declare was greeted by some with incredulity.

One internet user wrote: 'The commentators spoke of how Taylor had apparently passed a fitful, sleepless night. Why he failed to get much sleep was not explained in so many words — one can only assume that he was pondering the options. Trying to decide whether to go for personal glory, or make a bid, even against the odds, for a win for his side.

'That he choose the latter option is so typical of the man — he puts the team first, himself last. The quintessential team man, Taylor has done his thing quietly, in the shadows, letting his team mates hog the limelight, and corner all the glory — while he, thanks largely to his own self-effacing ways, has had to prove himself over, and over, again.'

David Gower was moved to say: 'It was an interesting decision to declare when he was on 334 not out. He won a lot of friends by doing that. The current set of Australians appear to have a keen sense of history. That was a selfless thing to do. Full credit to him.'

The Sunday Age had the good sense to contact Taylor's wife Judi and she recounted how, on the evening of the 334, he'd rung her and said he was 'tired but very happy'. She assured him that whatever he decided she would support. She did not tell him that the phone had been constantly ringing with people telling her to tell him to go for the record.

The Sunday Age also discovered that the Taylors had a family joke, and it went like this: rather than face constant banter during Taylor's difficult days when he was still captain but couldn't find runs, when their son William was being taken to school he'd be dropped off round the corner. Now, Judi had told Mark, 'we should be able to go through to the gates for nearly the whole term...'

All this was not the end of the story, however. Pakistan batted and helped themselves to the abundant harvest, reaching 580. Australia batted again and this time Taylor made 92 before the match was left drawn. That left Taylor with an aggregate of 426, second only to Gooch at Lord's.

The Third Test at Karachi was drawn (Taylor 16 and 68, incidentally) so that Australia won the series; and not everybody goes to Pakistan and does that.

There are a couple of postscripts. Reportedly, when the party got back to Australia Taylor visited Bradman in Adelaide and was thanked by him for not breaking the record (he'd also done this in a letter). This must have been Bradman at his diplomatic best because, as we shall see, he accepted that one day the record would inevitably go and he certainly wasn't clinging on to it as something untouchable. That in no way prevented him from thanking Taylor.

On 25 January 1999, Australian Prime Minister John Howard made a speech at the Governor's Dinner in the Sheraton Hotel, Brisbane, in honour of the Australian of the Year. In the context of this book, part of it deserves to be quoted extensively.

'Ladies and gentlemen, it gives me a very special degree of pleasure to say something of Mark Taylor, the Australian of the Year for 1999. As some of you may have discovered over the years, I have something of an interest in cricket. Like so many other Australians, I have great and abiding sporting passions. There's nothing that can simultaneously bind Australians together quite like sport and at the same time on certain occasions it can also push us apart, of course, in an entirely friendly fashion. We have many sporting loves as Australians. It remains one of the great wonderments of visitors to this country that a nation of 18 million people can have such diverse footballing tastes as we have. But there is of course one game that can truly be described as Australia's national sport and that is cricket.

'Mark Taylor to me, and I know to millions of Australians, epitomises the very best of what sport is all about. He's talented, he's a tremendous fighter, he's a tremendous achiever. There has been no prouder wearer of the baggy green, the Australian cricket cap, than Mark Taylor. Like any truly great sportsman, like any person who truly over a long period of time achieves what he or she sets out to achieve in life, he's had his moments of despair and his moments of receiving fierce criticism and his moments of wondering what was going to happen next. And I know that Mark went through, as all Australians know, a difficult time in his career until that marvellous innings that he played in the second innings of the first test of the Ashes series in 1997 [129 at Edgbaston], which really turned in the faces of all of his critics – their criticism – and left, I am very happy to say, hundreds of thousands of red faces around Australia and elsewhere in the world amongst his critics.

'But when he was going through a period of adversity, he wasn't blaming somebody else. He wasn't blaming the umpires, he wasn't blaming the journalists, he wasn't blaming his team mates, he wasn't blaming the selectors, he was accepting that he was going through a difficult period. He was facing up to it with square-jawed determination and displaying the grit that we like to believe has a special Australian character about it. And that to me stamped him as a man of very great decency and very great character. And to my immense joy and I know the immense joy of millions of

Australians, he worked his way out of that difficult period, he demonstrated what a champion he was because he was able to conquer adversity. He went on to play that marvellous innings last year on the Indian sub-continent. And I think it was not only the sheer personal achievement of that great innings but the sensitivity and the generosity that he displayed towards a great tradition of a great game that he chose to share that 334 with the greatest cricketer that Australia has ever produced, Sir Donald Bradman.

'And I remember the morning after that innings very well. I was down in Canberra on the Saturday morning putting together a new Cabinet after the election. Putting together Cabinets is not always the easiest things that comes the way of a Prime Minister, and I was very happy to take a few minutes off and to ring Mark and get him out of his breakfast at his hotel in Pakistan to say, convey my congratulations and I know the congratulations of the entire nation. And I asked him what he was going to do and he said, 'mate I think I'll pull up the stumps'. And he went on to do that and he, in a very special way, gave himself an immortal page in Australian cricket history.'

Notes

[1] In brief, cricket was convulsed in the late 1990s when stories, centred round South Africa in India, emerged that bookmakers had been involved and matches fixed. The tentacles of this seemed to reach widely.

[2] *cricinfo*

[3] *The Age.*

Pakistan v Australia
Played at Peshawar, 15, 16, 17, 18, 19 October 1998

AUSTRALIA

M.A. Taylor	not out	334	b Aamir Sohail		92
M.J. Slater	c Azhar Mahmood b Shoab Akhtar	2	lbw b Mushtaq Ahmed		21
J.L. Langer	c Moin Khan b Azhar Mahmood	116	c Yousuf Youhana b Mushtaq Ahmed		14
M.E. Waugh	c Salim Malik b Aamir Sohal	42	b Shoaib Akhtar		43
S.R. Waugh	c Moin Khan b Shoaib Akhtar	1	not out		49
R.T. Ponting	not out	76	lbw b Ijaz Ahmed		43
I.A. Healy	not out	14			
	l-b 9, w 3, n-b 16	28	l-b 4, n-b 9		13
	(4 dec)	599	(5 wkts)		289

Did not bat: D.W. Fleming, C.R. Miller, S.C.G. MacGill, G.D. McGrath.

	O	M	R	W		O	M	R	W
S. Akhtar	31	6	107	2		16	2	68	1
M. Zahid	16	0	74	0		10	2	42	0
M. Ahmed	46	3	153	0		20	1	59	2
A. Mahmood	23	2	82	1		3	0	18	0
A. Sohail	42	8	111	1		10	1	35	1
S. Malik	16	0	63	0		15	1	30	0
I Ahmed						14	1	33	1

PAKISTAN

Saeed Anwar	c Healy b Miller	126
Aamir Sohail	c Fleming b McGrath	31
Ijaz Ahmed	c Healy b MacGill	155
Inzamam-ul-Haq	c Healy b S R Waugh	97
Salim Malik	c Taylor b McGrath	49
Yousuf Youhana	c S R Waugh b MacGill	28
Moin Khan	c Healy b Ponting	0
Azhar Mahmood	c Langer b McGrath	26
Mushtaq Ahmed	not out	48
Mohammad Zahid	lbw b Fleming	1
	b 5, l-b 9, w 1, n-b 4	19
	(9 dec)	580

Did not bat: Shoaib Akhtar.

	O	M	R	W
McGrath	36	8	131	3
Fleming	35.1	6	103	1
MacGill	42	5	169	2
Miller	38	12	99	1
M.E. Waugh	8	0	32	0
S.R. Waugh	8	1	19	1
Ponting	5	1	13	1

MATCH DRAWN
Failed by 42 runs to beat the record.

Pakistan v New Zealand,
Lahore, May 2002

Inzamam-ul-Haq, born Multan, Punjab 3 March 1970.

*Test career (as at 3 May 2005), 1992–: 100 Tests,
7,453 runs, 21 centuries, average 50.02.*

The nicknames woven with alliteration, such as the Sultan from Multan and Gentle Giant, were hard to resist and, as is the way of nicknames, somehow seemed entirely appropriate. Multan is neither a large nor particularly lively town although it can be hellishly hot. As a boy Inzamam-ul-Haq was, as someone has remarked, chubby. When he reached adulthood and 6ft 2in, as someone else has remarked, he was burly. Oh, and gentle, of course, with a bat in his hand if he chose to be. He could hit the ball a long way or stroke the ball a long way, and was good enough to decide himself which delivery got which treatment.

He was spotted by the famous all-rounder Imran Khan as a 17-year-old and was in the Pakistan team by the early 1990s. He'd become the backbone of the team and so good that Imran said he played pace bowling better than any other batsman in the world.

In 2002 New Zealand made a brief tour of Pakistan with, inevitably, three one-day internationals (Pakistan won them all) and two Tests, the first at Lahore. It was early May, and Lahore would show it could be hot too, hellishly hot. The centrepiece of the Gadaffi Stadium – the pitch – was lifeless or, as the *New Zealand Herald* said, road-like. Captain Stephen Fleming called wrong and theoretically that was very ominous indeed: he said the toss would be particularly important; but opener Shahid Afridi edged the third ball from Daryl Tuffey and was caught behind, Pakistan 1 for 1.

The other opener, Imran Nazir, had been in prime form but proved vulnerable to Daniel Vettori, who might have had him twice in quick succession. Nazir, with Younis Khan, was forcing the pace of scoring but in Vettori's third over Khan played forward and the ball flipped up off the pad to Fleming at first slip. The appeal for a catch was upheld by umpire Rudi Koertzen. Pakistan were 57 for 2.

That brought 32-year-old Inzamam to the wicket and, as the heat rose – it touched 38 Celsius at midday as the earlier breeze stilled – so did the scoring rate. Inzamam began with a single off Vettori from the first ball he received, down on one knee and sweeping. Soon after he announced his intentions by straight-driving a Vettori full toss to the boundary. Inzamam did, however, survive a moment of alarm when he'd 32 and Chris Martin, a fast bowler recalled to the side, was confident he had him lbw. He hadn't.

By lunch Pakistan were 125 for 2 (Nazir 63, Inzamam 29 from 49 deliveries, five 4s). Pakistan had taken a mere 29 overs to reach it. Leg-spinner Brooke Walker had bowled three overs for 20 but would suffer later on.

The New Zealand bowling was tighter in the afternoon. Inzamam drove Tuffey to the boundary – uppish but safe, as they say – in the 45th over to get to his 50 off 111 deliveries (seven 4s).

New Zealand did restrict Pakistan to 84 off 31 overs in this afternoon session. At one point Martin bowled five maidens out of six overs and had another confident lbw appeal turned down when Inzamam was 73. None of that could prevent Pakistan cruising to 209 for 2 at tea and by then Nazir had reached his century off 171 deliveries. He'd moved into the 90s by straight-driving all-rounder Chris Harris for 6 and reached his century by hitting Harris into the stand, Nazir's third 6.

After tea Nazir went. Walker had been hammered for 19 off one over. Inzamam hit him over the long-leg boundary, swept him to the boundary, pulled him to the boundary and was into the 90s, Pakistan were past 250 and Walker was being taken off. Part-time seamer Craig McMillan replaced him and induced Nazir into error. Mark Richardson, at mid-on, ran, dived and caught the ball in one hand. The partnership had produced 204 in less than four hours.

Inzamam went to his century the over after when he pulled Vettori to the mid-wicket boundary. He'd got there in a minute under 4 hours facing 191 deliveries (a 6, 14 4s). It was his 16th and, in terms of centuries in Pakistan history, took him past Salim Malik. Only Javed Miandad, with 23, lay ahead.

Inzamam had already survived some rash strokes but was batting freely, his cutting and driving prominent. He cut loose and went to 150 from 49 deliveries – 36 in boundaries. He plundered Martin for two boundaries in an over and took three from Tuffey, although he could have gone at 110 off Vettori. The ball went towards Lou Vincent, fielding at backward point, but Vincent couldn't hold it. This was the only real chance he'd given.

With Yousuf Youhana, Inzamam increased the tempo again. The new ball was taken at 289 but the pair scored 66 from the final 10 overs of the day to put Pakistan on 355 for four, although Youhana was out in the last over, caught by Fleming at second slip off Martin. He and Inzamam had put on 94 together. Inzamam was 159.

He began slowly on the second and, in fact, across the first half an hour made only 4 from the 29 scored. The New Zealand bowling was altogether tighter, but Inzamam had time. He moved to the 10 runs he needed to become the second-highest run scorer in Pakistan Test history (passing Salim Malik, 5,768) but a long way behind, inevitably, Miandad who had 8,832 from 124 innings. In the morning session, Pakistan lost Abdul Razzaq, lbw to Tuffey, and Rashid Latif, beautifully caught-and-bowled by Harris, while 99 were added in 30 overs. Saqlain Mushtaq came in and was lucky to survive lbw appeals from Vettori and Walker.

Inzamam reached his double century shortly before lunch. Vettori was bowling, Inzamam turned him to mid-wicket and scampered a couple to get there and swept the next ball for another couple to make his highest Test score. He had cramp and for three overs had a runner. Saqlain Mustaq was 13 and they'd put on 55 already. The only real relief for the New Zealand bowlers was that cloud masked the sun.

After lunch, and on 211, Inzamam had cramp again but Fleming said no to a runner now. Inzamam explained that Fleming 'allowed the runner in the first session because only 12 minutes were left before lunch and he'd hoped that I would get the required treatment during the interval. I didn't improve and Fleming refused the runner when play began after lunch, but Fleming was within the laws of the game and I have no complaints. It's in the laws that one can't have a runner without the consent of the rival captain. Laws are made to be followed and that's exactly what Fleming did.'

As he went past 235, he beat the record Lahore Test score set by Zaheer Abbas 24 years before. He reached 250 with a single from McMillan to long-off (372 deliveries, 34 4s, three 6s) and that over McMillan bowled Saqlain middle stump. Saqlain had taken a wild swing at the ball and missed. Pakistan were 510 for seven. Waqar Younis

Thursday, May 2, 2002   Internet: www.nzherald.co.nz/sports

■ RUGBY

Player revolt at Pugh's match

International players, including All Blacks, are threatening to boycott the IRB's plan for a Northern v Southern Hemisphere clash.

by Wynne Gray

Irate international players are determined to red card the proposed Northern v Southern Hemisphere match at Twickenham as the International Rugby Board deals with their concerns.

The International Rugby Players' Association has questioned the motives, purpose and rationale behind the November 28 game.

It said its members had been screaming for some time about the dangers of a cluttered rugby season.

Players in New Zealand, Australia, South Africa, England and France are united in condemning the match and would refuse an invitation to be involved unless the IRB has a rethink.

Vernon Pugh

Pacific Lions side was to play several matches in New Zealand next month to help to raise funds for island rugby.

But IRB chairman Vernon Pugh decreed that his pet hemisphere match project was a better method of

Under the New Zealand collective agreement, the New Zealand Rugby Union cannot force players to participate in the hemisphere match and has apparently conceded that to the IRPA.

Originally, a raising that money and the Pacific Lions tour was cancelled.

The hemisphere match has been timed to follow the All Blacks tour to England, Wales and France.

Australia and South Africa will also tour Europe at that stage.

New Zealand association manager Rob Nichol made his players' objections clear several months ago when he labelled the game as "inflammatory."

"Within a suitable global season, this kind of game, with its focus on benefiting smaller rugby-playing and developing nations, may have some merit, but given the current demands on players it is nothing short of destructive.

"We have no doubts that if we are not successful in getting the situation

sorted out, international rugby will become plagued by frustrated, disillusioned and tired players who are continuously having their long-term careers jeopardised because of the excessive demands being placed on them."

Until the IRB dealt with the safety issues, the IRPA would not support the hemisphere contest.

It gave the IRB a detailed document last November highlighting worries about burnout and the high injury rates of fulltime professional players.

The Australian-based chairman of the IRPA, Tony Dempsey, said there had not been a satisfactory response from the IRB, which was in danger of abusing its duty to "promote, foster, develop, extend and

govern" rugby worldwide.

"This failure, coupled with the IRB's recent proposal to add yet another international fixture to an already cluttered playing schedule, might be interpreted by some players as having a blatant regard for the issues concerning player burnout and injury rates."

He said the IRB had to address all the problems and provide some plans for its members.

"It's not enough to simply refer these matters to medical advisory committees. History has shown this to be ineffectual.

"If the world's best players are constantly suffering burnout and injuries, then the game will suffer as a spectacle and thus be thwarted in its attempts to grow and prosper.

"The key decision-makers within world rugby need to get together and urgently sort out this matter so as to protect the game's most valuable resource, namely the players."

Dempsey said the IRB had suggested the North v South match was necessary to raise funds for the development of second-tier rugby nations.

"However, this begs the questions — what is being done with the A$130 million ($156.2 million) net profit the rugby World Cup made in 1999 and of the £50 million ($162.85 million) held by the IRB in reserve accounts?

"What is to be done with the millions to be made from next year's World Cup?"

■ Mains deals to slump   — Sport, B7

■ CRICKET

Pakistan head for big total in opening test

LAHORE — New Zealand's bowlers reined in the Pakistan batsmen after lunch, but the home side were still heading for a big total on the opening day of the first test in Lahore.

Thanks to young opener Imran Nazir, who clocked up his second test century in just his sixth match, Pakistan went through a wicketless second session to be 209 for two at tea after winning the toss.

Big Inzamam-ul-Haq was on 73 as he soldiered on towards his 16th century as the pair added an unbroken 152 for the third wicket on a flat, lifeless pitch.

The New Zealand bowlers, though, toiled much more effectively in the mid-afternoon heat than in the pre-lunch session when the home side raced to 125 for two off 29 overs.

Recalled paceman Chris Martin and allrounder Chris Harris did most of the work as Daniel Vettori looked below his best and legspinner Brooke Walker was not required after conceding 20 runs off three overs before lunch.

Pakistan added 84 off 31 overs in the middle session, with the only excitement for the tourists two confident leg-before shouts by Martin against Inzamam when he was on 32, both turned down by umpire Rudi Koertzen.

Martin managed to swing the ball on to the right-hander and bowled five maidens in his six-over spell after the break, conceding just one run.

After conceding 24 off his first five overs, Martin had none for 25 off 13 and was unlucky not to have a wicket.

Vettori took over, but there was a hint all was not well because he did not bowl with the zip and variation he showed before lunch.

SCOREBOARD

PAKISTAN
First innings

I. Nazir not out		100
S. Afridi c Hart b Tuffey		0
Y. Khan c Fleming b Vettori		27
Inzamam-ul-Haq not out		73
Extras (3b, 6nb)		9

Total (for 2 wkts, 60 overs) 209
Fall: 1/1, 2/57.
Bowling: D. Tuffey 13-2-49-1 (6nb), C. Martin 13-9-25-0, D. Vettori 17-2-61-1, B. Walker 3-1-20-0, C. Harris 13-1-50-0, C. McMillan 1-0-1-0.

He ended the session with one for 61 off 17.

Harris did the job of the absent Nathan Astle by plugging one end, but there was little likelihood of a breakthrough and he took some punishment late in the session.

IMRAN NAZIR: Second century.

Nazir was kept under wraps for the first hour after lunch, but then moved into the 90s with a straight six off Harris.

He repeated the dose in the last over before tea to bring up three figures off 171 balls, including 11 fours and three sixes.

Inzamam survived after several rash shots, but was also immovable, notching his 32nd half-century in his 81st test.

Earlier, captain Stephen Fleming said the toss would be hugely important and his head dropped immediately when he saw the coin flip up the wrong way.

But the tourists were celebrating

on just the third ball of the match when Daryl Tuffey got one to jag and lift to Shahid Afridi who gave debutant Robbie Hart a comfortable catch.

Then Vettori, after nearly removing Nazir twice with arm balls, had quick success in his third over when Younis Khan pushed forward on 27 and the ball ballooned off his pad to Fleming at first slip.

Umpire Koertzen obliged, despite there being doubt as to whether he had edged the ball.

New Zealand left out Ian Butler, Andre Adams, who had a back prob-

lem, Scott Styris and Mathew Sinclair.

Pakistan had the luxury of omitting 104-test veteran Wasim Akram, paceman Mohammad Sami, allrounder Shoaib Malik and batsman Misbah-ul-Haq.

Meanwhile, West Indies umpire Steve Bucknor paid tribute to England legend Dickie Bird after equaling his world umpiring record.

"It means a lot to me to go on par with Bird because I respect his umpiring. It's a matter of great achievement for me," said 55-year-old Bucknor, who hails from

Jamaica.

Bucknor, among the top eight international cricket umpires, was speaking just before the start of play as he reached Bird's record of officiating in 66 tests.

"I have been told he was ill so I wish him the best of health," said Bucknor, whose first test was between India and the West Indies in his home-town in 1987.

Bird, a Yorkshireman, took 23 years to take his tally to 66 and is now suffering eyesight problems.

"With the introduction of the ICC panel I will have more opportunities

and will learn even more in this period," Bucknor said.

The ICC announced an elite squad of eight umpires last month and test matches are now officiated by two neutral umpires from the panel.

A former high and triple-jumper, Bucknor has stood a record 25 matches in three World Cups and was also a football referee, having controlled a World Cup qualifying match in 1987.

Bucknor said the key to umpiring was remaining relaxed.

— NZPA

IN FORM: Inzamam-ul-Haq survived several rash shots on his way to 73.

---

came in but when he'd made 10, and Inzamam had advanced to 261, he hit a firm catch back to McMillan: Pakistan 534 for 8.

Shoaib Akhtar joined Inzamam and they put together the country's highest ninth wicket stand against New Zealand, 78.

The cramp made Inzamam amble his runs although, cannily, he circumvented the need to do it too often by hitting boundaries. One Vettori over illustrates this. To the first ball he advanced, checked his shot. To the second he advanced and hit the ball over long-on for 6. To the third he advanced and hit the ball over long-off for 6. (This took him to 282, beating Miandad's highest score in Pakistan, 280 against India). To the fourth he steered the ball towards mid-wicket and had enough time to amble a single.

At tea he'd made 287 off 409 deliveries (six 6s, 34 4s), Shoaib Akhtar 26. In the first over after it he pulled Harris to the boundary and took a couple of singles; the over after, he drove McMillan to the boundary and took a single to reach 298. He prodded Harris towards mid-on and that was 299. Shoaib took a single off the next delivery, and Inzamam prodded the one after that to backward point.

300.

The triple century had been made from 423 balls and Inzamam had created his own conjunction of circumstances. He'd say it himself: 'Once I reached 300, my target was to break Lara and Hanif Mohammad's record.' Hanif's 337 was important to Inzamam because it represented Pakistan's only triple century in Tests before and, by definition, the highest Test innings ever played by a Pakistani. More than that, it represented something almost unapproachable by several generations – Hanif made the runs 12 years before Inzamam was born. He was disarmingly honest when he said that even if he got beyond Hanif, that would not alter his view that Hanif 'remained the great batsman for me.'

The importance of Lara's 375 hardly needs stating.

So Inzamam set off, initially towards the 337.

Shoaib was stumped off Walker for 37 (Inzamam 302) and Pakistan were 612 for 9, which transferred pressure on to Inzamam: he had only the last batsman, Danish Kaneira, to rely on. Kaneira safely played out the two remaining deliveries of the over and then Inzamam pulled Harris to the boundary and hit him to the leg side boundary and took a single, leaving Kaneira to survive the final ball – which he drove straight for 4...

Inzamam 311.

The leg-spinner Walker was to bowl. Inzamam went on to one knee and smote the first ball of Walker's over for 6 to mid-wicket.

317.

He got a top edge to the next delivery but it landed safely. He smote the next for 6 over long-off.

323.

At this rate he was going to be past Hanif, and up, up, up and past Lara any minute now. The fourth ball was short and he pulled it for 6.

329.

He went for it again. He had to be tired. He had the cramp, that knotting of the muscle – in this case, the leg muscles – which can be absolute agony and leave you feeling that your leg has been clawed by hot irons. He'd say this did affect him. He had been at the crease for 20 minutes short of 10 hours and faced 435 deliveries, with 38 4s and, by now, nine 6s. He fully intended to make that 10 sixes off the fifth ball of Walker's over, this Walker who had conceded 97 runs in 14 overs.

Later, he'd see the folly of this, confess to impatience and 'threw my hard work down the drain. I should have trusted in the batting abilities of Kaneira.'

Inzamam smote the ball into the air but, just this once, his timing failed him. It went to Tuffey, fielding at deep mid-on, and he accepted the catch nicely – and gratefully – enough. He was only nine short of Hanif – another lusty blow and a 4 would have taken care of that – but the 47 to Lara was, in all the circumstances, a distant peak.

He said he wanted to dedicate the innings 'to my father,' who'd recovered from open heart surgery four months before. 'I can't give him more happiness than the way I batted today. He always took pride in me and now I am happy to dedicate this century to him. He has been my mentor and the driving force behind my success. I am glad that I have been able to repay him something. Obviously it's my best Test innings because scoring 329 runs is not an easy job.'

Inzamam now had 5,929 Test runs and the 329 had taken Pakistan to 643, beating their previous record against New Zealand of 616 for 5 declared at Auckland in 1988–9.

He returned to the context of Hanif. 'Even if I had gone on to break Hanif's record, I would never have been as good as he was. He is still an icon and probably the best batsman we have produced, but naturally it is a great feeling to achieve what only Hanif has achieved for this country.'

He understood the conjunction of circumstances. 'I had scored 15 centuries prior to this, but this is something special because you don't always get an opportunity to hit a triple.' He found an irony in that because, he felt, if he hadn't had the cramp, or he had had a runner, he might have beaten Lara's 375.

What he had done is score 206 of his runs in boundaries, which was second only to John Edrich (238 in his 310*), Hammond next on 196 of the 336*. Hanif, who hit 24 4s – 100 in boundaries – was eclipsed, at least in this one context. Interestingly, perhaps, Lara had made only (!) 180 in boundaries during his 375, which put him seventh on the list that May day in 2002.

The rest was strange to behold and sad to contemplate. Inzamam out and, the Pakistan innings over, New Zealand were brutalised by Shoaib Akhtar, who took 6 for 11. New Zealand sank to 58 for 6 at the close and went on to lose by an innings and 324 runs. It was the fifth-biggest victory in Test history, or the fifth-biggest defeat, depending on which side you were on.

And the Second Test, due to be played at Karachi, was never played. A car bomb killed 14 people outside the New Zealanders' hotel on the morning of the match and understandably they went home.

Pakistan v New Zealand
Played at Lahore, 1, 2, 3 May 2002

PAKISTAN

Imran Nazir	c Richardson b McMillan	127
Shahid Afridi	c Hart b Tuffey	0
Younis Khan	c Fleming b Vettori	27
Inzamam-ul-Haq	c Tuffey b Walker	329
Yousuf Youhana	c Fleming b Martin	29
Abdul Razzaq	lbw b Tuffey	25
Rashid Latif	c and b Harris	7
Saqlain Mushtaq	b McMillan	30
Waqar Younis	c and b McMillan	10
Shoaib Akhtar	st Hart b Walker	37
Danish Kaneria	not out	4
	b 1, l-b 8, w 1, n-b 8	18
		643

	O	M	R	W
Tuffey	25	7	94	2
Martin	31	12	108	1
Vettori	40	4	178	1
Walker	14.5	3	97	2
Harris	29	3	109	1
McMillan	18	1	48	3

NEW ZEALAND

M.H. Richardson	b Shoaib Akhtar	8	c Rashid Latif b Saqlain Mushtaq	32
M.J. Horne	b Shoaib Akhtar	4	c Rashid Latif b Waqar Younis	0
L. Vincent	c Rashid Latif b D Kaneria	21	c Rashid Latif b Danish Kaneria	57
S.P. Fleming	b Shoaib Akhtar	2	c sub b Danish Kaneria	66
C.Z. Harris	b Shoaib Akhtar	2	lbw b Abdul Razzaq	43
C.D. McMillan	c Shahid Afridi b Saqlain Mushtaq	15	lbw b Danish Kaneria	2
R.G. Hart	lbw b Waqar Younis	4	b Danish Kaneria	0
D.L. Vettori	c Waqar Younis b Saqlain Mushtaq	7	c sub b Abdul Razzaq	5
B.G.K. Walker	lbw b Shoaib Akhtar	0	not out	15
D.R. Tuffey	not out	6	c Younis Khan b Danish Kaneria	12
C.S. Martin	b Shoaib Akhtar	0	c sub b Saqlain Mushtaq	0
	l-b 1, n-b 3	4	b 4, l-b 6, n-b 4	14
		73		246

	O	M	R	W		O	M	R	W
W. Younis	10	6	21	1		9	1	38	1
S. Akhtar	8.2	4	11	6					
D. Kaneria	6	1	19	1		32	3	110	5
S. Mushtaq	6	1	21	2		17.3	3	38	2
A. Razzaq						14	2	47	2
A. Afridi						4	1	3	0

PAKISTAN WON BY AN INNINGS AND 324
Failed by 47 runs to beat the record.

Australia v Zimbabwe, Perth, October 2003

Matthew Lawrence Hayden, born Kingaroy, Queensland, 29 October 1971.

Test career (as at 3 May 2005), 1994–: 67 Tests, 5,721 runs, 20 centuries, average 53.46.

The arch of time: Hutton's 364 was, as we've seen, the last triple century until Hanif and Sobers; Lara's 375 might have lasted generations if it had been put together in the days when there weren't many tours and there weren't many Test matches. By the late 1990s and early 2000s cricket gave the appearance of happening everywhere all the time in a profusion of guises. Even following who was doing what and where in the most cursory way became a task of daily diligence and feat of memory. Some critics were even talking about an indigestible surfeit.

Once upon a time, to get to the tours and Tests which weren't being played in England you flicked through *Wisden* until, near the back, you reached *Overseas Cricket*. If you do that with the 1939 edition (covering winter 1937–8) you find not *Overseas Cricket* but *Cricket in the Empire* and there an account of Lord Tennyson's team in India, complete with the five Unofficial Test Matches. That, as it seems, was the only tour going on anywhere that winter.

If you look at the 1959 edition (covering winter 1957–8) you find Australia in South Africa, Pakistan in the West Indies and an MCC tour in East Africa.

If you look at the 2004 edition (covering winters 2002–3/2003–4) – these things depend on the Almanac's deadline – you find the World Cup in South Africa, England in Australia, England in Bangladesh and Sri Lanka, Bangladesh in South Africa, Australia in Pakistan, the West Indies in India and Bangladesh, Sri Lanka in South Africa, Pakistan in South Africa and Zimbabwe, Kenya in Zimbabwe, India in New Zealand, Sri Lanka in Australia, Australia in the West Indies, New Zealand in Sri Lanka, South Africa in Bangladesh, Sri Lanka in the West Indies, Bangladesh in Australia, Bangladesh in Pakistan, South Africa in Pakistan, New Zealand in India and eventually Zimbabwe in Australia (with New Zealand in Pakistan after that).

This is no place to examine the full implications of this enormous expansion, or what effect it had on the quality of the cricket being played, particularly by the newer Test playing countries, but it does seem reasonable to argue that, on the law of averages alone (if you can use such an expression in a cricket book), the chances of anything happening had to be increased, and that included triple centuries. Between Hutton and Hanif lay 20 years; between Jayasuriya and Hayden lay seven years and in that time four men did it. Two men did it again the following year.

This is not quite such an amazing compression when it is viewed against the enormous expansion, and there remained legitimate questions over the real strength of such teams as Zimbabwe, Kenya and Bangladesh. Short tours, courtesy of the jet age, might disguise that in exactly the same way as a full five-day five-Test tour of a major side would surely expose it. Setting nationalistic considerations aside – everybody likes to see their own country win – watching the strong pulverise the weak is very quickly uninteresting and then embarassing.

And one of those days among so many days as the jets delivered teams here, there and everywhere, gathered them and delivered them somewhere else, some batsman from a major Test playing country was going to get hold of one of the smaller sides and all records would be vulnerable, this particular smaller side being Zimbabwe. They were on a two-Test flying visit to Australia, shorn by retirements (Andy Flower, Henry Olonga, Guy Whittall) and injuries (Grant Flower, Douglas Hondo).

Sport

OUT OF THE BLUES STEPHEN SILVAGNI TO QUIT CARLTON BOARD SPORT 3

Hayden makes history

Chloe Saltau
Perth

Matthew Hayden has etched a new magic number, 380, into cricket history.

The bulking batsman from Kingaroy, once considered a legend in his own state but whose uncertain beginnings resulted in him taking six years to play eight Tests for his country, yesterday elevated himself into immortal company: first by passing the record score by an Australian, the 334 shared by Donald Bradman and Mark Taylor, and then by wiping Brian Lara's world record of 375.

Lara last night rang Hayden from the Caribbean to offer his congratulations, and Taylor hastened to the Australian dressing rooms to do the same.

Three balls before tea on the second day of the first Test against Zimbabwe, Hayden prodded a single to long-off and ambled into history. He held both arms aloft and was embraced by his batting partner, Adam Gilchrist, whose rapid and unbeaten 113 will be unfairly dwarfed by the sheer size of Hayden's achievement.

"I'm delighted and I can't quite believe it, to be honest I'm just thrilled that I was wearing the baggy green cap when the record was broken," said Hayden, who admitted he had been troubled by a bad back leading into the Test.

"I guess that's why you play cricket. We love the game and we cherish certain moments along the way. It (Lara's record) was eagerly awaited after 334, and I'm really privileged to be given the chance because of the way we play our game."

A curious peace, at odds with his brutal batting style, came over Hayden as he hit 38 boundaries and 11 sixes. Not long after his innings ended, the 31-year-old Queenslander spoke of the challenges ahead that include recapturing the form in India that finally secured his Test position on the subcontinent in 2001.

"I think I had a very nice temperament going in," Hayden said. "I spent so many years sitting on the beach wondering how I was ever going to get back into the Australian cricket team so I won't be wondering for a second. I'll be trying my guts out every time I go out and play."

Zimbabwe coach Geoff Marsh said his players were in remarkably good spirits last night. They were 1-79 at stumps after Steve Waugh declared at 6-735 upon Hayden's eventual dismissal and Don Ebrahim was bowled by Jason Gillespie for 29.

"I think Stephen had in his mind that he wanted to see the world record broken. I must admit I did feel a little greedy

though coming out after tea," said Hayden, who now deserves his place among the game's greats. Certainly, he has elevated a potentially ordinary match into something far more meaningful and provided a hostile welcome for a young African side.

Australian chairman of selectors Trevor Hohns said Hayden was "probably the best batsman in the world at the moment".

The score of 334 was made famous by Bradman at Headingley in 1930, and memorably matched by Taylor at Peshawar 68 years later, when the former Australian captain declared so as not to surpass the Don's record.

Hayden's 380 was defined by the ease and power with which he hit the quick bowlers back over their heads, and completed his remarkable rebirth. "I hung in there, I wanted to improve my game and I really wanted to prove to Queensland cricket as well that I was going to be a good Australian player."

His innings ended when Trevor Gripper had him caught after more than 10 hours at the crease, sweeping to Stuart Carlisle three balls after tea.

As if to signify his expansive mood, Hayden shed his conservative baggie through the first day and wore his easy-going cap. Although Zimbabwe's bowlers were valiant, they grew more ragged as the innings wore on and Gripper dropped Hayden in the outer for 99.

Earlier, Waugh led an impressive young team. Sean Ervine, who produced an inside edge from the Australian captain and threw himself forward to take a desperate catch. Ervine was one of the few Zimbabwean bowlers to keep his dignity, finishing with 4-146 from 31 overs.

After Ervine snaffled Darren Lehmann for 40, Gilchrist raced to 100 in 84 balls, at one stage unleashing an enormous six that landed on the roof of the pavilion. But this Test belongs unquestionably to Hayden.

Said Taylor: "I think Matthew Hayden's life probably changed a couple of years ago when he came back into the side and (since) he's been the player that we all saw in Sheffield Shield cricket. This will be the icing on the cake for him."

I MISS THE SLEDGING

En
all
for
re

Chloe Sal
Perth

Wearing his baggy green cap, Matthew Hayden drives powerfully on his way to a world-record 380.

SCOREBOARD

AUSTRALIA: 1st innings

		R	M	B	4s	6s
J Langer	b Ervine	26	42	36	5	
M Hayden	c Gripper b Gripper	380	622	438	38	11
R Ponting	lbw b b Ervine	37	91	65	6	
D Martyn	c Wishart b Gripper	53	96	75	9	
S Waugh	c and b Ervine	78	182	124	10	1
D Lehmann	c and b Ervine	30	61	48	3	1
A Gilchrist	not out	113	138	95	12	4
Sundries (4b, 10lb, 1w, 3nb)		18				
TOTAL (for six wickets declared)		**735**				

FALL: 43 (Langer), 192 (Ponting), 329 (Martyn), 516 (Waugh), 502 (Lehmann), 735 (Hayden). BOWLING: H Streak 26 6-1 121-0, A Ireland 26-3-115-0, Sean Ervine 31-4-146-4, R Price 36-5-187-0, T Gripper 25-3-0-132-2. BAT TIME: 622 minutes OVERS: 184.1

ZIMBABWE: 1st innings

		R	M	B	4s	6s

A DAY FOR THE RECORD BOOKS

HIGHEST INDIVIDUAL TEST SCORES

380	Matthew Hayden	Aust v Zim, Perth, '03-04	
375	Brian Lara	W Indies v Eng, St John's, '93-94	
365*	Gary Sobers	W Indies v Pak, Kingston, '57-58	
364	Len Hutton	England v Aust, The Oval, '38	
340	S. Jayasuriya	S Lanka v Ind, Colombo, '97-98	
337	H. Mohammad	Pak v W Indies, B'getown, '57-58	

FASTEST TONS BY AUSTRALIANS (BALLS FACED)

67	Jack Gregory	Aust v S Africa, Johannesburg, '21-22
84	Adam Gilchrist	Aust v Ind, Mumbai, '00-01
84	**Adam Gilchrist**	**Aust v Zim, Perth, '03-04**
88	Ray Lindwall	Aust v Eng, Melbourne, '46-47
91	Adam Gilchrist	Aust v S Africa, Cape Town, '01-02

FASTEST BY ANY PLAYER 56 Viv Richards (WI v Eng, St John's, '85-86)

We are at Perth, October 2003, and that batsman to whom everything would be vulnerable is Matthew Hayden.

It had been a hard road to here and all the sources proclaim it. He was selected for only eight Tests in six years: one against South Africa in 1993, three each against West Indies and South Africa in 1996 and one against New Zealand in 1999.

Kingaroy is evidently the 'land of wide skies, beef cattle and peanuts'.[1] From an early age Hayden found deep fulfilment in hitting a cricket ball hard and it would become a constant in his life. He was also born with a self-belief approaching the absolute and he was going to need that. As a teenager he wasn't selected for the gilded path to the Test side and didn't even get to the Australian Academy. His early Tests, when he was struggling to establish himself in the Australian side, were basically against the pace of South Africa and West Indies. Not easy for Hayden or a generation or two of other batsmen round the world before him. Paradoxically, this strengthened his self-belief. He felt he was 'gathering momentum'.[2] Others doubted his technique (which puzzled him because, as he'd say, he scored plenty of runs) but none doubted that the left-handed opener was a bludgeoner of bowling on his day.

He was finally recalled to the side in New Zealand in 2000, albeit only for the Third Test at Hamilton, where he made 2 and 37. In India it all came good. In the First Test he and Adam Gilchrist put on 197 in 32 overs of brutality, he made 97 and 67 in the next Test, 203 and 35 in the one after that. This wasn't mountain climbing, this was a volcano. He toured England in 2001: 35 in the First Test, 0 and 6 not out in the Second, 33 and 42 in the Third, 15 and 35 in the Fourth, 68 in the Fifth.

And so we come back to Perth, October 2003. Hayden had an injured back, was wearing a heavy vest and consequently ignored his favourite sweep shot. Instead he'd drive, mightily, mercilessly, majestically. He even felt that this injury might actually have helped him: 'I have found with injuries that your concentration tends to step up a notch, and I think I was able to use this to my advantage.'

He would not, however, set the seismographs trembling just yet. A five-day Test spreads an awful lot of time in front of a batsman going in first on day one.

The Zimbabwe captain, Heath Streak, won the toss, put Australia in and to use the word mistake hardly does the decision justice. These things are never done without reason, however, and the morning was blustery which might have helped his inexperienced bowlers and would certainly have helped the experienced Australian bowlers. As it turned out there were no devils in the wicket.

Streak himself opened the bowling with Arnoldus (Andy) Blignaut with less than 8,000 spectators in. Streak's first three overs cost 21 and, in the words of Peter Roebuck, 'to his dismay delivered one of the worst opening spells as the ball showed a marked reluctance to change course'.[3] Hayden survived a confident lbw appeal from Blignaut and proceeded cautiously.

Sean Ervine, right arm and medium-pace, was the first change and forced Justin Langer to play on after 42 minutes – he'd hit five 4s off 38 balls – to make Australia 43 for one.

Roebuck wrote: 'Alone among the Zimbabwean bowlers, Ervine held three batsmen in check. He did so by bowling in a style that has become unusual in the age of attacking cricket and fast food. Line and length were his bywords, a combination so old-fashioned that last winter England had to scan its list of veterans before finding anyone familiar with it. Ervine bowled full and straight, and to a field placed with this strategy in mind.'

Outright, defensive containment might or might not have been prudent tactics but what else could Streak – or Ervine, or Blignaut – do? If the situation got out of hand against this Australian batting side, the consequences would have been humiliation followed inexorably by destruction and ultimately annihilation.

Ricky Ponting spent 91 minutes making a steady 37 (six 4s) before he moved across a straight ball from Ervine and was lbw, Australia on 102. Damian Martyn was lively: his 53 came in 96 minutes (nine 4s) and when right-arm off-break bowler Trevor Gripper had him caught at first slip by Craig Wishart – who didn't take the ball cleanly and had to clasp it to his chest – Australia were 199. Steve Waugh was in and Hayden was moving towards 76 at tea.

He got to his century after more than 5 hours (and 208 balls). 'I really felt I was playing within myself for a long time,' he would say, 'but when I got the hundred I thought well, I'll start expanding and looking to play the way I've been telling myself for most of the day not to.'

The seismographs began to tremble.

Hayden struck Ray Price, left-arm spin, over mid-off for 6 and did the same to Gripper. He went from the century to 150 in 32 balls (35 minutes) and even, fleetingly, contemplated the possibility of a double hundred before the close. He wasn't slogging, he was using the drive, classical, orthodox, hard. He got as far as 183, with three 6s and 22 4s at the close, Waugh 61, Australia 372 for 3. As scenarios go, for the gallant young cricketers of Zimbabwe it could not have been more ominous. Next in was Darren Lehmann, then Andy Gilchrist for whom, when he wielded his bat, cricket grounds were too small and adjacent properties too vulnerable.

Hayden, Roebuck wrote in a lovely phrase, 'is a tall left-hander who looks like he could stand as a candidate for the governership of California'.

Before play on the second day Gilchrist asked Waugh what the tactics were. Here was a sub-plot, because Waugh had scored Test centuries everywhere but Perth. What Waugh told Gilchrist was that he thought Hayden could break Lara's record.[4] The conjunction was right: benign wicket, a bowling attack Hayden had at his mercy, plenty of support at the other end and time.

Hayden, however, wasn't thinking like that. He wanted, first, to get safely to the double century and then perhaps as far as a triple, 127 runs away. Lara was a great deal further on up, of course, but who knew? Hayden would say how important Waugh had been to him in the lean years when he'd been sitting, unselected, watching other Australians make the runs. Waugh, Hayden said, 'once told me when things were not going so well, "hang in there, because you are never out of my thoughts. I know you can do it".' It was exactly what Hayden had done and now here he was.

He'd taken the vest off which gave him more mobility. He moved to the double century after 8 minutes short of 7 hours, Streak could find nothing in the wicket and Blignaut couldn't find his line and length. In the morning session, however, Waugh went caught and bowled by Ervine for 78 – Ervine found the edge of Waugh's bat – and Lehmann, after scoring 30 in just over an hour, was caught and bowled by Ervine as well. That let Gilchrist in.

Hayden had reached 271 by lunch, punishing the attack moment by moment. He'd even take his helmet off and wear the famous green Australian cap instead, and it seemed to say to the bowlers 'I have nothing whatsoever to fear from you'.

Gilchrist was 13 at lunch and himself brimming – poised to erupt – with runs just as Hayden still was. The afternoon might bring anything and only one thing seemed certain: whatever it was, it wouldn't be long in coming.

As they walked out, Gilchrist asked Hayden how he felt and Hayden said he was totally relaxed throughout his whole body.[5] Gilchrist would feel that he had never seen any other batsman exercising such control and feeling at such ease.

The volcano was bubbling – he was striking the pace bowlers back over their heads.

He pounded his way towards the triple century and, at 299, drove Streak for a single. It had taken 6 hours 48 minutes with, between 200 and 300, five 6s – and, as Streak later reflected ruefully, some of them had been mis-hit. Hayden's power was as enormous as that.

Gilchrist pondered the extent of Hayden's control and ease, and wondered if it wasn't, in fact, the product of fatigue. He took it upon himself to approach Hayden a time or two to remind him that this chance might never come again: *be strong, keep focused*. Hayden, however, demonstrated that he wasn't tired by thumping the ball to the boundary.[6] *Wisden* noticed this paradoxical mood too: 'A curious calm had come over him.' The *Perth Advertiser* caught it as well: 'A curious peace, at odds with his brutal batting style, came over Hayden…'

He moved on Bradman's 334 which, of course, Mark Taylor had too. Taylor was watching from the Channel Nine commentary box. Bradman's son John was listening on the radio in Adelaide where the family had lived for a generation.

Hayden went past them by hitting a single, and handled this with sincerity and diplomacy. Bradman's place in Australian life, and his cricket career which still challenges credulity, meant that although others might equal and surpass some of his individual achievements that did not make them comparable. Hayden understood this. 'This sits uncomfortable for me, and so it should, but I guess I was never haunted by Bradman's record because I am sure that he would have an enormous amount of respect for anyone who had come close to any of his records.' Now the diplomacy. 'The fact is we wear the same Baggy Green. I am certain the 12 guys who are wearing the Baggy Green are as proud as The Don wearing it in his day.'

A run later Hayden's concentration faltered for the first time. He hit Ervine but Gripper at deep mid-wicket dropped it. Hayden responded by hitting a straight 6.

Gilchrist, meanwhile, was well into a hundred at faster than even time – it would occupy him a mere 1 hour and 24 minutes and include a 6 on to the pavilion roof – but, more than that, he fully intended to be at the other end when and if Hayden got past Lara.

Gilchrist was also helping with a little psychology, offering his congratulations as each landmark came and went then stepping back to leave Hayden alone at centre stage. He'd say to Hayden 'savour these moments to the full, it goes away too fast'.[7]

Hayden showed no trace of nerves as he moved away from the 334 and on through 350. As someone remarked, Hayden's energy levels are high and that was proved now by the way he and Gilchrist kept on running between the wickets like eager teenagers.

The triple centurions were all behind him now except Hutton, Sobers and Lara. Hayden hit another straight 6 to go to 364 and a single took him to Sobers. He didn't tarry there. Off the fifth ball of a Gripper over, he drove the ball and took a single.

366.

Next over, being bowled by Price, Gilchrist was on strike and stroked the ball away for a single. Hayden took a single, Gilchrist took a single and then Hayden swept the ball to the boundary.

371.

Off the fifth ball of the next over, Hayden drove Gripper to long-on and they ran a brisk couple.

373.

Now Price to Gilchrist, a single into the deep. Hayden played a back-foot defensive shot to the next ball then worked the ball square of the wicket.

375.

Hayden didn't score off the next then drove the ball to long-off for a single. As someone said, Hayden ambled into history.

376.

He took his cap off and kissed it. He raised his bat. His smile was so broad it could have been seen in Queensland. His bat had been broader than that. Gilchrist came up and bear-hugged him, this Gilchrist who wanted Hayden to 'accept and understand the scale of his achievement, let it into his heart and soul'.[8]

Wisden wrote that 'there was also something reverent about his reaction – especially when he touched the black band wound round his bicep in remembrance of the 88 Australians killed in the Bali attacks a year earlier'.[9]

Taylor sought out the context of the achievement. It should not be judged, he said, by the fact that it was done against a weak and now shattered Zimbabwe side. To get as far as Hayden had done 'takes special concentration. It takes fitness – we always knew Matthew Hayden had that. Even though the attack wasn't great, you still have to bat for a long time, face a lot of balls and not make mistakes'.

Hayden now felt that Waugh wanted to see the record broken and Gilchrist found the dressing room 'a buzz.' Hayden himself 'felt a bit greedy coming out after tea'. He drove the second ball after it – from Gripper – over long-on to the boundary and the place where nobody had ever been before now extended to 380. It did not extend further. Hayden swept the third ball to Stuart Carlisle at deep backward square leg.

In the starkest terms, he had laboured over the first hundred then gone from it to 200 in 1 hour 44 minutes, from 200 to 300 in 1 hour 57 minutes and made the final 80 in 1 hour 33 minutes. Stark, yes: he'd been scoring virtually a run a minute for the equivalent of a day, and, in the latter part, Gilchrist had simultaneously made 113 in 2 hours 18 minutes.

Hayden had batted for 10 hours 22 minutes, faced 437 balls and hit 11 6s and 38

4s. As he came off, the team came on to greet him and that was, all else aside, the final gesture of his acceptance, if any was needed by now. He'd put aspects of that into words. 'We play a unique game in a lot of ways. We enjoy scoring runs quickly, and then love putting sides under pressure. This is a great moment not just for me, but for the way our team plays. I am really pleased it has happened to us because we live our moments together.' Yes, he was an insider not an outsider now.

Hayden wasn't sure if he'd ever really grasp his achievement. 'What can I say? I am delighted – I cannot quite believe it. I hope some of those people involved in the Bali tragedy can take something from that. It is very hard to describe my feelings. I was really privileged to be given a chance because of the way we play our game. This is the sort of opportunity that may never come along again.'

Waugh declared immediately and Zimbabwe fought it out gamely enough, making 239 and 321. It gave Australia the match by an innings and 175 runs.

Australia's oldest living Test player, 91-year-old Bill Brown, said he felt sure Bradman would have appreciated Hayden's innings. An arch of time was at work here. Brown had not toured England in 1930, but in 1934 he'd opened at Headingley in the innings where Bradman got 304. John Bradman felt his father would have been delighted Hayden had beaten the 334, 'and then to go and get the world record... what a magnificent effort. I have never met Matt, but from what I have been told he is a very good person and he showed what a terrific cricketer he is with that innings. I'm sure that my dad would have been proud if he were here to witness it'.

John explained that his father was 'anything but petty when it came to his records. He was not precious about that kind of thing at all. My father knew when he set them that they were milestones that would be reached and he was happy for that to happen. It would be nice to meet Matthew. I would just shake his hand and have a chat to him about what he had done and what the moment was like'.

Lara telephoned from the West Indies offering his congratulations. He got through to the dressing room a couple of hours after Hayden's innings had ended. 'His sentiments were pretty simple,' Hayden exlained. 'He said great things happen to good cricketers, and that he really enjoyed the way we play our game, so he was pleased to see the record go to the Australian side.'

Brian Lara had not, however, spoken his final word on climbing Mount Everest.

Notes

[1]   *Wisden,* Almanac 2003, page 68.
[2]   *Wisden,* Almanac 2003, page 69
[3]   *The Age,* Melbourne.
[4]   *Sydney Morning Herald* website.
       http://www.smh.com.au/cgibin/common/popupPrintArticle.pl?path.../1065917348483/htm
[5]   Ibid.
[6]   Ibid.
[7]   Ibid.
[8]   Ibid.
[9]   *Wisden,* Almanac 2004, page 1258. A terrorist bomb in a nightclub on the Indonesian island of Bali in 2002 killed more than 200 people, including 88 Australians.

Australia v Zimbabwe
Played at Perth, 9, 10, 11, 12, 13 October 2003

AUSTRALIA

J.L. Langer	b Ervine	26
M.L. Hayden	c Carlisle b Gripper	380
R.T. Ponting	lbw b Ervine	37
D.R. Martyn	c Wishart b Gripper	53
S.R. Waugh	c and b Ervine	78
D.S. Lehmann	c and b Ervine	30
A.C. Gilchrist	not out	113
	b 4, l-b 10, w 1, n-b 3	18
	(6 dec)	735

Did not bat: A.J. Bichel, B. Lee, J.N. Gillespie, S.C.G. MacGill.

	O	M	R	W
Streak	26	6	131	0
Blignaut	28	4	115	0
Ervine	31	4	146	4
Price	36	5	187	0
Gripper	25.3	0	142	2

ZIMBABWE

D.D. Ebrahim	b Gillespie	29	b Gillespie	4
T.R. Gripper	c Lehmann b Lee	53	c Gilchrist v Gillespie	0
M.A. Vermeulen	c Hayden b MacGill	38	c Gilchrist b Lee	63
S.V. Carlisle	c Hayden b MacGill	2	c Hayden b Lehmann	35
C.B. Wishart	c Gilchrist b Bichel	46	lbw b Bichel	8
C.N. Evans	b Bichel	22	b Lehmann	5
T. Taibu	lbw b Gillespie	15	c Gilchrist b Bichel	3
H.H. Streak	b Lee	9	not out	71
S.M. Ervine	c Waugh b Gillespie	6	b Birchel	53
A.M. Blignaut	lbw b Lee	0	st Gilchrist b Lehmann	22
R.W. Price	not out	2	c Waugh b Bichel	36
	l-b 10, w 2, n-b 5	17	b 4, l-b 6, w 5, n-b 6	21
		239		321

	O	M	R	W		O	M	R	W
Lee	14	4	48	3		35	8	96	1
Gillespie	25.3	9	52	3		3	0	6	2
Bichel	21	2	62	2		28.2	15	63	4
MacGill	21	4	54	2		3.4	1	10	0
Lehmann	2	1	3	0		31.2	15	61	3
Waugh	5	1	10	0		8	2	26	0
Martyn						13	5	34	0
Ponting						5	1	15	0

AUSTRALIA WON BY AN INNINGS AND 175 RUNS

New world record by 5 runs. The old record stood for 9 years and 7 months.

India in Pakistan, Multan, March 2004

Virender Sehwag, born 20 October 1978, Delhi.

Test career (as at 3 May 2005), 2001–: 36 Tests, 3,079 runs, 10 centuries, average 55.98.

Sehwag, someone wrote, is easy to sum up. All he does is stir a certain confusion, a certain irritation, a sort of amusement and downright awe in about the same quantities. Of all triple centurions, he is the only one such a description fits.

Perhaps it fitted him from the beginning because he didn't come from a background of money. Quite the contrary. He came from an extensive family (there is talk of 16 cousins) but his parents – his father a contractor in a flour mill – just about managed to give him enough for cricket lessons. Nobody expected much and evidently his grandmother referred to him as *bholi*, meaning a simple fellow of good heart.

At 13 he impressed a coach by his determination to perfect a stroke. The coach was bowling to him at the end of the day but Sehwag wanted to go on and on until he got it right. The coach thought 'this is potentially something special'.[1]

He was. He played for his school and then the Delhi under-19's, although reportedly he had to take two-hour bus journeys to and from the ground. By 2001 the right-hand opener had made the Indian team and, in a one-day Coca-Cola Cup match at Colombo against New Zealand, scored a century off 69 balls (one 6, 19 4s). It was the second-fastest by an Indian and the seventh-fastest by anyone in a one-day international. He had modelled himself on Sachin Tendulkar who, as every Indian will tell you insistently, was the best batsman in the world.

Sehwag is iconic in a different way because cricket lifted him to a place he couldn't have expected to reach any other way, and it is reflected in his popularity among advertisers and his earning power. Amid talk that he'd bought the family a new home in a desirable area away from the crowded Najafgarh in south-west Delhi where he grew up, he remained touchingly close to his mother.

We've already had politics in this book: the aftermath of the Bali bomb, the car bomb at Karachi and now the delicate matter of India touring Pakistan with the dispute over Kashmir constantly simmering, religious differences and so on. In the event, the tour did more than pass without incident. It proved George Orwell – who said that if you want to create enmity between nations, let them play sport against each other – quite wrong.

The sadness was that the crowds packed the stadiums to watch the one-day matches but stayed away from the three Tests. They missed a feast, and none more so than the First at Multan. Sehwag was about to show the Pakistani spectators who did attend what he could really do, and not waste any time doing it either.

Sourav Ganguly had a back injury, Rahul Dravid took over the captaincy and won the toss. The wicket, Sehwag would conclude, clearly favoured batsmen although you had to work for your runs. He opened with Aakash Chopra to the bowling of Shoaib Akhtar and Mohammad Sami, and Sehwag's reading of the pitch was correct. Chopra took a couple off the second ball to start his innings, and next over Sehwag turned Sami off his legs to the mid-wicket boundary to begin his. By the end of the sixth over Sehwag was on 16 and had hit two more 4s. In another couple of overs he'd struck two more, a thwack to the point boundary off Sami and a deft turn off Akhtar to the fine-leg boundary. Sehwag's innings threatened to catch fire.

The 50 came up in the 17th over and Akhtar was bowling bouncers to relieve his frustration. Meanwhile Shabbir Ahmed bowled a short ball outside the off-stump and Sehwag carved it over third man for 6. It would not be the last. Saqlain Mustaq came on with his spinners and bowled an over to Chopra. Sehwag went to his own 50 in the over after that (off 60 deliveries, that 6, nine 4s) and then to a respectable delivery from Saqlain – straight, well pitched up – he thumped it over the mid-wicket boundary for his second 6.

Chopra cast himself in a supporting role and played that solidly. It gave Sehwag the freedom of movement he needed and by lunch, while Chopra had made his way to 25, Sehwag was 76 already, although he'd given a chance at 68. Sehwag hit Saqlain towards mid-on and Sami ran in towards the ball, caught it but couldn't hold it. Sehwag gave another chance just after lunch when, at 77, he flicked a ball from Shoaib Akhtar and Saqlain, diving, couldn't hold it.

Chopra nibbled and chipped into the afternoon, while Sehwag suddenly savaged Saqlain. Off the second ball of an over he heaved the ball high beyond mid-wicket for 6; made room and stroked the next into the covers for a couple; spooned the next towards square leg for another couple; flayed the next one – flighted up at him – to the point boundary and pushed the final ball for a single. He'd started the over on 78, finished it on 93. There seemed to be a mood on him. After a couple of singles he stroked Shoaib Akhtar to the third man boundary and went to the century in proper style, a 6. The century had come off only 107 deliveries (four 6s, 14 4s). When Sehwag had reached 111, Chopra went, edging Saqlain Mushtaq to Imran Farhat.

Dravid, in next, didn't get far – 6 – before Sami had him caught by Yasir Hameed at square leg off a mis-hit. This was a genuine surprise because Dravid's style and inclinations ought, on a pitch like this, to have led to a major score. That was 173 for 2 and Tendulkar came in. This would decide the shape and direction of the innings and, wisely, Tendulkar judged that his role, like Chopra's, was to give support – and advice.

With Sehwag in this mood, and scoring at the pace he was, support was tactically shrewd, although Tendulkar fully intended that wickets would not fall. He calmed Sehwag but, even so, at 122 Sehwag couldn't resist hitting Saqlain for another 6, this one off the front foot. A couple of overs later he took three boundaries from Shabbir, a consummate flick, a cover drive, another consummate flick. That brought him to 143.

Sehwag went to his 150 by straight-driving Shoaib Akhtar to the boundary and it had come in even time off 150 deliveries (five 6s, 20 4s). By then India were 210. At tea he had 155 and Tendulkar a circumspect 17, the total 228 for 2 off 57 overs. In defence, Tendulkar – like many great players – seemed impregnable, while Sehwag might offer a chance at any moment, despite Tendulkar's ministrations. Sehwag would say that whenever he 'made a mistake or played a false shot,' Tendulkar indicated for him to stick around, wait for the loose deliveries to come along.

After tea Sehwag turned his attention to Abdul Razzaq, driving him to the long-off boundary; taking a couple off the next; pulling the next to the mid-wicket boundary and the one after that; then prodding a comfortable single into the off-side. He'd started that over on 156, finished it on 171. India were 244.

Sehwag quietened, began to score in singles and 2s, and was content to leave some and block others. He took seven overs to go to 189 and then went single, then single again, then played a maiden to Abdul Razzaq; 3 off Sami, dot ball, dot ball, single; dot ball, dot ball; and from Saqlain, dot ball, dot ball, and a sweep to the boundary.

He was 199, and the innings became agony to watch.

He played a maiden to Shabbir Ahmed. Off the second ball of Abdul Razzaq's next over, Tendulkar took a single. Sehwag played the first back down the wicket, stroked the next to mid-wicket where it was fielded and hit the next to mid-off. He had been on 199 for nine long deliveries.

Was he nervous in the 190s? Not at all. With disarming honesty he said he was simply waiting for a loose delivery because, echoing those Tendulkar ministrations, he understood how important it was not to give his wicket away. That allowed him to expand on his philosophy: in one-day cricket the pressure is on you to score immediately – certainly in the first 15 overs – whereas in Test cricket you play a waiting game until those loose deliveries come along and, consequently, hitting boundaries is easier.

From the 10th ball of the sequence he moved from 199 past the double century by steering Abdul Razzaq out into the on-side. This was the fastest double century anyone had ever put together on the sub-continent, in 222 deliveries (five 6s, 26 4s). India ticked on. They reached 300 in the 76th over and after that Tendulkar, still subdued and careful, went to his half century off 112 deliveries (seven 4s).

At 221, Sehwag moved past the Indian record score against Pakistan, Sanjay Manjrekar's 218 at Lahore in December 1989 (in 8 hours 31 minutes, 401 balls, 28 4s). It was beautifully done. Shabbir Ahmed bowled outside the off-stump and Sehwag cover-drove it classically.

He finished the day on 228, made off 271 deliveries (compare Manjrekar getting to 218) with 30 4s and the five 6s. He and Tendulkar had made 183 together and at 356 for 2 India were already in a strong position. Unless the Pakistani bowlers could find something on the second day that strong position would become impregnable.

Sehwag felt this was his best innings in Tests and said he intended to go for the triple century. It seemed amazing that India had produced a dynasty of great batsmen and none of them had ever achieved that.

During the evening Sehwag spoke to his mother Krishna and she congratulated him but added that she hoped he would stay at the crease when play resumed.

The second day was in a very real sense a continuation of the first with both batsmen going carefully. By now people were gathering round the Sehwag home in Najafgarh. They had drums to beat whenever he scored a boundary and sweets to pass out. TV crews were fed on them as they waited to record the reaction if and when Sehwag reached the triple century.[2]

Shoaib Akhtar opened the bowling to Tendulkar who took a single off the fourth ball. Sehwag took a single out on the off-side from the sixth, and the day was under way. Tendulkar in particular would demonstrate his mastery of what to hit and what to leave alone but Sehwag was moving to other rhythms. Mohammad Sami bowled the second over and Sehwag flicked him to the boundary, two balls later hammered him to the off-side boundary and nipped the final ball to third man to retain the bowling. That took him to 238 and now he quietened. The scoreboard was moving in singles here and there, and Sehwag needed a further six overs to reach 250. Neither batsman was venturing much and the Pakistani bowling was tighter than it had been the day before.

Virender Sehwag, right, is congratulated by Sachin Tendulkar after reaching his 300 for India in Multan yesterday. Photograph: Arko Datta/Reuters

Sehwag hits India's first 300

Rahul Bhattacharya
at Multan Cricket Stadium

**India 675-5 dec
Pakistan 42-0**

In this age of run lust Virender Sehwag rewrote the history of Indian batting here yesterday with a devilish innings of 309. For a nation with so rich a lineage of batsmen, from CK Nayudu in the 30s down to the electric middle order of the current side, it had become a point almost of embarrassment that a triple hundred had eluded all.

"It was needed," said Sehwag's idol Sachin Tendulkar, himself left on 194 not out on a day when India continued their domination of Pakistan, amassing 675 for five before declaring towards the end of the second day of this first Test. "A fabulous innings. It's a big moment for Indian cricket."

This was an innings of sustained and violent brilliance, though not without its iffy moments. There was an edge between slip and the keeper on either side of VVS Laxman's previous Indian record of 281, and in all there were 3½ chances. As much as anything, these things are a matter of destiny.

Sehwag provokes confusion, irritation, amusement and awe in equal measure. No one knows what to make of him. He cares not to look at the pitch before a match: "How's it going to help?" He likes to say

that he has never faced a special bowler: "Anyway, you face a ball, not a bowler."

Everything about Sehwag seems natural, as if it has simply always been there. And yet plenty of invisible work has gone into his rise as a Tendulkar clone in the bylanes of Najafgarh, a grain-stocking satellite of Delhi. Before the current tour he was doing what was for him a familiar drill: facing eight bowlers at the nets for stints of over an hour. "He shouldn't get time to even straighten his back," his coach once said.

In the days before he had access to the choicest of gyms Sehwag strengthened his forearms by performing a thousand swings of a bat placed inside a cloth casing filled with sand. To prevent his foot from slipping out of the crease against spinners, his rear leg would sometimes be tethered to the back of the net. Not that it taught Sehwag to think twice before dancing down the pitch.

He heralded his triple century yesterday with a primal blast over wide long-on off Saqlain Mushtaq. Michael Slater, the former Australian opener, a kindred spirit and a commentator here, was heard gushing: "Six for the triple. It tells you all need to know."

Tendulkar said: "It's impossible to predict with Veeru but still I knew that on 295 he would go for a big one." What advice did the master have for the protégé? "Well, we talked

about not playing rash strokes. Of course, he hears me but I'm not sure if he ever listens."

Sehwag finally fell in the 127th over as he edged a Mohammad Sami delivery to Taufeeq Umar at first slip.

Among innings for which balls faced are known Sehwag's 300, off 363 deliveries, was just one slower than Matt Hayden's effort against Zimbabwe last year, when the Australian went on to make his world-record 380.

Sehwag rated this innings the best he has played. That in itself is a worthy tribute, for look at some of his previous deeds. On his Test debut, at Bloemfontein against South Africa in November 2001, he constructed a superbly

rounded century from 68 for four on a pitch so bouncy that Tendulkar's pet shot was the upper cut. Against England on the first day at Trent Bridge in 2002, with the ball swinging about a foot, he made 106 in only his second Test as opener.

In Australia in December Sehwag struck 195 after being clunked twice on the helmet in the opening session and eventually fell trying to move to his double century with a six. "Nobody knows what the blighter might try next," Peter Roebuck then observed, "including himself and his opponents."

For Tendulkar, who had batted meticulously since Sunday afternoon, there was to be a savage twist towards close of play. On the fall of the fifth wicket, of Yuvraj Singh, the stand-in captain Rahul Dravid pulled the plug on the innings to leave his bowlers 16 overs in the evening. Pakistan negotiated them, though not without trouble, to finish at 42 without loss.

"It's a real disappointment," Tendulkar said of the declaration. "I was surprised by it. I wasn't sure of the plan but I thought we could have continued for three to four overs." This would have been Tendulkar's fourth double. Only Dravid and Sunil Gavaskar among Indians, with four each already, have more.

And so the parting note on a day which offered the team much celebration was one of muted discontent.

Triple centuries in Tests

380 Matthew Hayden (Australia, right) v Zimbabwe, Perth, 2003	Mohammad (Pakistan) v West Indies, Bridgetown, 1958	**325** Andy Sandham (England) v West Indies, Kingston, 1930
375 Brian Lara (West Indies) v England, St John's, 1994	**336*** Wally Hammond (England) v New Zealand, Auckland, 1933	**311** Bobby Simpson (Australia) v England, Manchester, 1964
365* Garfield Sobers (West Indies) v Pakistan, Kingston, 1958	**334*** Mark Taylor (Australia) v Pakistan, Peshawar, 1998	**310*** John Edrich (England) v New Zealand, Leeds, 1965
364 Len Hutton (England) v Australia, The Oval, 1938	**334** Don Bradman (Australia) v England, Leeds, 1930	**309** Virender Sehwag (India) v Pakistan, Multan, 2004
340 Sanath Jayasuriya (Sri Lanka) v India, Colombo, 1997	**333** Graham Gooch (England) v India, Lord's, 1990	**307** Bob Cowper (Australia) v England, Melbourne, 1966
337 Hanif	**329** Inzamam-ul-Haq (Pakistan) v New Zealand, 2002	**304** Don Bradman (Australia) v England, Leeds, 1934
		302 Lawrence Rowe (West Indies) v England, Bridgetown, 1974

* indicates not out

'Nothing new' in Murali's doosra

David Harbord

Muttiah Muralitharan's "doosra" delivery that turns to the off-spinner reported for having a suspect action is not new according to Sri Lanka Cricket's chief executive Duleep Mendis.

The offending delivery spins in the opposite direction to his stock ball, was referred to the International Cricket Council on Sunday by match referee Chris Broad.

"There is no such thing as new delivery," Mendis said yesterday. "Murali has been bowling this ball in international cricket for over five years. The only difference between then and now is that he has perfected the delivery, making it more effective and accurate.

Stories suggesting that Murali had developed a supposed new ball, nicknamed the "doosra" — an Urdu word meaning "other" — began to appear last year.

The latest investigation into Murali's action, applies only to his alleged new delivery — the bowling, already the most analysed in the history of the game, was cleared by the ICC following a complaint from Australian umpire Darrell Hair in Melbourne in December 1995.

"We have to follow ICC procedures now that this has been reported," said Mendis, a former Sri Lanka captain and coach.

He said that Sri Lanka had started the ICC's two-year process for dealing with illegal bowling actions and will appoint an ICC-approved human movement specialist who will work with a five-man committee before reporting to the ICC within six weeks.

Bruce Elliott, the University of Western Australia biomechanist who was part of the original investigation into Murali's action, said yesterday he was not surprised by the latest report.

Elliott said: "Where we tested before he didn't bowl that ball. It's not something that we've looked at.

"This guy along with Shane Warne are the best two spin bowlers of all time. And I think from his perspective it would be good if he came down in history with restrictions over his action."

The South African captain Graeme Smith and the medium-fast bowler Andre Nel were adjudged guilty of dissent on the fourth day of the third Test against New Zealand in Wellington.

Nel was fined 75% of his match fee and Smith 30% by the match referee Clive Lloyd after they disputed an lbw decision by the umpire Aleem de Silva. Smith remonstrated with De Silva over the decision while Nel snatched his cap from the umpire at the end of the over. South Africa, needing for three, chasing 324 needed for victory to clinch the three-match series

Sehwag got to the 250 by driving Shoaib Akhtar to the mid-on region and running 3. It had taken him 4 minutes under 7 hours and come off 299 balls (32 4s, the five 6s).

The next target was the 281 of V.V.S. Laxman's highest Indian Test score set in 2001 against Australia at Kolkata (made in 10 hours 31 minutes, 452 balls, 44 4s).

At 252 Sami made one move sharply away and it completely beat Sehwag. The scoreboard was moving in singles here, although, at 261, he stroked Abdul Razzaq to the mid-wicket boundary and now the partnership was worth 250. Sehwag worked on through singles towards Laxman but then, typically and gloriously, he cut loose again. This was, in the words of Rahul Bhattacharya writing in *The Guardian*, 'an innings of sustained and violent brilliance'.

Laxman, due to bat at number five, was watching, no doubt intently.

Sehwag reached 274, Shabbir Ahmed bowling. He played defensively to the first ball, sending it easily towards mid-on. He drove and edged the second just wide of Taufeeq Umer at first slip – although Umer was able to touch it, and some say it was a real chance. Was Sehwag nervous? No. He cut the next ball viciously to the boundary and was 282. Laxman's record had gone. Nervous? Well, maybe a little. He edged the next and although Moin Khan dived he couldn't lay a glove on it – if the ball had been only a little closer he would have done. It went to the boundary. Nervous? Off the ball after that, Shabbir roared an appeal but the umpire (Simon Taufel of Australia) turned it down.

Sehwag would say he never felt any pressure, that he was just made like that.

286.

He took a single from Saqlain, a gorgeous flick to the leg side boundary off Shabbir Ahmed, then a single and that was 292. It was also lunch.

When they came back out Shoaib Akhtar opened to Sehwag and he took a single. For a couple of overs Tendulkar had the bulk of the strike before Sehwag edged a ball towards square leg. He saw the chances of making it into 2 and sprinted the second one.

295.

There was a context to that because in Melbourne against Australia the previous December he'd reached his highest Test score, 195, and tried to get to 200 with a 6. Clearly he'd be more prudent this time wouldn't he?

The clock moved towards one o'clock.

Tendulkar watched intently, he was on strike to Saqlain, and had suspicions that, knowing Sehwag's character and impulses, when Sehwag got the strike for himself he'd abandon prudence altogether and want to get to 300 with 'a big one.' They'd discussed the discipline of not playing rash strokes. Sehwag, Tendulkar would conclude, 'hears me but I'm not sure he ever listens'.

Saqlain bowled and Tendulkar left the ball alone as it went down the leg side.

Saqlain bowled and Tendulkar, going back, pushed a single on the leg side.

Saqlain bowled and Sehwag played defensively.

Saqlain bowled, just two or three short steps and a roll of the arm. As the ball left his hand, Sehwag's back-lift had begun. As the ball spun towards him he moved his weight on to his left foot, the body coming forward. Now his back-lift was so urgent and pronounced that he almost lifted himself off the ground. He moved his left foot

Pakistan v India
Played at Multan, 28, 29, 30, 31 March, 1 April 2004

INDIA

A. Chopra	c Farhat b Mushtaq	42
V. Sehwag	c Omar b Sami	309
R. Dravid	c Hameed b Sami	6
S.B. Tendulkar	not out	194
V.V.S. Laxman	run out	29
Y. Singh	c & b Farhat	59
	b 8, l-b 20, w 1, n-b 7	36
	(4 dec)	675

Did not bat: P.A. Patel, A. Kumble, Z. Khan, L. Balaji, I.K. Patham.

	O	M	R	W
Akhtar	32	4	119	0
Sami	34	4	110	2
Ahmed	31	6	122	0
Mushtaq	43	4	204	1
Razzaq	15	3	61	0
Farhat	6.5	0	31	1

PAKISTAN

Imran Farhat	lbw b Balaji	38	c Patel b Kumble		24
Taufeeq Umar	c Dravid b Pathan	23	lbw b Kumble		9
Yasir Hameed	c Patel b Patham	91	c Sehwag b Y Singh		23
Inzamam-ul-Haq	c Chorpa b Kumble	77	run out		0
Yousuf Youhana	c Patel b Khan	35	c Dravid b Pathan		112
Abdul Razzaq	c Patel b Pathan	47	c Chopra b Kumble		22
Moin Khan	b Tendulkar	17	lbw b Pathan		5
Saqlain Mushtaq	c Khan b Pathan	5	lbw b Kumble		0
Mohammad Sami	b Kumble	15	lbw b Kumble		0
Shoaib Akhtar	c & b Tendulkar	0	c Laxman b Kumble		4
Shabbir Ahmed	not out	19	not out		0
	b 4, l-b 26, n-b 10	40	b 4, l-b 5, w 1, n-b 2, pen 5		17
		407			216

	O	M	R	W		O	M	R	W
Khan	23	6	76	1					
Pathan	28	5	100	4		21	12	26	2
Kumble	39.3	12	100	2		30	10	72	6
Balaji	20	4	54	1		11	3	48	0
Sehwag	2	0	11	0		3	0	8	0
Tendulkar	14	1	36	2		6	2	23	0
Y. Singh						6	1	25	1

INDIA WON BY AN INNINGS AND 52 RUNS
Failed by 72 runs to beat the record.

wide and he had room. The ball pitched. As it rose, Sehwag hit it a fearful blow on the up and it soared over the mid-wicket boundary.

The television camera, tracking its trajectory, panned across the vast, virtually empty grandstands. This stroke, this innings and this man demanded an audience of teeming thousands instead of echoes across shadowland.

Tendulkar embraced him and, playfully and lightly, he tapped Tendulkar's shoulder, a gesture of great affection. He'd taken only 364 balls to become the first Indian to reach a Test triple century (six 6s, 38 4s).

Sehwag adjusted his thinking towards Hayden's 380, the sort of thing – going for a specific target rather than just batting – he wouldn't normally have done, but this was Hayden and this was the 380.

He took a single and a 4 off Shoaib, a single from Saqlain.

307.

He scampered a single off Sami – the fielder's throw missed the stumps at the bowler's end.

308.

He drove Saqlain into the deep and took a single.

309.

Tendulkar played out the last two balls of the over and now Sehwag faced Sami who bowled on line with the off stump. Sehwag was trying to steer it but it flicked the edge of the bat and lobbed to Taufeeq Umar at first slip, who caught it.

The innings had lasted 375 deliveries over 8 hours 51 minutes (six 6s, 39 4s).

The streets of Najafgarh were silent.

'I don't normally think about what I have missed,' Sehwag would say, but, aiming for Hayden, 'I was disappointed to get out'. He and Tendulkar had put on 336 together, an Indian record. There was more, of course. Tendulkar went on to 194 and the Indian total at the declaration, 675 for 5, was the highest against Pakistan.

Mark Slater, who was at the stadium commentating and who had opened with Mark Taylor at Peshawar in 1998, said he was happy to see Chopra and Sehwag in action because 'they play the same way as we did'. Slater judged that the conditions were similar for Taylor's 334* and Sehwag's 309, although the innings were 'very different in character'. A comparison could not be made between Sehwag's 309 and Hayden's 380 because the strength of the Zimbabwe bowling, and the conditions, were not at all the same. Slater did find a similarity, however, in 'the concentration level and the aggression shown over two days'.

Mum Krishna was happy enough with the 309 but felt this was only the start. 'The world record will follow soon,' she said, as mums do.

India won the Test by an innings and 52, Pakistan levelled the series with a 9-wicket win in the Second, but India finished it off with an innings and 131 win in the Third.

Notes

[1]   *TIMEasia* profile by Brian Bennett, 28 April 2003.

[2]   http://www.newkerala.com/news-
      daily/news/features.php?action=fullnews&id=7959

West Indies v England, Antigua, April 2004

Brian Charles Lara

A decade after taking the record from Sobers, Lara was now poised to become the second man – after Bradman – to score a triple century in a Test match. Then he'd keep on going...

The days when the West Indies were a feared, fearsome side were memory now. It was as if a great wheel had turned full circle. By April 2004, as England's tour there drew to a close, the First Test at Kingston had been won by 10 wickets, the Second at Port of Spain by seven, the Third at Bridgetown by eight. More than that, at the age of 34, Lara was captaining the West Indies and, as a consequence of the three defeats, was under the most intense pressure. To add to it, his form with the bat had gone.

'The next five days,' he would say, 'are very important in terms of my future as captain. No one wants to go down as the first to lose all the Tests in a series in the Caribbean. You hope that when you fail somebody else will step in. We batted well in South Africa, these are proven performers and what is happening in this series is baffling.'[1]

The Fourth Test, at Antigua, demonstrated that the wheel had turned full circle. People spoke of England being ruthless just as they spoke of crisis in the West Indies; England captain Michael Vaughan spoke of a whitewash and, of the team which had suffered Lara's 375 10 years before, only Graham Thorpe remained.

Lara won the toss and batted, although Vaughan said he'd have been tempted to put West Indies in if he'd won it, for psychological reasons: having suffered against the England bowlers so acutely up to here, it made sense to maintain that pressure on the West Indian batsmen as soon and as directly as possible. This theory would have confronted a terrible reality if it had been tested. Luckily for Vaughan, it wasn't...

The pitch was so good that only changes of pace by the bowlers or mistakes by batsmen offered any realistic hope. Mike Atherton and Angus Fraser, who had played in 1994, gave their opinions that this pitch and that pitch were very similar.

The West Indies did not begin promisingly. Opener Daren Ganga moved across – a shuffle really – to a ball that Andrew Flintoff slanted in and pitched up. Ganga was lbw for 10, the score 33. Chris Gayle was batting freely and now Lara came out to join him. With nine runs added, Lara survived a stifled appeal by Steve Harmison for lbw but the ball was missing the leg stump and on the same total he survived a raucous, jubilant appeal for caught behind, also off Harmison. This was the only false shot for a long time. Lara had yet to score but he did moments after. Harmison bowled a slightly short delivery well outside the off-stump and lifting. Lara half-drove, half-steered it through gully, taking his left hand off the bat as he did so.

Gayle went to 69 but Flintoff had limped off and now off-spinner Gareth Batty bowled the last over before lunch. Gayle attempted to turn the fifth ball on to the leg side but spooned it back to Batty. The West Indies were 98 for 2 at lunch, Lara 17.

Rain fell hard and three hours were lost. When play resumed Lara clicked. He cut Matthew Hoggard to the boundary – gave himself room, rolled the wrists as he smacked the ball, and that represented an omen. If he hadn't been completely fluent until this moment he was after it. He was quickly to his 50 with a hook from outside the off-stump, which sent the ball bob-bob-bobbing across the damp outfield. He had needed only 61 deliveries and 118 minutes to get there.

At the other end Ramnaresh Sarwan scored briskly too, while Lara played a couple of exquisite cuts using his supple, strong wrists to angle the ball fine enough to beat the field. By now the shadows had lengthened. Lara brought the 200 up by chipping

Harmison to deep square leg in the 50th over of the innings. Lara and Sarwan had, in the space of 26 overs, added 110 and the West Indies closed on 208 (Lara 86, Sarwan 41) because the light had deteriorated. Lara's innings had contained 11 4s so far. He had refound his balance, refound his control and he was in the mood.

In the mood? Next day he drove the first ball – full length and from Hoggard – to the extra-cover boundary. The stroke was beautiful in its ease and certainty, the movement of the body classically proportioned. This ball didn't bob along, it bounded.

That set the mood. Within five overs and 25 minutes he'd reached his century. On 94 Hoggard bowled him a ball of full length and he flicked it imperiously through mid-wicket to the boundary. The timing gave the ball a kick as it left the bat. Lara's genius gave the ball its direction, bisecting mid-on and square leg. Then Hoggard bowled a rising ball outside the off-stump and Lara slash-cut it for a couple. That, of course, was 13 boundaries in his innings now. The century had taken 195 minutes and came from a mere 131 deliveries. Lara acknowledged it in a slightly subdued, understated way. He removed his helmet and raised his bat as if moving by rote and from memory. He was sweating freely. He had the air of a man who must have known – everyone at the ground, including the England players must have known, too – that there was plenty more to come. The question, already, was how much?

Part of the answer seemed to come straight after when Hoggard, bowling round the wicket, pitched one a long way outside the off-stump and Lara hauled it to the mid-wicket boundary easy as you like.

By now the records and the statistics were coming in to focus. He had played 106 Tests and this was his 25th century, and seventh against England. He was now past Vivian Richards's 24 and only Sobers's 26 lay ahead.

The pitch was benign, it was dry and any humidity in the air had been pushed away by a gentle wind.

He was tap-dancing to Batty, up the wicket and driving through the covers, rocking back and steering into gaps on the off-side, sweeping fine and even one-handed.

He might have been out at 127 when he opened the face of the bat to a delivery from Simon Jones and guided the ball deftly towards Hoggard, fielding at third man. Lara ran two but on completing the second Hoggard threw down the wicket. The umpire called for the television replay and the slow-mo showed Lara's bat creeping over the line to safety as Hoggard's astonishing throw was about to hit the stumps.

Sarwan had started slowly but when Batty plied his off-spin he accelerated, striking him into the Andy Roberts stand.

Lara was still in the mood. He steered Jones for a couple to the leg side and had 151 from 199 deliveries. He did, however, hit Hoggard in the air and not far from Mark Butcher in the covers: an academic chance, nothing more.

Sarwan went, an edged catch to Trescothick at first slip off Harmison at 330. Ricardo Powell, re-called to the West Indies side after four years, was known as a one-day specialist who liked to crack the ball about and he started to do that now. Lara went to lunch at 165, with the West Indies on 342. Directly after lunch Lara cracked Hoggard's first ball to the cover boundary, but there was another dimension to the stroke. Lara moved into position for the cut as he habitually did – fast – and then waited for the ball to come for its cracking. If he could do that before his eye was in again, the afternoon lay at his mercy already. The impression strengthened against Harmison. A ball well pitched-up, angling across to the off-stump and beyond, Lara up on to his toes, his body so agile that he could rise on his feet and create space at the same instant, and another cracking to the boundary.

Soon after the partnership went to 50, but Powell tried to hook Simon Jones and was caught in the deep by Nasser Hussain. West Indies were 380 and Ryan Hinds joined Lara, who was now moving imperiously against a flagging attack. His placing of the ball was precise, the precision born of the time he had to play each ball. He seemed to be constantly within himself and which bowler bowled at him, or what they bowled, seemed curiously irrelevant. For instance, when Lara was on 189 Batty came on to bowl. Lara took a step back, then a step forward and drove him high for a straight six. Perhaps somebody found it on the neighbouring island of Barbuda.

He swept Batty to the square leg boundary, leaning down and in to the stroke, ticked a ball on middle-and-leg for the most comfortable of singles and he'd reached 200 off 260 balls, so that the second hundred had taken him only 129. It was only the 49th over of the day. He took this second hundred as he had taken the first, in a slightly subdued, under-stated way, as if great cares were falling away from him and great questions were being answered without any need for histrionics – there was still plenty of work to do. He straight-drove Batty for another six.

Vaughan had a bowl with his spinners and repeatedly Lara lapped him between square leg and fine leg. He was 224 at tea (Hinds 28) and batting like a man who had revindicated his whole career. As Colin Bateman wrote in the *Daily Express,* 'he dealt ruthlessly with the ill-directed bowling served up at him, pounding the advertising boards which ring the hotch-potch Recreation Ground'. He hit Batty out of the ground 'and into the bus depot […] but in general it was an innings of huge concentration and control'.

He lost that for a moment against Harmison, missing a ball that pitched outside the leg stump. It thumped into Lara's pad and Harmison gave more of a heartfelt plea than an appeal. It was refused. The next ball he pulled him to the mid-wicket boundary.

Hinds went caught and bowled off Batty, and Ridley Jacobs came in to stay with Lara until day's end. Lara was more cimcumspect against Batty, tap-dancing into position but only lofting him straight for 4. That took Lara to 246. He tap-danced one pace up the wicket and retreated one pace – all in a single, fluid movement – and now had the whole of the off-side spread before him. He off-drove Batty with the ball well outside the leg stump: an entirely orthodox stroke in its execution. It went fast to the extra-cover boundary and that was 250 from 323 deliveries. He straight drove Batty along the ground and the West Indies were 500.

He was playing demonstration cricket, playing the finest of leg-glances and late cuts, pulling from outside the off-stump, even changing his mind – and stroke – in mid delivery from the persistent (and undaunted) Batty. Not everything, of course, went to the boundary and he seemed content with that: the singles and 2s mounted and

CROSSQUIZ

THE Express Crossquiz is a two-in-one challenge to test your sports knowledge. Answer each question and then arrange the letters that fall in the shaded squares into a well-known sportsword or the surname of a famous sporting personality. The last letter of each answer will be the first letter of the next.

The solution will be published tomorrow, or call 0901 567 5665. Calls cost 60p a minute from a BT landline.

ACROSS

1. Name the burly New Zealand all-rounder who took 16 wickets in the 1983 Test series in England (6).

2. What is the surname of Facundo, the Argentinian striker who joined Fulham from Gimnasia for £2 million in 2002? (4).

6. Who played on the left-wing for Tottenham Hotspur's double winning team and scored twice in the 1963 European Cup-Winners' Cup final? (5).

7. Which American golfer won the 1985 US Open at Oakland Hills? (5).

11. Complete the name of Gunter, the German midfield maestro who played for Borussia Moenchengladbach and Real Madrid? (5).

12. Who won the 1954 Australian Open men's singles title? (4).

DOWN

1. What is the name of the American football team from Kansas City? (6).

3. Which word usually describes a tall southpaw boxer with a long reach? (7).

4. Which American heavyweight fought Bruce Woodcock, Joe Louis and Rocky Marciano? (6).

5. In what do Chelsea now have strength? (5).

6. Which Scottish football referee officiated at World Cup 2002? (6).

8. What is Ricky Hatton's nickname? (3,3).

9. Which non-League team knocked Coventry City out of the FA Cup in 1989? (6).

10. Strikers like to see the ball do what in the net? (6).

SPORTSWORD CLUE: *You may be snookered!*

YESTERDAY'S SOLUTION

ACROSS: 1 Costa. 2 Anglo. 6 Cook. 7 Knibbe. 11 Greb. 12 Bares. DOWN: 1 Colomba. 3 Opener. 4 Abo. 5 Rotate. 6 City. 8 Equaliser. 9 Yearling. 10 RM.

SPORTSWORD: (Paul) Sturrock.

Compiled by MICHAEL GILLER

---

10 TO TACKLE

1. Which Sunderland player received his marching orders in the recent FA Cup semi-final against Millwall?

2. Which 14-year-old footballer made his Major League Soccer debut in America playing for DC United against San Jose recently?

3. Which snooker player's soon-to-be-released autobiography is entitled 'Double or Quits'?

4. Which three jockeys have ridden Grand National winners for trainer Ginger McCain?

5. Which bowler abandoned his normal medium pace to bowl off-spin, and take 13-156 for England in the fifth Test of the 1974 series in the West Indies?

6. Which football club's two FA Cup final appearances resulted in wins in 1900 and 1903?

7. Name the only golfer to win The Open on six occasions.

8. Which Australian in 1997 became the first batsman to score a century in each of his first three Ashes Tests?

9. Which Welshman lost on points to Joe Louis in a world heavyweight title fight?

10. Which year in the Eighties saw the first athletics World Championships?

RATINGS: 0-3 poor, 4-6 average, 7-9 good, 10 world class.

ANSWERS: 1 Jason McAteer. 2 Freddy Adu. 3 Willie Thorne. 4 Brian Fletcher, Tommy Stack and Graham Lee. 5 Tony Greig. 6 Bury. 7 Harry Vardon. 8 Greg Blewett. 9 Tommy Farr. 10 1983.

FOURTH TEST: West Indies skipper be[...]

Lara's pie[...]

COLIN BATEMAN
in Antigua

BRIAN LARA and England were both on their knees yesterday – Lara giving thanks as he kissed the bountiful Antigua pitch, while England were simply begging for mercy from the world's finest batsman.

Lara scored an unbeaten 400, the highest Test score ever seen in the history of the game, and the West Indies made 751-5, the biggest total ever made against an England side – surpassing Australia's 729 at Lord's in 1930.

In reply, after two-and-a-half days in the field at the mercy of Lara, England inevitably stumbled up the mountain confronting them.

Openers Michael Vaughan and Marcus Trescothick were out cheaply again, and when Nasser Hussain was the third batsman dismissed with the score on 54, the follow-on target of 552 looked about as fanciful as asking for a cup of Earl Grey in a rum shack.

Mark Butcher responded with a half-century, but England lost two wickets with the score on 98. First Butcher was bowled by Pedro Collins for 52, and in the next over Graham Thorpe was caught on the boundary off Fidel Edwards for 10.

As glorious gestures go, they do not come more spectacular than Lara's 13 hours of batsmanship during which he never gave a chance. He was ridiculously good. It was a fabulous 400.

But thankfully for England, that's all it was: a gesture. Lara said: "It's a great feeling, but it is dampened by the series result."

That is what England have to cling to over the last two days in Antigua as they battle for the draw: the comfort of knowing that they will be going home triumphant, the first English side to win a series in the Caribbean for 36 years.

For Lara, though, yesterday was Salvation Day. With three defeats and only 100 runs to his name in the first three Tests, the series had become the 'Strife of Brian'.

Antigua could have been his last Test in charge had it gone the way of the others but instead it was turned into a celebration of Lara's sublime talent. And he was clearly after Matthew Hayden's mantle yesterday. Lara had made the highest score in Test cricket with his 375 against England in 1994, beating Sir Garfield Sobers' 365. It was a record held for close on 10 years until October 10 last year, when Hayden hit 380 off Zimbabwe in Perth.

Hayden, though, was allowed only 185 days as king. Yesterday, setting off on 313, Lara relentlessly and ruthlessly picked off the English bowling.

He equalled Hayden's 380 around 20 minutes before lunch by lofting off-spinner Gareth Batty back over his head for a six into the first tier of the Sir Vivian Richards' Pavilion. The next ball he swept for four and pandemonium broke out.

Lara almost did a lap of honour and out into the middle, flanked by TV cameras and security men, came Antigua's new Prime Minister, Baldwin Spencer, to hail the hero. Every England player embraced Lara, who then dropped to his knees. He knew pitches like this are only made in heaven.

Lara said it was hard to believe that he had achieved the feat for a second time, admitting: "When I scored it before, I didn't know what to expect. This time it was very tiring, but I'm here again.

"Ten years ago the match ended in a draw but this time we're looking for a result."

Ten years ago it was Andrew Caddick, Angus Fraser, Chris Lewis and Phil Tufnell who suffered, and yesterday England's resources were frighteningly thin.

Matthew Hoggard was back in the team hotel with a bug and within an hour Steve Harmison had been banned from bowling by umpire Darrell Hair after his third warning for running on the pitch.

Simon Jones had a torrid time, bowling inaccurately and conceding 32 runs off five overs with the third new ball. Andrew

---

HOW BRIAN GOT ON TOP OF THE V[...]

SCOREBOARD

WEST INDIES: First Innings
(Overnight 595-5)

	Mins	Balls	Runs
B Lara not out	1707	582	400
R Jacobs not out	307	207	107
B4 lb5 w2 nb5			16
Total (5 wkts, dec 202 overs)			**751**

Fall: 33, 98, 330, 380, 469.
Bowling: Hoggard 18-2-82-0, Harmison 37-6-92-1, Flintoff 35-8-109-1, Jones 29-0-146-1, Batty 52-4-185-2, Vaughan 13-0-60-0, Trescothick 18-3-68-0.

ENGLAND: First Inns

	Mins	Balls	Runs
M Trescothick c Jacobs b Best	71	34	16
(flat-footed push edged to keeper)			
M Vaughan c Jacobs b Collins	19	17	7
(played around straight ball)			
M Butcher b Collins	128	83	52
(late on off-stump straight)			
N Hussain b Best	19	15	3
G Thorpe c Collins b Edwards	62	35	10
(pulled to deep backward square leg)			
A Flintoff not out	11	9	0
G Jones not out	4	3	0
Lb2 w1 nb8			11
Total (5 wkts , 31.2 overs)			**99**

Fall: 8, 45, 54, 98, 98.
Bowling: Collins 9.2-2-24-2, Edwards 9-1-34-1, Collymore 8-3-15-0, Best 4.3-1-20-2, Hinds 0.3-0-4-0.
Umpires: A Dar & D Hair.

HIGHEST INDIVIDUAL SCORES

Name	Score	For
B.C. Lara	400*	WI
M.L. Hayden	380	AUS
B.C. Lara	375	WI
G.St A. Sobers	365*	WI
L. Hutton	364	ENG
S.T. Jayasuriya	340	SRI
Hanif Mohammad	337	PAK
W.R. Hammond	336*	ENG
M.A. Taylor	334*	AUS
D.G. Bradman	334	AUS
G.A. Gooch	333	ENG
Inzamam-ul-Haq	329	PAK
A. Sandham	325	ENG
R.B. Simpson	311	AUS
J.H. Edrich	310*	ENG
V. Sehwag	309	IND
R.M. Cowper	307	AUS
D.G. Bradman	304	AUS
L.G. Rowe	302	WI

Emmett pride aft[...]

EMMETT: Brave recovery

SEAN EMMETT could hardly pull off his racing gloves to collect the winner's trophy, after pushing himself to the limit to win the second race of the second round of the British Superbike Championship at Brands Hatch.

The MonsterMob Ducati rider had fallen heavily in a tangle with Glen Richards on the

SUPERBIKES
By David Fern

second lap of the opener, but bravely opted to carry on.

"My feet came off the peg, I was out of the seat, but I held on and thought I had corrected it. Then Glen cannoned into me, it was a racing incident," said Emmett. Before the second race, he wrapped a bag of frozen peas around injured hand to re[...] the swelling.

After reeling in leader Yukio Kaga[...] he took the lead o[...] second lap.

"That was my [...] hope," said Emme[...] was too weak t[...] involved in a scra[...] had to get my [...] down, get ahead, [...] hope I could hold [...] was riding on [...]

ce of history

WORLD BEATER:
Brian Lara celebrates
after breaking
Matthew Hayden's
highest Test score
record of 380

D AGAIN

ET:		
nce	Date	
ohn's	12/04/2004	
rth	18/10/2003	
rth'y	06/04/1991	
gton	28/07/1958	
Oval	20/08/1938	
o (RFS)	02/03/1997	
stown	17/03/1958	
land	31/03/1913	
haam	14/10/1998	
rds	11/07/1930	
ds	28/07/1900	
xxe	01/08/2002	
gton	03/04/1930	
afford	23/07/1984	
nlley	08/07/1985	
ourne	28/03/2004	
ourne	11/07/1986	
ugby	20/07/1914	
tttown	06/03/1974	

PITCH PERFECT:
Lara kisses wicket
after breaking
Hayden's record

ed away manfully but
an and Trescothick
ore than cafeteria
o yourself – to Lara.
y Jacobs he added
o the overnight score,
nbroken sixth-wicket
o 282, another West
I.

hird Test century
unnoticed, but the
an again proved his
ide in the No2 role.
ndies bowlers came
at the leash, suddenly
g look difficult again.
eparted for seven
head at the caught
on given against him
s' third over.
swished Tino Best to
the same bowler
r Hussain for three.
more wickets fell in
ion before reaching
land must have been
t Lara was still

n fall

line. After the
race I was
ointed, but to
e back was great."
ael Rutter
t his HM Plant
Fireblade in just
cs behind, with
Reynolds, the
of the opening
a third place.
ON VINCENT won
second round of
itish Supersport

COMMENT
BY COLIN BATEMAN

NO OTHER player has achieved
what Brian Lara did yesterday in
Antigua in regaining his crown as
the holder of the highest score in
Test cricket.

In doing so he also became the
first player to reach 400 in a Test,
to add to his highest first-class
score, his 501 for Warwickshire
against Durham in 1994.

Those crown jewels of batting
now belong to the 34-year-old
Trinidadian, but they do not make
him the best batsman of all time.

Comparing sportsmen from
different eras is a futile task. Sir
Don Bradman is generally
regarded as the greatest with his
Test average of 99.94, but is Lara
better than Sir Vivian Richards,
Sunil Gavaskar, Javed Miandad,
Wally Hammond or WG Grace?

What is certain is that Lara
played the greatest innings of his
life yesterday in his 106th Test.

It was more impressive than
the 375 he scored against
England on the same ground 10
years ago simply because he
came into the match under
immense pressure; his captaincy,
his ability, and his future being
questioned. It was an immense
sporting achievement.

mounted. One from Flintoff, a drive of dramatic intent and execution, did go to the boundary and now he on-drove Flintoff to the boundary too.

He moved through the 280s (and survived an lbw appeal, the ball well outside the leg stump). On 293 he blasted the ball back at Batty who didn't catch it any more than he could have caught a shell out of a gun barrel. He had his hands in the right place but the ball exploded through them and went to the boundary undisturbed. He steered Jones for a leg side single and got to the triple century by steering Batty out for a single on the off-side. It was the 98th over of the day. He leapt far into the air. He had joined Bradman as a double triple-centurion. He'd needed no more than 144 deliveries to get there from the double century. This, at last, was intoxication. The whole crowd was on its feet, everyone beaming with pleasure and satisfaction.

He tap-danced up the wicket to Vaughan, gave him the Barbuda treatment, and finished on 313. From 426 deliveries he'd hit 34 4s and three 6s. He had set up a chance, a very real chance, to achieve something no man ever had before.

He couldn't sleep much, was up and lively at three o'clock and, because of the time gap, ringing friends in England to talk to get his mind off it. He didn't go near a golf course next morning but instead had a knock-up in front of one of the stands. Vaughan could take the new ball in four overs and Lara had initially to concentrate on surviving against that before the day spread before him.

The England bowling would be fully stretched during this third day. Hoggard was in the team hotel with a stomach bug, and Harmison didn't complete the day – a third warning for running on the pitch took him out of the attack.

Lara leg-glanced Trescothick to the boundary to bring up the 600 (Lara 319), cut Batty through the off-side and already it seemed like a continuation of all that had gone on the day before. He edged Harmison to the boundary through where third slip would have been: Harmison had only a first slip. Harmison was distinctly lively hereabouts with the new ball, brushing Lara's shoulder as he got out of the way of one, striking him high up on the thigh with another. Lara reached his 350 off 494 balls with a couple off Batty, controlled and along the ground. He acknowledged the crowd, waved his bat briefly and didn't even take his helmet off. Jacobs came along and they embraced in a matter-of-fact way. There was not only work still to be done, there was the real work to be done.

He swatted Jones to the leg boundary to reach 355, worked Batty here and there, sliced Vaughan into the deep, chipped Vaughan to third man and that made him 364. He swept a single.

365.

He flicked Vaughan off his toes.

367.

He tucked Batty to deep square leg into an ocean of space but they could run no more than a single.

368.

Vaughan, bowling a good length and actually restraining Lara, brought up his deep mid-on to try and increase the pressure. Lara tap-danced and struck the ball to exactly where deep mid-on had been.

372.

Vaughan drew a forward defensive stroke from him and pursed his lips. Next ball Lara came up the wicket and drove the ball gently into a gap in the off-side.

373.

Batty now beat him. The ball spun outside the off-stump, Lara missed and wicketkeeper Jones appealed for the catch. 'Not out!' Lara permitted himself the ghost of a smile. There had been a distinctive sound, but that was bat on the ground not bat on the ball. Lara composed himself again. He tried to sweep Batty, didn't connect with it properly and remained on one knee, gloves held in front of his helmet visor. The pressure was suddenly on him like a great weight and Vaughan was still drawing forward defensive strokes out of him. He glanced Vaughan.

374.

Batty bowled. Lara tap-danced up the wicket, opened his shoulders and hit the ball high and clean into the Sir Vivian Richards stand.

380.

In this one stroke – more a sublime gesture – Lara equalled Hayden. It was some 20 minutes before lunch. Jacobs, then on 92, came up and said something. Lara nodded. He adjusted his arm guard, played a cut at an imaginary ball, pumped his left hand as if he was telling himself do it, do it. Vaughan was setting the field, bringing it in, tightening it. Lara walked briskly up and down keeping his body loose, losing himself in the motion.

Batty to bowl. It was on the leg stump and, carefully, he swept it to the boundary.

384.

He did a circle of honour, helmet off, the biggest smile you've seen. Three policeman marched a spectator away from the rim of the square. Jacobs hugged him. More policemen pursued another spectator. Flintoff, big-boned, ambled up to congratulate Lara. Then the England team were patting his back and Butcher was saying something that gave them both the biggest smiles you've ever seen. The newly-elected Prime Minister of Antigua, Baldwin Spencer, came out with an entourage and shook his hand. A policeman in the middle distance applauded. Still the crowd roared their approval.

Then he did as he had done in 1994, kissed the ground and batted on. At 394 he straight drove Batty to the boundary and then took a single.

397.

Lara cut Flintoff for a single; a moment or two later Flintoff bowled him a lifter outside the off-stump and Lara cheekily poked it towards third man.

399.

That was the final ball of that over. Batty was bowling and induced a false shot, Lara feeling for the ball and edging it to deep square leg. He signalled that there was a problem with the sightscreen which ought to have moved back to white after displaying a red advertisement when the bowling was from the other end. When Batty did bowl Lara swept it for a single.

400.

He declared and came off through a guard of honour, bats up-raised over him. He spoke rather modestly of how happy he had been 'for the game' when Hayden had beaten his 375 and how he was sure Hayden would be happy for him. He wasn't sure if Hayden had rung to congratulate him but said he'd be checking his messages.

Inzamam-ul-Haq, whose 329 now seemed – and was – even further away from the record, summed it all up nicely enough. Lara, he said, is a truly wonderful batsman to watch. He added: 'I know records are meant to be broken but I can't see anyone else getting to 400 in my lifetime.'

Nor was Inzamam-ul-Haq alone in having his great innings diminished. That April day it had been done to them all, Sandham and Bradman, Hammond and Hutton, Hanif and Sobers, Simpson and Edrich, Cowper and Rowe, Gooch and Jayasuriya, Taylor and Hayden and Sehwag.

All of them had achieved the monumental and some of them had redefined the possibilities of a man and a bat. Brian Lara achieved something else. He had moved the beautiful game to a place where it had never been before. It was a lovely place.

Notes

1   Quoted in *The Independent on Sunday*.

West Indies v England
Played at Antigua, 10, 11, 12, 13, 14 April 2004

WEST INDIES

C.H. Gayle	c & b Batty	69
D. Ganga	lbw b Flintoff	10
B.C. Lara	not out	400
R.R. Sarwan	c Trescothick b Harmison	90
R.L. Powell	c Hussain b Jones	23
R.O. Hinds	c & b Batty	36
R.D. Jacobs	not out	107
	b 4, l-b 5, w 2, n-b 5	16
	(5 dec) 751	

Did not bat: T.L. Best, P.T. Collins, C.D. Collymore, F.H. Edwards.

	O	M	R	W
Hoggard	18	2	82	0
Harmison	37	6	92	1
Flintoff	35	8	109	1
Jones	29	0	146	1
Batty	52	4	185	2
Vaughan	13	0	60	0
Trescothick	18	3	68	0

ENGLAND

M.E. Trescothick	c Jacobs b Best	16	c Sarwan b Edwards	88
M.P. Vaughan	c Jacobs b Collins	7	c Jacobs b Sarwan	140
M.A. Butcher	b Collins	52	c Gayle b Hinds	61
N. Hussain	b Best	3	b Hinds	56
G.P. Thorpe	c Collins b Edwards	10	not out	23
A. Flintoff	not out	102	c Lara b Sarwan	14
G.O. Jones	b Edwards	38	not out	10
G.J. Batty	c Gayle b Collins	8		
M.J. Hoggard	c Jacobs b Collins	1		
S.P. Jones	lbw b Hinds	11		
S.J. Harmison	b Best	5		
	b 1, l-b 5, w 4, n-b 22	32	b 4, l-b 7, w 3, n-b 16	30
		285	(5 wkts) 422	

	O	M	R	W		O	M	R	W
Collins	26	4	76	4		8	2	34	0
Edwards	18	3	70	2		20	2	81	1
Collymore	19	5	45	0		18	3	58	0
Best	10.3	3	37	3		16	1	57	0
Hinds	17.3	7	29	1		38	8	83	2
Sarwan	7	0	18	0		12	2	26	2
Gayle	1	0	4	0		17	6	36	0
Powell						8	0	36	0

MATCH DRAWN

New world record by 20 runs. The old record stood for 7 months.

3 1 7

Last Man In

Christopher Henry Gayle, born Kingston, Jamaica, 21 September 1979.

Test career (as at 3 May 2005), 1999–: 50 Tests, 3,364 runs, 7 centuries, average 40.05

Then, from nowhere, there was a strange, almost haunting, sequence of links with the past. Chris Gayle, the left-hander from Jamaica, might decimate any attack in the world with his brutally powerful strokes – or fail completely. Nobody ever knew which it would be, including, as it seems, the man himself.

In the 2005 series against South Africa he'd been failing, and, in the Fourth and final Test at Antigua, fielded while South Africa made 588 for 6 declared, an innings that lasted an hour into the third day. That time in the field had exacted a toll on Gayle who felt slightly tired.

He knew perfectly well that pressure was on him having, as he said, 'played two Test matches and not scored any runs'. He gazed at the wicket, still so bountiful with runs, and told himself *dig deep, cash in.* Wavell Hinds was out for a duck and Ramnaresh Sarwan, who had batted with Lara during the 400, came out to join him. Here was the first link.

It's always been tempting to regard West Indians as intuitive cricketers but Gayle had been working on his technique with Sobers in the indoor nets, and that was ironic because he'd find himself eyeing up the Sobers 365. Gayle said he'd been working hard with Sobers 'basically about balance and trying to get your momentum going'. Gayle, too, would discipline himself to stand still while the ball was delivered rather than move about, as he had been doing.

He and Sarwan began the long journey towards the South African total, and however deep he dug he was not to deny himself all the habits of a lifetime: he took 33 off the first 4 overs. He went to 50 in even time (nine 4s and a 6) and his 100 off 97 balls (15 4s, three 6s). One of those 6s went full into the crowd over long-off. By close of play on that third day he'd reached 184 (257 balls, 26 4s, the three 6s), Sarwan on 103 but the follow-on still 90 runs away.

On the fourth day they took their partnership to 331, and Gayle went to 200 (off

293 balls) before Sarwan was brilliantly caught in the covers. That brought Lara in – another link. What might Lara do here of all places? He'd made 4 when he was out caught behind.

Shivnarine Chanderpaul came in and, of course, he'd been partnering Lara when the 400 was made...

Soon enough Gayle took the West Indies past the follow-on with a boundary off South African skipper Graeme Smith. The ball was short and outside the off-stump, Gayle had plenty of time and hammered it to the leg side boundary. The fielders didn't move. He took his time moving through the 240s to 250 and got there off 369 balls in 8 hours 14 minutes (33 4s and 3 6s) by belting Makhaya Ntini through the covers. At this point West Indies were 416 for 3 and, because the match was essentially dead (and the series, South Africa leading 2-0), Gayle sensed he had time to do something exceptional. In simple terms, that meant the rest of this fourth day and the whole of the fifth, and at the rate he'd been maintaining that could take him far, far beyond Everest.

He was travelling forward in singles and 2s now, and the statistics of the day reveal that: he'd make 133 off 226 deliveries with 11 4s, in starkest contrast to the day before when, no thoughts of records in anyone's mind, he'd given full freedom to his power.

By now, travelling away from 250, records were in many people's minds, as well as his. He reached 298 with a single to mid-wicket off Shaun Pollock, edged Smith and wicketkeeper Mark Boucher dropped it; reached 299 with a cover drive off Smith and reached 300 with an onside nudge off A.B. de Villiers, an occasional off-spinner. It had taken 463 balls and was the highest ever against South Africa. That had been set by Bradman with 299* for Australia at Adelaide in 1931–32, of course. Here, for Gayle and our story, was another link. He'd got there in 9 hours 58 minutes (34 4s and three 6s.)

At the moment he completed the single he did more than elevate himself, becoming the fourth West Indian with a triple, he elevated Lara into a strange position too. Since the beginning of our story with Andy Sandham, only one other man – Hammond – had made a triple century himself and also batted while someone else was doing it. Here, then, was another link, and there were more. He reached 300 five balls before tea and, shortly after it, drove fast bowler Monde Zondeki to the boundary at extra cover to move past Rowe's 302. He'd say, with disarming candour, that 'the only record I was thinking about was the 400. I was trying to get as close as possible to 400'. That was the notional plan for this fourth day – moving up, in a West Indian context, past the established base camps of Sobers 365 and Lara 375, towards the summit. Then he'd have the fifth day stretching before him like an invitation to eternity. Chris Gayle is unusual in our story in that, amid so much understandable reticence and modesty from 1930, he *was* thinking about Everest and he *did* say he was thinking about it.

And then, so soon afterwards, the great truth that nobody knows what the next ball will bring asserted itself. He'd been at the crease for 32 minutes since the 300 and played what has been described as a lazy shot, possibly induced by fatigue, against Zondeki. He was trying to cut but edged the ball, head high, to Smith at slip. In raw statistics, 10 hours 30 minutes, 483 balls, 37 4s and those same three 6s...

He was philosophical. A new record could have happened, it didn't happen and, overall, he was satisfied but he did muse on two subjects. The first: to do it all again from

0 would be a long way to go. The second: 'When will I reach this stage again?' They could all have wondered that, and all but Bradman and Lara didn't reach it – so far.

Anyway, after all the noise and thunder at Antigua, after all the adulation and the links, Christopher Henry Gayle did something very private and very human.

He rang his mum.

She was proud and she was right to be. Her son was now a member of the very best company and, like the 17 other triple centurions, always would be.

West Indies v South Africa
Played at St John's, 29, 30 April, 1, 2, 3 May 2005

SOUTH AFRICA

A.B. de Villiers	c Browne b Best	114	c Washington b Best		12
G.C. Smith	c Washington b Powell	126	not out		50
H.H. Dippenaar	run out	5	not out		56
J.H. Kallis	c Washington b Powell	147			
H.H. Gibbs	c Deonarine b Gayle	23			
A.G. Prince	c Browne b Bravo	131			
M.V. Boucher	not out	11			
S.M. Pollock	not out	13			
	b 4, l-b 1, w 5, n-b 8	18	b 1, w 1, n-b 7		9
	(6 dec)	588	(1 wkt)		127

Did not bat: M. Zondeki, M. Ntini, N. Boje.

	O	M	R	W		O	M	R	W
Powell	32	3	137	2		8	2	27	0
Best	26	4	116	1		5	0	31	1
Washington	22	3	73	0		7	1	20	0
Bravo	27		97	1		3	0	12	0
Gayle	31	11	65	1		1	0	3	0
Hinds	6	0	24	0		3	1	10	0
Deonarine	18	1	69	0		3	1	20	0
Sarwan	1	0	2	0		1	0	3	0

WEST INDIES

C.H. Gayle	c Smith b Zondeki	317
W.W. Hinds	c & b Ntini	0
R.R. Sarwan	c Prince b Zondeki	127
B.C. Lara	c Boucher b Zondeki	4
S. Chanderpaul	run out	127
N. Deonarine	c Boucher b Smith	4
D.J.J. Bravo	c Prince b Boucher	107
C.O. Browne	lbw b Smith	0
D.B. Powell	b de Villiers	12
T.L. Best	c Gibbs b de Villiers	5
D.M. Washington	not out	7
	b 2, l-b 9, w 3, n-b 23	37
		747

	O	M	R	W
Pollock	34	5	111	0
Ntini	33	3	106	1
Zondeki	25	4	120	3
Kallis	36	6	96	0
Boje	30	6	76	0
Smith	43	3	145	2
de Villiers	21	6	49	2
Prince	9	1	22	0
Dippenaar	2	1	1	0
Boucher	1.2	0	6	1
Gibbs	1	0	4	0

MATCH DRAWN

Failed by 84 runs to beat the record.

The Comparison

That's a slight misnomer because the chapter title implies that a valid comparison between the triple centuries can be made but it can't. The England attack at Leeds in 1930 that Bradman broke can in no way be compared with the Zimbabwean attack that Hayden broke, and even that does not take into account the state of the various wickets and the state of the various matches. For instance, Hammond's mauling of an indifferent New Zealand attack in a match where he felt he could indulge himself without worrying about getting out gives monstrous statistics if it is overlaid with Hanif's 16-hour trek towards eternity. At the same striking rate as Hanif's 337, Hammond would have been 1,008. So the table below is purely for interest.

PLAYER	INNINGS	TIME		6s	4s
Sandham	325	10 hours			28
Bradman	334	6 hours	23 minutes		46
Hammond	336*	5 hours	18 minutes	10	34
Bradman	304	7 hours	10 minutes	2	43
Hutton	364	13 hours	17 minutes		35
Hanif	337	16 hours	13 minutes		24
Sobers	365*	10 hours	14 minutes		38
Simpson	311	12 hours	42 minutes	1	23
Edrich	310*	8 hours	52 minutes	5	52
Cowper	307	12 hours	6 minutes		20
Rowe	302	10 hours	12 minutes	1	36
Gooch	333	10 hours	28 minutes	3	43
Lara	375	12 hours	46 minutes		45
Jayasuriya	340	13 hours	19 minutes	2	36
Taylor	334*	12 hours		1	32
Inzamam	329	9 hours	40 minutes	9	38
Hayden	380	10 hours	22 minutes	11	38
Sehwag	309	8 hours	51 minutes	6	39
Lara	400*	12 hours	53 minutes	4	43
Gayle	317	10 hours	30 miutes	3	37

Bibliography

Altham, H.S. and E.W. Swanton *A History of Cricket* George Allen & Unwin, London, revised edition, 1938.

Arlott, John *Cricketing Lives: Maurice Tate* Phoenix House, London, 1951.

Barker, Ralph *Ten Great Innings* Chatto & Windus, London, 1964.

Batchelor, Denzil *The Book of Cricket* Collins, London, 1952.

—— *The Test Matches of 1964* Epworth Press, London, 1964.

Bowes, Bill *Express Deliveries* Stanley Paul, London, undated.

Bradman, Don *My Cricketing Life* Stanley Paul, London, 1938.

—— *Don Bradman's Book* Hutchinson & Co., London, undated.

—— *Farewell to Cricket* Hodder & Stoughton, London, 1950.

Cardus, Neville *The Essential Neville Cardus* Jonathan Cape, London, 1949.

Clarke, John *With England in Australia* Stanley Paul, London, 1966.

Dexter, Ted *Ted Dexter Declares* Stanley Paul, London, 1966.

Docker, Edward Wyberg *Bradman and the Bodyline Series* Angus & Robertson, Brighton, 1978.

Edrich, John and David Frith *Runs in the Family* Stanley Paul, London, 1969.

Fender, P.G.H. *Kissing the Rod* Chapman & Hall, London, 1934.

—— *The Tests of 1930* Faber & Faber, London, 1930.

Gooch, Graham, and Frank Keating *Gooch: My Autobiography* CollinsWillow, London, paperback edition, 1996.

Hammond, Walter R. *Cricket My Destiny* Stanley Paul, London, undated.

Hobbs, J.B. *The Fight for The Ashes 1932-33* Harrap, London, 1933.

—— *The Fight for The Ashes 1934* Harrap, London, 1934.

Hutton, Len *Just My Story* Hutchinson & Co., London, 1956.

James, C.L.R. *Beyond a Boundary* Hutchinson, London, second impression, 1966.

Jardine, D.R. *Ashes and Dust* Hutchinson & Co., London, 1934.

Lara, Brian and Brian Scovell *Beating the Field* Partridge Press, London, 1995.

Martin-Jenkins, Christopher *Testing Time* Macdonald, London, 1974.

Paynter, Eddie and Alan Buckley *Cricket All The Way* A. Richardson, London & Leeds, 1962.

Richardson, V.Y. *The Vic Richardson Story* Angus & Robertson, London, 1968.

Sobers, Gary *Cricket Crusader* Pelham Books, London, 1966.

Tebbutt, Geoffrey *With the 1930 Australians* Hodder & Stoughton, London, 1930.

Thomson, A.A. *Cricket my Pleasure* The Sportsmans Book Club, London, 1954.

Tyson, Frank *The Century-Makers* Sidgwick & Jackson, London, 1980.

Valentine, Barry *Cricket's Dawn That Died* Breedon Books, Derby, 199).

Wakley, B.J. *Classic Centuries in the Test Matches between England and Australia* Nicholas Kaye, London, 1964.

Warner, P.F. *The Fight for the Ashes 1930* George Harrap, London, 1930.

Wellings, E.M. *Simpson's Australians* Robert Hale, London, 1964.

Wyatt, R.E.S. *Three Straight Sticks* Stanley Paul, London, 1951.Abbas, Zaheer 152

Index